THE FOLGER GUIDE
TO TEACHING *MACBETH*

The Folger Guides to Teaching Shakespeare Series
— Volume 2 –

Peggy O'Brien, Ph.D., General Editor

Folger Shakespeare Library

WASHINGTON, DC

Simon & Schuster Paperbacks

NEW YORK   LONDON   TORONTO   SYDNEY   NEW DELHI

100 YEARS
SIMON &
SCHUSTER
PAPERBACKS

1230 Avenue of the Americas
New York, NY 10020

First Simon & Schuster trade paperback edition November 2024

SIMON & SCHUSTER and colophon are registered trademarks of Simon & Schuster LLC

For information about special discounts for bulk purchases, please contact Simon & Schuster Special Sales at 1-866-506-1949 or business@simonandschuster.com.

The Simon & Schuster Speakers Bureau can bring authors to your live event. For more information or to book an event, contact the Simon & Schuster Speakers Bureau at 1-866-248-3049 or visit our website at www.simonspeakers.com.

Manufactured in the United States of America

1   3   5   7   9   10   8   6   4   2

Library of Congress Cataloging-in-Publication Data is available upon request.

ISBN 978-1-9821-0567-9
ISBN 978-1-6680-1760-9 (ebook)

THE FOLGER SHAKESPEARE LIBRARY

The Folger Shakespeare Library makes Shakespeare's stories and the world in which he lived accessible. Anchored by the world's largest Shakespeare collection, the Folger is a place where curiosity and creativity are embraced and conversation is always encouraged. Visitors to the Folger can choose how they want to experience the arts and humanities, from interactive exhibitions to captivating performances, and from pathbreaking research to transformative educational programming.

The Folger seeks to be a catalyst for:

Discovery. The Folger's collection is meant to be used, and it is made accessible in the Folger's Reading Room to anyone who is researching Shakespeare or the early modern world. The Folger collection has flourished since founders Henry and Emily Folger made their first rare book purchase in 1889, and today contains more than 300,000 objects. The Folger Institute facilitates scholarly and artistic collections-based research, providing research opportunities, lectures, conversations, and other programs to an international community of scholars.

Curiosity. The Folger designs learning opportunities for inquisitive minds at every stage of life, from tours to virtual and in-person workshops. Teachers working with the Folger are trained in the Folger Method, a way of teaching complex texts like Shakespeare that enables students to own and enjoy the process of close-reading, interrogating texts, discovering language with peers, and contributing to the ongoing human conversation about words and ideas.

Participation. The Folger evolves with each member and visitor interaction. Our exhibition halls, learning lab, gardens, theater, and historic spaces are open to be explored and to provide entry points for connecting with Shakespeare and the Folger's collection, as well as forming new pathways to experiencing and understanding the arts.

Creativity. The Folger invites everyone to tell their story and experience the stories of and inspired by Shakespeare. Folger Theatre, Music, and Poetry are programmed in conversation with Folger audiences, exploring our collective past, present, and future. Shakespeare's imagination resonates across centuries, and his works are a wellspring for the creativity that imbues the Folger's stage and all its programmatic offerings.

The Folger welcomes everyone—from communities throughout Washington, DC, to communities across the globe—to connect in their own way. Learn more at folger.edu.

All Shakespeare used in this book is taken from the Folger Shakespeare editions of the text. Available in paperback and for free at folger.edu/folgershakespeare.

IMAGE CREDITS

Diego Valadés, "The Great Chain of Being" in his *Rhetorica christiana*. Perugia: Petrus Jacobus Petrutius, 1579. Second page following gathering EE. (Getty Research Library Special Collections BV4217 .V34 1579)

Ramberg, Johann Heinrich. *Macbeth*, IV, 1, Macbeth in witches' cave (1829).

Gilbert, Frederick. *Macbeth*, IV, 3, the witches' cauldron (1859).

Du Guernier, Louis. *Macbeth*, act IV, scene 1 (London, 1714).

Rhead, Louis. *Macbeth*, act IV, scene I (1918).

Rhodes, Richard. Macbeth . . . Shall never vanquish'd be, untill Great Birnam wood to high Dunsinane Hill shall come against him, act 4 scene 1 (London, 1813).

Thew, Robert. *Macbeth*, act IV, scene 1, a dark cave (London, 1801).

If you are a teacher,
you are doing the world's most important work.
This book is for you.

CONTENTS

THE FOLGER GUIDE
TO TEACHING *MACBETH*

Shakespeare for a Changing World

Why Shakespeare?

Michael Witmore

You have more in common with the person seated next to you on a bus, a sporting event, or a concert than you will ever have with William Shakespeare. The England he grew up in nearly 400 years ago had some of the features of our world today, but modern developments such as industry, mass communication, global networks, and democracy did not exist. His country was ruled by a monarch, and his days were divided into hours by church bells rather than a watch or a phone. The religion practiced around him was chosen by the state, as were the colors he could wear when he went out in public.

When Shakespeare thought of our planet, there were no satellites to show him a green and blue ball. The Northern European island where he grew up was, by our standards, racially homogeneous, although we do know that there were Africans, Asians, Native Americans, Muslims, Jews, and others living in London in the early 1600s—and that Shakespeare likely saw or knew about them. The very idea that people of different backgrounds could live in a democracy would probably have struck him as absurd. What could an English playwright living centuries ago possibly say about our changed and changing world? Would he understand the conflicts that dominate our politics, the "isms" that shape reception of his work? What would he make of debates about freedom, the fairness of our economies, or the fragility of our planet?

The conversation about Shakespeare over the last 250 years has created other obstacles and distance. Starting around that time, artists and promoters put Shakespeare on a pedestal so high that he became almost divine. One such promoter was an English actor named David Garrick, who erected a classical temple to Shakespeare in 1756 and filled it with "relics" from Shakespeare's life. Garrick praised Shakespeare as "the God of our idolatry," and in his temple included a throne-like chair made of wood from a tree that Shakespeare may have planted. Today, that chair sits in a nook at the Folger Shakespeare Library. The chair's existence reminds us that the impulse to put Shakespeare in a temple has been at times overwhelming. But temples can exclude as well as elevate, which is why the Folger Shakespeare Library—itself a monument to Shakespeare built in 1932—needs to celebrate a writer whose audience is contemporary, diverse, and growing.

While Shakespeare was and is truly an amazing writer, the "worship" of his talent becomes problematic as soon as it is expected. If Shakespeare's stories and poetry continue to be enjoyed and passed along, it should be because we see their value, not because we have been told that they are great. Today, if someone tells you that Shakespeare's appeal is "universal," you might take away the idea that his works represent the experience of everyone, or that someone can only be fully human if they appreciate and enjoy his work. Can that possibly be true? How can one appreciate or enjoy the things in his work that are offensive and degrading—for example, the racism and sexism that come so easily to several of his characters? What about such plays as *The Merchant of Venice*, *Othello*, or *The Taming of the Shrew*, where the outcomes suggest that certain kinds of characters—a Jew, an African, a woman—deserve to suffer?

When we talk about Shakespeare, we have to confront these facts and appreciate the blind spots in his plays, blind spots that are still real and reach beyond his specific culture. In acknowledging such facts, we are actually in a better position to appreciate Shakespeare's incredible talent as a writer and creator of stories. Yes, he wrote from a dated perspective of a Northern European man who was a frequent flatterer of kings and queens. Within those limits, he is nevertheless able to dazzle with his poetry and offer insights into human motivations. We are not *required* to appreciate the language or dramatic arcs of his characters, but we can appreciate both with the help of talented teachers or moving performances. Memorable phrases such as Hamlet's "To be or not to be" are worth understanding because they capture a situation perfectly—the moment when someone asks, "Why go on?" By pausing on this question, we learn something at a distance, without having to suffer through everything that prompts Hamlet to say these famous words.

Had Shakespeare's plays not been published and reanimated in performance over the last few centuries, these stories would no longer be remembered. Yet the tales of Lady Macbeth or Richard III still populate the stories we tell today. They survive in the phrases that such characters use and the archetypal situations in which these characters appear—"out, out damned spot" or "my kingdom for a horse!" Marvel characters and professional politicians regularly channel Shakespeare. When a supervillain turns to the camera to brag about their evil deeds, we are hearing echoes of King Richard III. When the media criticizes a leader for being power-hungry, some version of Lady Macbeth is often implied, especially if that leader is a woman.

While they are from another time, Shakespeare's characters and situations remain exciting because they view life from a perspective that is both familiar and distant. The better able we are to recognize the experiences described in Shakespeare's plays in our lives, the broader our vocabulary becomes for understanding ourselves. We see and hear more when the plays dramatize important questions, such as:

- What does a child owe a parent and what does a parent owe their child? Why must children sometimes teach their parents to grow up? *King Lear*, *Hamlet*, and *Henry IV, Part 1* all ask some version of these questions.

- Are we born ready to love or is the capacity to love another something that is learned? Shakespeare's comedies—*Twelfth Night*, *As You Like It*, *Much Ado About Nothing*—are filled with characters whose entire stories are about learning to accept and give love.

- How does one deal with an awful memory or the knowledge of a brutal crime? Hamlet is burdened with both, just as many are today who are haunted by trauma.

These questions get at situations that anyone might experience at some point in their life. If you are a teenager whose mad crush is turning into love, you will have to go out on that balcony, just like Juliet. Will you be confident or afraid? If a "friend" who knows you well is feeding you lies, you will be challenged to resist them—as Othello is when faced with Iago. Will you be able to think for yourself? These questions come up in any life, and the answers are not predetermined. A goal in any humanities classroom is to improve the questions we ask ourselves by engaging our specific experiences, something very different from looking for "timeless truths" in the past.

Do not believe that you must master Shakespeare in order to appreciate literature, language, or the human condition. Do, however, be confident that the time you and your students spend with these plays will result in insight, new skills, and pleasure. Shakespeare was a deeply creative person in a deeply polarized world, one where religious and economic conflicts regularly led to violence. He used that creativity to illustrate the many ways human beings need to be saved from themselves, even if they sometimes resist what they need most. He also understood that stories can change minds even when the facts cannot. If there was ever a time to appreciate these insights, it is now.

The Folger Teaching Guides are the product of decades of experience and conversation with talented educators and students. The Folger continues to offer teachers the best and most effective techniques for cultivating students' abilities in the classroom, starting with Shakespeare but opening out on the great range of writers and experiences your students can explore. We invite you to visit the Folger in person in Washington, DC, where our exhibitions, performances, and programs put into practice the methods and insights you will find here. And we extend our gratitude to you for doing the most important work in the world, which deserves the dedicated support we are providing in these guides.

Good Books, Great Books, Monumental Texts—Shakespeare, Relevance, and New Audiences: GenZ and Beyond

Jocelyn A. Chadwick

"People can find small parts of themselves in each character and learn what it may be like to let the hidden parts of themselves out. Regardless of personal background, everyone can relate to the humanity and vulnerability that is revealed in Shakespeare's works." (Student, 2023)

" 'To me, there is no such thing as black or yellow Shakespeare,' Mr. Earle Hyman, a celebrated African-American actor said. 'There is good Shakespeare or bad Shakespeare. It's simply a matter of good training and opportunity.' " ("Papp Starts a Shakespeare Repertory Troupe Made Up Entirely of Black and Hispanic Actors," *New York Times*, January 21, 1979)

"The question for us now is to be or not to be. Oh no, this Shakespearean question. For 13 days this question could have been asked but now I can give you a definitive answer. It's definitely yes, to be." (President Volodymyr Zelenskyy's speech to the UK Parliament, March 8, 2022)

"I, at least, do not intend to live without Aeschylus or William Shakespeare, or James, or Twain, or Hawthorne, or Melville, etc., etc., etc." (Toni Morrison, "Unspeakable Things Unspoken: The Afro-American Presence in Literature," *The Source of Self-Regard*, 2019)

How have William Shakespeare's brilliant and probing plays about the human condition come to an *either/or* to some contemporary audiences? The preceding quotes reveal appreciation, understanding, and metaphorical applications along with definitions of the playwright's depth and breadth. And yet, a misunderstanding *and* sometimes *conscious cancellation* of the man, his work, and his impact have undergone substantial *misunderstanding and misinterpretation*.

For as long as any of us can or will remember, William Shakespeare has continued to be with us and our students. True, this is a bold and assertive declarative statement; however, in the 21st century, is it and will it continue to be accurate and still *valid*?

In 1592, playwright Robert Greene, a contemporary of William Shakespeare, did not think much of Shakespeare's work or his talent:

> There is an upstart Crow, beautified with our feathers that with his Tygers hart wrapt in a Players hyde, supposes he is as well able to bombast out a blank verse as the best of you: and being an absolute Johannes factotum is in his owne conceit the onely Shake-scene in a country. (Robert Greene, *Greene's Groats-Worth of Wit*, 1592)

Clearly, Greene was jealous of Shakespeare's popularity and talent.

Interestingly, what Greene objects to parallels some 21st-century perspectives that at this writing recommend removal of Shakespeare's plays and poetry from curricula throughout the country—*just because*. For Greene, the objection was Shakespeare's talent, his appeal to his contemporary audience, his rising popularity, and cross-cultural exposure—not only angering Greene but also resulting in his undeniable jealousy.

Today, however, the primary argument is that Shakespeare's texts are old and dated; he is white and male—all of which from this perspective identify him, his time, and his work as disconnected from the realities of 21st-century students: antiquated, anachronistic, even racially tinged. These arguments persist, even though without doubt, Shakespeare's London was metropolitan, multicultural, and influenced by the city's international trade—imports as well as exports.

And further, to be clear, as Toni Morrison and so many other scholars, writers, *and* readers have asserted, the *durability of* a text lies with its present *and* future audiences. I should add here that Morrison was engaging with, and "talking back to," Shakespeare's play *Othello* when she wrote her play *Desdemona* in 2011.

At this writing, there are a number of contemporary catalysts pointing out the necessity of rethinking, reflection, and consubstantiation of such texts that have long been a part of the canon. We are experiencing not only that resurgence but also a book-banning tsunami in schools and public libraries. The result of such movements and actions indeed causes us to rethink; they have also compelled educators at all levels, parents, librarians, writers, and GenZ students to speak up and out.

To illustrate concretely students' responses, this introduction necessarily includes the perspectives and voices from some high school students (grades 9–12), who attend Commonwealth Governors School (CGS) in Virginia. I asked a number of them what they thought about Shakespeare, and they told me. Their statements are in *their own words*; I did no editing. In addition, the students within the CGS system represent the panoply of inclusion and diversity.

> It's the big ideas that make Shakespeare relevant to myself and other students. Everyone loves, and everyone feels pain, so while we each might experience these feelings at different points in our lives, in different degrees, and for different reasons than others, I think Shakespeare's work is enough out of our times so that all students can connect to his themes and imagine themselves in the positions of his characters. (Student, May 2023)

And . . .

> I feel his general influence; I feel like he created a lot of literary words, and musicians like Taylor Swift draw from the works of earlier people, and Shakespeare continues to be relevant. (Student, 2023)

Interestingly, students *tapestry* what they read and experience in Shakespeare's works into their contemporary world, concomitantly, reflecting Umberto Eco's assertion about the import, impact, and protean qualities of a text's life: students create their own meaning and connections—building onto and extending Shakespeare's words, expression, characters, and challenges, ultimately scaffolding into their present realities, experiences, and challenges.

With all of these developments and conversations in mind, this Folger series of teaching guides provides that crossroad and intersection of analysis and rethinking. The central question that joins both those who see at present limited or no redeemable value in Shakespeare and those who view these texts as windows of the past, present, and, yes, the future is *"Do William Shakespeare's plays resonate, connect, and speak to 21st-century readers of all ages, and especially to our new generations of students?"*

Let us consider Eco's assertion: each time playwrights, directors, and artists reinterpret, every text undergoes a disruption, thereby reflecting new audiences. To *re-see* a character or setting when producing Shakespeare's plays is with each iteration a kind of disruption—a disruption designed to bring Shakespeare's 16th-century texts to audiences from multiple perspectives and epochs. The term *disruption* here takes on a more modern definition, a more protean and productive definition: Every time a reader enters a text— one of Shakespeare's plays, to be specific—that reader can meld, align, interweave experiences, memories, thoughts, aspirations, and fears, and yes, as the first student quote alludes, empower the reader to *identify* with characters, and moments and consequences. This reading and/or viewing is indeed a positive kind of disruption—*not to harm or destroy*; on the contrary, a positive disruption that expands and interrelates both reader and viewer with Shakespeare and each play. Past *and* present intersect for each generation of readers. In this positive disruption texts remain relevant, alive, and *speak verisimilitude*.

Similarly, we ask 21st-century students studying Shakespeare to bring their *whole selves* to the work, and to come up with their own interpretations. Allowing and privileging 21st-century students to compare and contrast and then examine, inquire, and express their own perspectives and voices remains the primary goal of English language arts: independent thinking, developed voice, and ability to think and discern critically for oneself. Both the primary text and adaptations are reflections *and* extended lenses:

> *The man i' th' moon's too slow—till new-born chins*
> *Be rough and razorable; she that from whom*
> *We all were sea-swallowed, though some cast again,*
> *And by that destiny to perform an act*
> *Whereof what's past is prologue, what to come*
> *In your and my discharge.* (The Tempest 2.1, 285–89)

Just as the past continuously informs and reminds the present, the present—each new generation—brings new eyes, new thoughts, new perspectives. Of course, each generation sees itself as unique and completely different; however, the echoes of the past are and will always be ever-present.

In so many *unexpected* ways, the 21st-century Shakespeare audience in school—students, teachers, and others—share far more with William Shakespeare and his time than we may initially recognize and acknowledge. From his infancy to his death, Shakespeare and his world closely paralleled and reflects ours: upheavals and substantial shifts culturally, sociopolitically, scientifically, and religiously, as well as the always-evolving human condition. Each of the plays represented in this series—*Hamlet, Macbeth, Othello, Romeo and Juliet*, and *A Midsummer Night's Dream*—illustrates just how much William Shakespeare not only observed and lived with and among tragedy, comedy, cultural diversity, challenges, and new explorations, but also, from childhood, honed his perspective of both past and present and—as Toni Morrison expresses—*rememoried* it in his plays and poems. Tragedy and Comedy is rooted in the antiquities of Greek, Roman, and Greco-Roman literature and history. William Shakespeare uniquely crafts these genres to reflect and inform his own time; more importantly, the plays he left us foreshadow past and future connections for audiences to come—audiences who would encounter cross-cultures, ethnicities, genders, geography, even time itself.

More than at any other time in our collective history experienced through literature, the past's ability to inform, advise, and even "cushion" challenges our students' experiences today. It will continue to do so into the foreseeable future and will continue to support and inform, and yes, even protect them. Protecting, meaning that what we and our students can read and experience from the safe distance literature provides, allows, even encourages, readers to process, reflect, and think about how we respond, engage, inquire, and learn.

> The play . . . *Macbeth* . . . is about pride; there are lots of common human themes. He's the basis for a lot of literature like *Hamlet* is just the *Lion King*; it is just *Hamlet*, but it's lions. (Student, May 2023)

One fascinating trait of GenZ readers I find so important is *the how* of their processing and relating canonical texts with other contemporary texts and other genres around them: TV, movies, songs, even advertisements. What I so admire and respect about *students' processing* is their critical thinking and their ability to create new and different comprehension pathways that relate to their own here and now. In this new instructional paradigm, we *all* are exploring, discovering, and learning together, with William Shakespeare as our reading nucleus.

Although many writers and playwrights preceded William Shakespeare, his scope and depth far exceeded that of his predecessors and even his peers. His constant depiction and examinations of the human condition writ large and illustrated from a myriad of perspectives, times, cultures, and worlds set Shakespeare decidedly apart. The result of his depth and scope not only previewed the immediate future following his death, but more profoundly, his thematic threads, characters, settings, and cross-cultural inclusions continue to illustrate *us to us*.

The pivotal and critical point here is GenZ's continued reading and experiencing of William Shakespeare's plays. As they experience this playwright, they take bits and pieces of what they have read and experienced directly into other texts they read and experience in classes and daily living. In fact, in the "tidbits" they experience initially through Shakespeare, students will connect and interpret *and make their own meaning and connections*, even *outside* of textual reading. Malcolm X, in fact, provides us with an example of how that works:

> I read once, passingly, about a man named Shakespeare. I only read about him passingly, but I remember one thing he wrote that kind of moved me. He put it in the mouth of Hamlet, I think, it was, who said, "To be or not to be." He was in doubt about something—whether it was nobler in the mind of man to suffer the slings and arrows of outrageous fortune—moderation—or to take up arms against a sea of troubles and by opposing end them. And I go for that. If you take up arms, you'll end it, but if you sit around and wait for the one who's in power to make up his mind that he should end it, you'll be waiting a long time. And in my opinion the young generation of whites, blacks, browns, whatever else there is, you're living at a time of extremism, a time of revolution, and now there has to be a change and a better world has to be built, and the only way it's going to be built—is with extreme methods. And I, for one, will join with anyone—I don't care what color you are—as long as you want to change this miserable condition that exists on this earth. (Oxford Union Queen and Country Debate, Oxford University, December 3, 1964)

Like Malcolm X, GenZ students turn toward the wind, staring directly and earnestly into their present and future, determined to exert their voices and perspectives. Their exposure to past and present literature, sciences, histories, and humanities allows, even empowers, this unique generation to say, "I choose my destiny." And the myriad texts to which we expose them informs, challenges, and compels them to always push back and move toward a truth and empowerment *they* seek. Some of us who are older may very well find such empowerment disconcerting—not of the "old ways." But then, just what is a comprehensive education for lifelong literacy supposed to do, if not expose, awaken, engage, even challenge and open new, prescient doors of inquiry, exploration, and discovery? This is the broad scope of not just education for education's sake but of reading and experiencing for oneself *devoid of outside agendas—whatever they may be or from wherever they may emanate.*

A student put this succinctly:

> Elements of his writing are still relevant in today's films and books, like his strong emotional themes, tropes, and character archetypes. Shakespeare's works are quoted often by common people [everyday people] and even by more influential individuals, including civil rights leader Martin Luther King Jr., who was known to quote Shakespeare often. I believe the beautiful and unique work by William Shakespeare is still greatly relevant and appreciated now and will go on to remain relevant for centuries more. (Student, May 2023)

The plays comprising this series represent curricula inclusion around the country and also represent the angst some parents, activists, and politicians, even some fearful teachers, have about our continuing to include Shakespeare's works. That said, there are many, many teachers who continue to teach William Shakespeare's plays, not only allowing students from all walks of life to experience the man, his time, and the sheer scope of his thematic and powerful reach, but also privileging the voices and perspectives GenZ brings to the texts:

> We can see in Shakespeare our contemporary and sometimes frightening range of humanity today—I am specifically thinking of our current political turmoil—is not unique, and that just like the evil monarchs such as Richard III appear in Shakespeare's plays, they are always counterbalanced by bright rays of hope: in *Romeo and Juliet*, the union between the Montagues and Capulets at play's end restoring peace and civility . . . It is impossible for me to watch any performance or read any Shakespeare play—especially the tragedies—without leaving the theatre buoyed up by hope and respect for humankind, a deeper appreciation of the uses of the English language, and a feeling that I have been on a cathartic journey that leaves my students and me enriched, strengthened, and hopeful. (Winona Siegmund, Teacher, CGS)

> I'm going to be honest, I'm not very knowledgeable on the subject of Shakespeare . . . I never really went out of my way to understand and retain it. All I know is that I can't escape him. No matter how hard I try, and trust me, I try, he will always be somewhere, running through the media with his "art thous" and biting of thumbs. Perhaps people see themselves in the plays of Shakespeare. Maybe Shakespeare is a dramatization of the hardships we experience every day . . . Shakespeare has stained my life. One of those annoying stains that you can't get out. A bright, colorful stain that's easy to notice. But who cares? It was an ugly shirt anyway; might as well add some color. (Student, May 2023)

> Taylor Swift's "Love Story." I LOVE the STORY of *Romeo and Juliet*. See what I did there? But in all honesty, there are so many Shakespeare-inspired works (*Rotten Tomatoes, West Side Story, Twelfth Grade Night*, etc.) that I liked and remained relevant to me, and prove that Shakespeare will always be relevant. The first Shakespeare play I read was *Macbeth* when I was twelve and going to school in Azerbaijan. And even as a preteen studying in a foreign country, I loved the story and found it morbid, funny, and wise all at the same time. My Azerbaijani classmates liked it, too. Due to this unique experience, I think that anyone can enjoy and identify with Shakespeare's works, no matter their age or country of origin. (Student, May 2023)

The five plays in this Folger series represent the universal and social depth and breadth of all Shakespeare's poetry and plays—verisimilitude, relevance, *our* human condition—all writ large in the 21st century and beyond. Through characters, locations, time periods, challenges, and *difference*, William Shakespeare takes us all into real-life moments and decisions and actions—even into our *not yet known or experienced*—to illustrate the human thread joining and holding us all as one.

> Despite being several hundred years old, Shakespeare's works have yet to Become antiquated. There are several reasons for this long-lasting relevance—namely the enduring themes. Shakespeare's themes on humanity, morality, loss, and love remain relatable for people across all walks of life. (Student, May 2023)

In sum, a colleague asked me quite recently, "Jocelyn, why do you think students just don't want to read?" To add to this query, at this writing, I have tracked an increasing, and to be honest, disturbing sentiment expressed on social media: some teachers positing, essentially, the same perspective. My response to both is the same: our students— elementary through graduate school—*do* read and write every day. They will also read what we assign in our classes. However, this generation of students first thinks or asks outright—*Why?* What do I *get* if I invest the time and effort? Most assuredly, direct inquiries with which many veteran teachers *and* professors are unfamiliar—perhaps even resentful. But let's be honest. Our students of a now-patinated past most likely felt the same way. Remember the plethora of *CliffsNotes* and *Monarch Notes*? I know I threw my share of students' copies in the trash—wanting them to read for themselves.

Just like adults, our students, especially today, have a right to ask us *Why?* What *do* they *get* if they invest their time in reading assigned texts? Umberto Eco brilliantly answers why our students *must* continue reading and experiencing texts—for this series, William Shakespeare's plays—and learning through performance:

> Now a text, once it is written, no longer has anyone behind it; it has, on the contrary, when it survives, and for as long as it survives, thousands of interpreters ahead of it. Their reading of it generates other texts, which can be paraphrase, commentary, carefree exploitation, translation into other signs, words, images, even into music. ("Waiting for the Millennium," *FMR* No. 2, July 1981, 66)

To illustrate Eco's assertion, I will leave it to one student and two people with whom all teachers and many students are familiar:

> Shakespeare's work is relevant because his legacy allows people from all walks of life to understand that they can make a difference. Although people from all walks of life may not always relate to his works, the impact that he made on modern literature and theater is undeniable. The lasting dreams that his works have provided for young people lay the groundwork for our future. Shakespeare's living works are proof that one small man with one small pen can change the future of everything around him. (Student, May 2023)

> I met and fell in love with Shakespeare . . . It was a state with which I felt myself most familiar. I pacified myself about his whiteness by saying after

all he had been dead so long it couldn't matter to anyone anymore. (Maya Angelou on her childhood introduction to and love of Shakespeare in *I Know Why the Caged Bird Sings*, 1969)

and, as Malcolm X proclaimed:

I go for that. (Oxford Union Queen and Country Debate, Oxford University, December 3, 1964)

Why This Book?

Peggy O'Brien

First, let's start with YOU: If you are a schoolteacher, know that you are the most precious resource in the world. In every school, town, city, state, country, civilization, solar system or universe, there is none more valuable than you. It is hard, hard work and yet . . . you are doing the most important work on earth. Period.

At the Folger Shakespeare Library, we know this well and deeply, and that's why you are a clear focus of our work. If you teach Shakespeare and other complex literature—and particularly if you are a middle or high school teacher—it is our mission, passion, and honor to serve you. Therefore . . . welcome to *The Folger Guides to Teaching Shakespeare* and our five volumes on teaching *Hamlet, Macbeth, Othello, Romeo and Juliet,* and *A Midsummer Night's Dream.*

Here's why this book: our overall purpose. We know that many of you find yourselves teaching plays that you don't know well, or that you've taught so often that they are beginning to bore you to death. (You talk to us, and we listen.) So, these books give you fresh information and hopefully meaningful new ideas about the plays you teach most frequently, along with a very specific way to teach them to *all* students—highfliers, slow readers, the gamut. We see the Shakespeare content and the teaching methodology as one whole.

We often get these questions from y'all. You may recognize some or all of them:

- How on earth do I even begin to think about teaching a Shakespeare play? No one has really ever taught me how to teach Shakespeare and my own experience with Shakespeare as a high school student was . . . not great.

- How can Shakespeare possibly make sense in this day and age? In this changing world? Old dead white guy?

- Shakespeare can't possibly be engaging to *all* my students, right? I mean, it's true that really only the brightest kids will "get" Shakespeare, right?

- SO . . . what's the Folger Method and how does it fit into all of this?

- I have to teach the "10th-grade Shakespeare play"—whatever it is—and I haven't read it since high school, or maybe I have never read it.

- I'm a schoolteacher and don't have extra time to spend studying up before I teach this stuff.

- Doesn't using those watered-down, "modernized" Shakespeare texts make it easier? Aren't they the most obvious way to go?

- Can learning and teaching Shakespeare really be a great experience for my kids and for me too?

Our *Folger Guides to Teaching Shakespeare* are hopefully an answer to these questions too.

Here's why this book: the Folger Method. At the Folger, not only are we home to the largest Shakespeare collection in the world but we have developed, over the last four decades or so, a way of teaching Shakespeare and other complex texts that is effective for *all* students. We're talking well-developed content and methodology from the same source, and in your case, *in the same book.* Imagine!

The Folger Method is language-based, student-centered, interactive, and rigorous, and provides all students with ways into the language and therefore into the plays. Our focus is words, because the words are where Shakespeare started, and where scholars, actors, directors, and editors start. Shakespeare's language turns out to be not a barrier but *the way in.* The lessons in this book are sequenced carefully, scaffolding your students' path. They will find themselves close-reading, figuring out and understanding language, characters, and the questions that the play is asking. All of this when they may have started out with "Why doesn't he write in English?" It's pretty delicious. If you want to know more about the Folger Method right this minute, go to the chapter that starts on page 37.

A couple of things I want you to know right off the bat:

- Because the Folger Method involves lots of classroom work that is interactive and exciting (and even joyful), sometimes teachers are tempted to pull a few lessons out of this book and use them to spruce up whatever they usually do. Oh resist, please. Take the whole path and see what your students learn and what you learn.

- There is no "right" interpretation of any play (or work of literature, for that matter).
  In working with the Folger Method principles and essentials, your students come up with their own sense of what's going on in *Macbeth*. Their own interpretation. Not yours, or the interpretation of famous literary critics, but their own. And then they bring it to life. Exciting! That's what we're after, because the skills that they'll develop in doing this—close-reading, analysis, collaboration, research—they will use forever.

- The Folger Method may call on you to teach differently than you have before. Be brave! You are not the explainer or the translator or the connector between your students and Shakespeare. You're the architect who sets up the ways in which Shakespeare and your students discover each other . . . and we'll show you very explicitly how to do that.

Here's why this book: parts of the whole. Each of these guides is organized in the same way:

- **Part One is the big picture:** Folger director Michael Witmore and Jocelyn Chadwick both take on the "Why Shakespeare?" question from very different angles. And Jocelyn brings students into the conversation too. Delicious!

- **Part Two is *YOU* and *Macbeth*.** Through a set of short takes and one delicious long take, you'll get a stronger sense of the play. The shorts are some speedy and pretty painless ways to learn both the basics and a few surprises about both *Macbeth* and Shakespeare.

The long take is "*Macbeth* and the Pleasure of Puzzling Uncertainty," an essay written for you by Ayanna Thompson, an accomplished and celebrated Shakespeare scholar. We know that you have no "extra" time ever, but we also know that schoolteachers find connecting with new scholarship to be enlivening and compelling. New ways to look at old plays—new ways most often sparked by the changing world in which we live—continue to open up many new ways to look at Shakespeare. What you take away from Thompson's essay may show up in your teaching soon, or maybe at some point, or maybe never—and all of those are good. You may agree with or grasp her perspective on *Macbeth,* or you may not; she will get you thinking, though—as she gets us thinking all the time—and that's what we're about.

- **Part Three is you,** *Macbeth,* **your students, and what happens in your classroom.**

  - The Folger Method is laid out clearly—and bonus: with the kind of energy that it produces in classrooms—so that you can get a sense of the foundational principles and practices before you all get into those lessons, and your own classroom starts buzzing.

  - A five-week *Macbeth* unit, day-by-day lessons for your classes, with accompanying resources and/or handouts for each. We know that the people who are the smartest and most talented and creative about the "how" of teaching are those who are working in middle and high school classrooms every day. So, working schoolteachers created all of the "What Happens in Your Classroom" section of this book. They do what you do every day. While these writers were writing, testing, and revising for you and your classroom, they were teaching their own middle and high school kids in their own. And I am not mentioning their family obligations or even whispering the word *pandemic.* At the Folger, we are in awe of them, and for many of the same reasons, are in awe of all of you.

  - Two essays full of practical advice about two groups of students whom teachers ask us about often. The first details and demonstrates the affinity that English Learners and Shakespeare and *Macbeth* have for one another. The second focuses on the deep connections that can flourish between students with intellectual and emotional disabilities and Shakespeare and *Macbeth.* No barriers to Shakespeare anywhere here.

  - The last essay is packed with information and examples on pairing texts—how we make sure that students are exposed to the broad sweep of literature while at the same time are busy taking Shakespeare right off that pedestal and into conversations with authors of other centuries, races, genders, ethnicities, and cultures. This is where magic starts to happen!

And now . . . YOU! Get busy! And as Macduff says in Act 4 (and, OK, in a completely different context), get busy "in one fell swoop"! A joyful and energized journey of mutual discovery is at hand—for you and your students. Get it all going in Scotland! And tell us how it goes. As always, we want to know *everything.*

PART TWO

Getting Up to Speed, or Reviving Your Spirit, with *Macbeth*

Ten Amazing Things You May Not Know About Shakespeare

Catherine Loomis and Michael LoMonico

The basics: Shakespeare was a playwright, poet, and actor who grew up in the market town of Stratford-upon-Avon, England, spent his professional life in London, and returned to Stratford a wealthy landowner. He was born in 1564—the same year Galileo was born and Michelangelo died. Shakespeare died in 1616, and Cervantes did too.

1. In the summer of 1564, an outbreak of bubonic plague killed one out of every seven people in Stratford, but the newborn William Shakespeare survived.

2. In Shakespeare's family, the women were made of sterner stuff: Shakespeare's mother, his sister Joan, his wife, Anne Hathaway, their daughters, and granddaughter all outlived their husbands. And Joan lived longer than all four of her brothers. The sad exception is Shakespeare's younger sister, Anne. She died when she was seven and Shakespeare was fifteen.

3. Shakespeare appears in public records up until 1585, when he was a 21-year-old father of three, and then again in 1592, when he turns up in London as a playwright. During those lost years, he may have been a schoolmaster or tutor, and one legend has him fleeing to London to escape prosecution for deer poaching. No one has any idea really, but maybe there is a theatrical possibility: An acting company called the Queen's Men was on tour in the summer of 1587, and, since one of their actors had been killed in a duel in Oxford, the town just down the road, the company arrived in Stratford minus an actor. At age 23, did Shakespeare leave his family and join them on tour?

4. Shakespeare wrote globally: in addition to all over Britain, his plays take you to Italy, Greece, Egypt, Turkey, Spain, France, Austria, Cyprus, Denmark and, in the case of *The Tempest*, pretty close to what was to become America.

5. Shakespeare died of a killer hangover. The Reverend John Ward, a Stratford vicar, wrote about Shakespeare's death on April 23, 1616, this way: "Shakespeare, [Michael] Drayton, and Ben Jonson had a merry meeting, and it seems drank too hard, for Shakespeare died of a fever there contracted."

6. On Shakespeare's gravestone in Stratford's Holy Trinity Church is a fierce curse on anyone who "moves my bones." In 2016, archaeologists used ground-penetrating radar to examine the grave, and . . . Shakespeare's skull is missing.

7. Frederick Douglass escaped slavery and as a free man became a celebrated orator, statesman, and leader of the American abolitionist movement—and he was a student and lover of Shakespeare. Visitors to Cedar Hill, his home in DC's Anacostia neighborhood, can see Douglass's volumes of Shakespeare's complete works still on his library shelves and a framed print of Othello and Desdemona on the parlor wall. In addition to studying and often referencing Shakespeare in his speeches, Douglass was an active member of his local Anacostia community theater group, the Uniontown Shakespeare Club.

8. Shakespeare is the most frequently produced playwright in the U.S. Despite this, *American Theatre* magazine has never crowned him America's "Most Produced Playwright," an honor bestowed annually based on data from nearly 400 theaters. He always wins by such a large margin—usually there are about five times more Shakespeare productions than plays by the second-place finisher—that the magazine decided to just set him aside so that other playwrights could have a chance to win.

9. While Nelson Mandela was incarcerated on South Africa's Robben Island, one of the other political prisoners retained a copy of Shakespeare's complete works, and secretly circulated it through the group. At his request, many of the other prisoners—including Mandela—signed their names next to their favorite passages.

> *Cowards die many times before their deaths;*
> *The valiant only taste of death but once.*
> *Of all the wonders that I yet have heard,*
> *It seems to me most strange that men should fear,*
> *Seeing that death, a necessary end,*
> *Will come when it will come.*

These lines from *Julius Caesar* were marked "N. R. Mandela, December 16, 1977." Nelson Mandela was released from prison in 1990.

10. The Folger Shakespeare Library is in Washington, DC, and houses the largest Shakespeare collection in the world, just a block from the U.S. Capitol. We are Shakespeare's home in America! We are abuzz with visitors and audience members from our own DC neighborhoods, from across the country and around the world: teachers and students, researchers and scholars, lovers of the performing arts, all kinds of learners, and the curious of all ages and stages. Find us online at folger.edu/teach—and do come visit our beautiful new spaces. Be a part of our lively and accessible exhibitions and programs, explore rare books and other artifacts, join a teaching workshop, and enjoy the magic of theatre, poetry, and music. We're waiting for you, your classes, and your families!

Ten Amazing Things You May Not Know About *Macbeth*

Catherine Loomis and Michael LoMonico

1. Math Facts: *Macbeth* is 5 acts, 28 scenes, and 17,121 words in total, and yet it is Shakespeare's shortest tragedy—at only 2,453 lines. The actor playing Macbeth has 681 lines. By way of comparison, the play *Hamlet* has 4,167 lines, and the actor playing Hamlet has more than 1,400 lines.

2. In 1603, King James of Scotland became King James I of England. He was a man very interested in witchcraft—he had even written a book about it (*Daemonologie*, 1597)—and Shakespeare was a very smart businessman. Probably in 1606, he wrote *Macbeth*, a play set in Scotland in which a trio of witches drive much of the action. It was performed for the public at The Globe in 1611, but it was first performed in 1606—at court, for King James himself.

3. Most scholars believe that what have come to be called "the Hecate scenes" in *Macbeth*—3.5 and 4.1—were added later to printed versions of *Macbeth*. Most agree that they were not written by Shakespeare at all but by Thomas Middleton, another playwright. Many stage productions of *Macbeth* leave these scenes out, and you should feel free to do this too.

4. In the theatre world, there is a superstition that the word *Macbeth* is cursed and that, except as part of a performance, it should never be spoken. And if it is spoken, it is thought terrible disasters will occur. No one really knows for sure where this belief comes from, but it is why—for hundreds of years now—many actors do not say "Macbeth" and, instead, call *Macbeth* "the Scottish play." Part of the superstition includes how to break the curse: If you do say "Macbeth," you must run outside of the theater, spin around three times, and spit over your shoulder.

5. *Macbeth* has caused rioting in the streets! In 1849, two different productions of *Macbeth*—one American and one British—were onstage in New York City at the same time. The American actor playing Macbeth, Edwin Forrest, and the English actor playing Macbeth, William Macready, were rivals, and they each had dedicated fans who were also rivals. During the run of both plays, a riot broke out among their fans in Astor Place, a street near the theatres. More than 20 people died, and more than 100 were injured, in what we now call the Astor Place Riot.

6. *Macbeth* was President Abraham Lincoln's favorite Shakespeare play. As a young lawyer, he carried a copy of the play in his back pocket, and as president, he was an ardent reader of the plays, but *Macbeth* was his favorite. In an August 1863 letter to an American actor, he wrote, "Some of Shakespeare's plays I have never read; while others I have gone over perhaps as frequently as any unprofessional reader. Among the latter are Lear, Richard Third, Henry Eighth, Hamlet, and especially Macbeth. I think nothing equals Macbeth. It is wonderful."

7. Five days before he was assassinated, Lincoln read long passages from *Macbeth* to a group of people who were traveling with him from Richmond, Virginia, to Washington, DC. He was fascinated by the verses after Duncan's assassination and read them aloud over and over—he focused on Macbeth's ultimate envy that King Duncan in his grave was freed from what Lincoln called the "torments of the mind" that tortured Macbeth, the murderer.

8. John Wilkes Booth, the actor who assassinated President Lincoln at Ford's Theatre in Washington, DC, appeared in 39 different productions of *Macbeth*.

9. In 1936, Orson Welles, with the support of the Negro Theatre Unit of the Federal Theatre Project, directed in Boston and in Harlem an all-Black production of *Macbeth*, often referred to as the *Voodoo Macbeth*. Welles moved the setting from Scotland to a fictional Caribbean island, the cast numbered 150 people, and only four were professional actors. The Federal Theatre Project Negro Unit was a subsidiary of the Works Progress Administration and was specifically designed to employ and train African Americans in theatrical production, supporting creativity and creating jobs at the same time.

10. The Folger Shakespeare Library brings you *Macbeth* in many ways. The Folger has 542 copies of *Macbeth* in 39 different languages from Afrikaans to Xhosa, and these include Arabic, Hebrew, Ukrainian, and Esperanto. On our Elizabethan stage, we have produced *Macbeth* five times. Of continuing popularity is the 2008 magic-filled production co-directed by Aaron Posner and Teller, the celebrated magician (and Shakespeare fan). The Folger has also staged Davenant's *Macbeth*—a rarely performed version of the play rewritten in 1664 by William Davenant. The result of an extraordinary collaboration between actors and scholars, it played to sold-out houses. At our festivals for elementary and secondary school students, we are treated to endless—and endlessly wonderful—scenes from *Macbeth*. Witches are always a frequent favorite! We teach thousands of middle and high school teachers how to teach *Macbeth*. The Folger serves lovers of *Macbeth* from around the U.S. and the world. Since 1992 and as of this writing, the Folger Shakespeare paperback edition of *Macbeth* has sold 3.3 million copies. Online, free Folger Shakespeare copies of *Macbeth*—plus additional information about the play—have been requested more than 2 million times. Find us online (folger.edu) and come visit us! We'll have you onstage with lines from *Macbeth* too!

What Happens in This Play Anyway?

A Plot Summary of *Macbeth*

Macbeth, set primarily in Scotland, mixes witchcraft, prophecy, and murder. Three "Weïrd Sisters" appear to Macbeth and his comrade Banquo after a battle and prophesy that Macbeth will be king and that the descendants of Banquo will also reign. When Macbeth arrives at his castle, he and Lady Macbeth plot to assassinate King Duncan, soon to be their guest, so that Macbeth can become king.

After Macbeth murders Duncan, the king's two sons flee, and Macbeth is crowned. Fearing that Banquo's descendants will, according to the Weïrd Sisters' predictions, take over the kingdom, Macbeth has Banquo killed. At a royal banquet that evening, Macbeth sees Banquo's ghost appear covered in blood. Macbeth determines to consult the Weïrd Sisters again. They comfort him with ambiguous promises.

Another nobleman, Macduff, rides to England to join Duncan's older son, Malcolm. Macbeth has Macduff's wife and children murdered. Malcolm and Macduff lead an army against Macbeth, as Lady Macbeth goes mad and commits suicide.

Macbeth confronts Malcolm's army, trusting in the Weïrd Sisters' comforting promises. He learns that the promises are tricks, but continues to fight. Macduff kills Macbeth and Malcolm becomes Scotland's king.

What Happens in This Play Anyway?

A PLAY MAP OF *MACBETH*

Mya Gosling and Peggy O'Brien

What happens in **MACBETH?**

Art by Mya Lixian Gosling
of goodticklebrain.com
Concept by Peggy O'Brien

Duncan is King of Scotland!

But Scottish nobleman **Macbeth** and his friend **Banquo** meet **three witches** who tell them:

Macbeth's wife says this means they should:

Who's Who in Scotland

DUNCAN
King of Scotland.

LADY MACBETH   married   **MACBETH** Thane of Glamis.   friends   **BANQUO**

BLOODY GHOST
Whose is it?

MALCOLM & DONALBAIN
Heirs to the throne.

THE THREE WITCHES
What do they predict? Who listens to them, and why?

FLEANCE

MURDERERS
Who do they work for? Who do they kill?

MACDUFF
Thane of Fife. Whose side is he on?   married   **LADY MACDUFF**

ROSS, LENNOX, ANGUS, CAITHNESS, & MENTEITH
Assorted Thanes. Whose side are **they** on?

THE PORTER
Is he the inventor of the knock-knock joke?

Questions to Ask

Should you believe a trio of witches?

Who's the boss here? Mac or Lady Mac?

Should you get to keep what you take by force?

Can a forest move?!?

Is there a doctor in the house?

Macbeth and the Pleasure of Puzzling Uncertainty

Ayanna Thompson

I have always loved *Macbeth*, and I continue to love it with each new encounter. For many, *Macbeth* serves as a type of gateway drug into a full-fledged Shakespeare addiction. I first read the play when I was a witch-obsessed eight-year-old girl. When my mother informed me there were witches who cast spells in *Macbeth*, I snuck into my closet with a flashlight and a copy of the play, hoping to learn something about how to harness otherworldly powers. While I managed to scare myself when I read the witches' incantations, I didn't really understand anything else in the play. I needed a guide into the text to reveal just how scared I should have been in that dark closet. *Macbeth* is eerie, spooky, dangerous, and terrifying when someone guides you through it thoroughly. You, amazing teacher, can be that guide for your students.

Unlike the plots of some of Shakespeare's plays, the plot of *Macbeth* is fairly straightforward. Aided by the traitorous Scottish thane Macdonald, Norway invades Scotland. Macbeth and Banquo, two Scottish thanes, manage to defeat Macdonald and drive out the Norwegians. To reward Macbeth for cutting off the invading army and for cutting an enemy combatant in half and decapitating him ("unseamed him from the nave to th' chops, / And fixed his head upon our battlements" [1.2.24–25]), the Scottish king, Duncan, gives Macdonald's title, Thane of Cawdor, to Macbeth.

Before Macbeth can learn this officially, he is told that he shall be the Thane of Cawdor and the "king hereafter" by three mysterious women whom he and Banquo encounter on the heath (1.3.53). Banquo asks about his own fate and is told that he will father a line of kings, "though thou be none" (1.3.70). Once Macbeth learns that he is indeed the Thane of Cawdor from the king's official messengers, he reveals in a soliloquy that he is already thinking about killing the king so that the prophecy will come true. He writes a letter to his wife about the prophecy, and she reacts in a similar fashion—she, too, believes that they must make the prophecy come true by killing the king.

Fortunately for the Macbeths, King Duncan decides to spend that night at their castle, and together they plot to kill him that evening. They get Duncan's guards so drunk that they pass out, and then Macbeth stabs Duncan in his sleep and Lady Macbeth smears the blood on the guards to frame them for the murder. When the murder is discovered in the morning, Duncan's two sons, Malcolm and Donalbain, flee to England and Ireland to protect themselves ("The near in blood, / The nearer bloody" [2.3.165–66]).

Despite the fact that Macbeth is made king, and despite the fact that no one suspects his guilt in Duncan's murder, Macbeth is not content because the prophecy declared that Banquo's heirs will rule as well. Macbeth decides that he is not safe on the throne while Banquo's son is alive ("To be thus is nothing, / But to be safely thus" [3.1.52–53]), so he orders the murders of Banquo and his son, Fleance. The murderers manage to kill Banquo but not Fleance, and Macbeth's paranoia increases ("I had else been perfect" [3.4.23]). He is even haunted by the ghost of Banquo at a banquet he hosts at his castle. Lady Macbeth has to cover for him, making excuses to the guests that Macbeth is often afflicted in this manner ("My lord is often thus / And hath been from his youth" [3.4.64–65]).

Act 4 opens with the famous cauldron scene, and the witches cooking a deadly brew. Macbeth decides that he has to visit them again to get greater clarity about their prophecy, and he charges them to "answer me / To what I ask you" (4.1.63–64). Out of the cauldron come three different apparitions: the first is "an armed head" that tells Macbeth to "Beware Macduff" (4.1.81); the second is a "bloody child" that tells Macbeth that he cannot be harmed by any "of woman born" (4.1.91); and the third is a "child crowned with a tree in his hand" who declares that Macbeth is safe until the Birnam Wood moves to Dunsinane Hill. Deciding that he must kill the entire Macduff family to be safe, Macbeth is even more resolute, declaring that he will never delay in action again ("From this moment / The very firstlings of my heart shall be / The firstlings of my hand" [4.1.166–68]). The next scene shows Ross warning Macduff's wife and son to flee, but they resist leaving without Macduff and then they are murdered. Meanwhile, Macduff has gone to England to try to persuade Malcolm, Duncan's son, to return to Scotland to contest Macbeth's reign. In one of the more bizarre scenes in the play, Malcolm tests Macduff's loyalty by lying about his craven habits and desires. When Macduff passes Malcolm's test ("Fit to govern? / No, not to live.—O nation miserable" [4.3.120–21]), Malcolm reveals that he has an English army ready to help them overthrow Macbeth. Macduff's celebration is cut short, however, when he learns that his entire family has been killed by Macbeth.

The last act—Act 5—opens with Lady Macbeth sleepwalking, reenacting the murder of Duncan in action and words. Despite the fact that her lady-in-waiting has called a doctor to help alleviate her affliction, the doctor says, "More needs she the divine than the physician" (5.1.78). Malcolm, Macduff, and the English army descend upon Birnam Wood in Scotland, and they cut down branches from the trees to conceal the size of the army. Lady Macbeth kills herself as the English army advances upon Dunsinane. Outnumbered and seeing that the invading army holds branches from the Birnam Wood, Macbeth faces the fight with resolution because he remembers the other prophecy ("I bear a charmèd life, which must not yield / To one of woman born" [5.8.15–16]). Macduff, however, reveals that he was born via a cesarian section ("Macduff was from his mother's womb / Untimely ripped" [5.8.19–20]). Macduff kills Macbeth and returns to the stage with Macbeth's decapitated head. Malcolm takes the throne at the end of the play.

I have given you this plot summary here—and there is another one elsewhere in this book—because the plot is the least interesting thing about the text/play of *Macbeth*. Your students should have the plot summary so they don't get lost, unable to see the forest for the trees. While the plot of Shakespeare's play is largely taken from Raphael Holinshed's *Chronicles of England, Scotland, and Ireland* (1577 and 1587)—a source Shakespeare turned to for the plots of several of his plays—the way Shakespeare reimagines the plot with a tighter time frame; the way he includes unexplained repetitious words and phrases; and the way he creates an over-abiding question about who or what is propelling the events—people, fate, or unseen metaphysical entities—are the elements that make *Macbeth* a gripping play that people want to return to throughout their lives.

You might have heard *Macbeth* referred to as "the Scottish play" by actors, directors, and theater practitioners. The play is thought to be cursed, and there are lots of anecdotes about unlucky occurrences when staging this show: actors dying, theaters burning, props gone missing, etc. To ward off the supposed curse, the title of the play is not uttered within the walls of a theater, and many carry this belief beyond the bounds of the theater itself, only ever referring to *Macbeth* as "the Scottish play." The idea that the play is cursed should come as no surprise, however, because the play is about liminal states—thresholds between two different worlds or states of being, or the point below conscious awareness in which something cannot be fully or clearly experienced or felt.

For instance, who or what are the witches? We know that Shakespeare wrote *Macbeth* in 1606 in an attempt to appeal to the new king of England, King James I, who assumed that crown in 1603. James had already been the king of Scotland, and as such he wrote a book in 1597 denouncing witches called *Daemonologie*. In it, James wrote, "The fearfull abounding at this time in this countrie, of these detestable slaves of the Devill, the Witches or enchaunters, hath moved me (beloved reader) to dispatch in post, this following treatise of mine . . ." Clearly, Shakespeare was tapping into a topic that was near and dear to the new king's heart, a play that was set in the country of the king's birth, a play that traced the king's family's bloodline as descendants of Banquo, and a play that presented witches as nefarious forces of evil.

While in the *dramatis personae*, the list of characters, the women on the heath are listed as "First Witch," "Second Witch," and "Third Witch," they refer to themselves as "sisters" (1.3.33), Macbeth calls them "hags" (4.1.48), and Banquo states, "You should be women, / And yet your beards forbid me to interpret / That you are so" (1.3.47–49). The play forces us to ask if they are older female siblings, intersex, bearded women, or demonic witches. There is also a textual dispute. While most modern editions refer to the sisters as "weïrd," a word that stems from the Old English word *wyrd*, meaning fate, the first printing of *Macbeth* (in the 1623 First Folio) refers to them as "weyward" and "weyard," meaning weird, fated, fateful, perverse, intractable, willful, erratic, unlicensed, fugitive, troublesome, and wayward. The very essence of the women on the heath, thus, is rendered questionable and potentially unknowable.

If we understand the three sisters to be the embodiment or personification of fate, then their words can be interpreted as being prophetic—their words reveal what fate has already determined will occur. Macbeth and Lady Macbeth sometimes speak as if they understand the "weïrd sisters" as operating in this fashion, as entities that speak what fate has preordained. For instance, when Macbeth explains to Lady Macbeth what was said on the heath, he writes, "This have I thought good to deliver to thee, my dearest partner in greatness, that thou might'st not lose the dues of rejoicing by being ignorant of what greatness is promised thee" (1.5.10–13). Macbeth wants his wife to know that the "weïrd sisters" have revealed what has been "promised" to her, that Lady Macbeth will be queen. And Lady Macbeth responds by clearly indicating that she understands the sisters to be voicing "fate," what will occur in the future (1.5.32)

Yet, the Macbeths also speak and act as if they understand the "weïrd sisters" in an entirely different manner—as entities that give voice to the Macbeths' innermost, secret desires. For instance, the "weïrd sisters" and Macbeth seem to speak the same language. The women begin the play chanting together, "Fair is foul, and foul is fair," (1.1.12), and Macbeth's first line in the play is, "So foul and fair a day I have not seen" (1.3.39). Macbeth could not have heard the sisters' words earlier in the play; nonetheless, he seems to echo them. More than just the linguistic echoes, though, the sisters' words seem to tap into Macbeth's true desires. Macbeth's first reaction upon being greeted with his new title is to imagine killing the king: "why do I yield to that suggestion / Whose horrid image doth unfix my hair" (1.3.147–48). Clearly Macbeth is ambitious, and the women on the heath unleash that unbridled ambition. Can we understand the "weïrd sisters" then as externalized representations of Macbeth's psyche? Likewise, Lady Macbeth's first reaction is to wonder if Macbeth's nature is "too full o'th' milk of human kindness / To catch the nearest way" to achieve the crown (1.5.16–17). Desiring the crown above all else, Lady Macbeth plans to spur Macbeth to action so that nothing will stand in the way of achieving "the golden round, / Which fate and metaphysical aid" have made possible (1.5.31–32).

In this context, *metaphysical* means supernatural, and the play cleverly allows the reader, audience, and your students to ponder if the "weïrd sisters" are actually agents of the devil. When Macbeth is officially given the title Thane of Cawdor by the king's emissaries, Banquo asks, "What, can the devil speak true?" (1.3.113). Banquo's question invites us all to wonder if the "weïrd sisters" are the devil's agents on earth. Thus, the play dances around the distinctions and differences between understanding the sisters as the voice of fate, the embodiment of desire, and the agents of the demonic. In the scenes in which the "weïrd sisters" operate alone, after all, they are involved in some creepy scheming and cooking. There is the scene in which they plot revenge upon a sailor's wife, whose sole crime is her refusal to share her chestnuts, and one sister produces the thumb of a ship's pilot, the man who steers the ship, ensuring that the woman's husband will be "tempest-tossed" and lost at sea (1.3.26). Later in the play, in the famous cauldron scene ("Double, double toil and trouble" [4.1.10]), the "weïrd sisters" collectively cook a stew of toads, snakes, newts, frogs, bats, dogs, adders, worms, lizards, dragons, wolves, sharks, and goats. Yet mixed into the animal stew are also the "Liver of blaspheming Jew" (4.1.26), the "Nose of Turk" (29), the "Tartar's lips" (29), and the finger of an aborted baby ("Ditch-delivered by a drab" [31]). A dramatic anti-feast, the ingredients in the cauldron not only explore the limits of what are considered edible animals but also the limits of the "normal" racialized body. Foreign and racialized bodies, as well as the unborn, unbaptized dead, are included in this mix, marking them as outside the bounds of Christianity. It is important not to gloss over these references because race is clearly being explored as one of the elements that demarks a liminal space. The suggestion of the sisters' demonic status is tied to these racialized bodies to which the "weïrd sisters" have both access and proximity. Are they too close? the play asks.

If *Macbeth* invites questions about who/what the witches are, it also invites questions about who/what the Macbeths are. The old joke is that the Macbeths are the happiest married couple in Shakespeare's canon. After all, there are not a lot of intact marriages in Shakespeare's plays; instead, there are lots of single parents who appear to be widowed, like King Lear. The marriages that are represented in Shakespeare's plays do not look particularly amicable (think of Juliet's parents in *Romeo and Juliet*, for instance), and while Shakespeare's comedies typically end in marriages, those marital relationships are not depicted—they will develop in the future that occurs after the play itself (think, for example, of *Much Ado About Nothing* or *A Midsummer Night's Dream* or *Twelfth Night*). Unlike these other marriages, the Macbeths are oddly, often disturbingly, in tune. When Macbeth is promoted, for instance, he writes to his wife immediately and calls her his "dearest partner of greatness" (1.5.11). Likewise, both Macbeth and Lady Macbeth react in the exact same way to the witches' prophecies—they both imagine that murder is the fastest way to achieve their desired ends. The Macbeths are one of the earliest literary examples of a power couple; that is, a relationship in which both parties are equally ambitious and power hungry. The Macbeths match each other not only in their desires for power but also in the immoral, yet expedient, methods they are willing to deploy to achieve that power.

At first Lady Macbeth seems to guide Macbeth toward action, and she frames action in explicitly gendered terms, saying, "When you durst do it, then you were a man" (1.7.56). Likewise, during the banquet when Macbeth sees the ghost of Banquo, Lady Macbeth is there asking, "Are you a man?" (3.4.70). She then chides him for thinking he has seen a ghost because in her estimation ghosts are only believed in "A woman's story at a winter's fire, / Authorized by her grandam" (3.4.78–79), and then she claims that Macbeth is "unmanned in folly" (3.4.88). Macbeth seems to agree with Lady Macbeth's assessment, declaring that if he continues in such behavior he should be called "The baby of a girl" (3.4.128) and that he is resolved to be a "man again" (3.4.131). He even says that Lady Macbeth should "Bring forth men-children only" (1.7.83).

While Lady Macbeth worries that Macbeth is "too full o'th' milk of human kindness" to kill the king, she also worries that she needs to be transformed to help enact such violence. When she learns that Duncan will visit their castle, Lady Macbeth calls upon "spirits" to "unsex me here / And fill me from the crown to the toe top-full / Of direst cruelty" (1.5.48–50). She then asks these spirits to "Make thick my blood" and to "take my milk for gall" (1.5.50, 55). While scholars have traditionally read these lines as being in accord with Early Modern medical theories about unhealthy blood conditions, feminist scholars have noted that Lady Macbeth seems to be asking for her biological femininity to cease—that she desires to lose her ability to menstruate and lactate. Either way, she is requesting a physical change that she assumes will enable her to act like the "man" she wants her husband to be.

The question is, does she? Why does Lady Macbeth's role dwindle as the play progresses? It is fair to ask how much Macbeth needs his "partner" in "greatness" once Duncan is actually murdered. Why is she less and less of an interlocutor with Macbeth as the plot advances? Do the "weïrd sisters" replace Lady Macbeth as Macbeth's "partner" once he has killed for the first time? Has Macbeth become a "man," and is that an essence/identity that has no need for a partner? Macbeth's reaction to Lady Macbeth's death allows for a wide range of interpretive readings. By the time that Lady Macbeth dies, Macbeth is clearly in a nihilistic mood, noting that he cannot be scared by anything because he has "supped full with horrors" (5.5.15). He then declares that life itself has no meaning: "It is a tale / Told by an idiot, full of sound and fury / Signifying nothing" (5.5.29–31). But Macbeth's immediate reaction to learning that Lady Macbeth is dead is, "She should have died hereafter" (5.5.20). Macbeth's "should" can be interpreted as "ought to," meaning, Lady Macbeth ought to have lived longer. Yet, his "should" can also be interpreted as "would," meaning, Lady Macbeth would have died at some point. The text allows for both contradictory interpretations to exist simultaneously. There is no way to fix just one of the meanings. There is no way to pin certainty onto this text. *Macbeth* as a play sits in liminal spaces.

Ambiguity—the sense that words and phrases can contain multiple, potentially conflicting, meanings—resonates throughout *Macbeth*. And a particular type of ambiguity known as equivocation—the use of ambiguous language to mislead, conceal, or avoid a clear meaning—is central to *Macbeth*'s plot, design, and structure. Think, for example, about the "weïrd" sisters' prophecies to Macbeth—that he cannot be harmed by a man born from a woman, and that he is safe until the woods move up a hill. While Macbeth assumes that the sisters are telling him that his power and position are secure, they are prevaricating, speaking in an evasive way that is intended to mislead and misdirect.

The short, comic scene with the porter after Macbeth has killed Duncan (2.3) is often used to explore the Early Modern understanding of equivocation. The house is quiet and everyone is asleep after a night of heavy drinking (and quiet murder), and Macduff is knocking to be admitted to Macbeth's castle. Slowly walking to open the door, the porter jokes about being the "porter of hell gate" (2.3.2). He alludes to medieval religious plays in which hell was figured as a castle, and he jokes about the devilish inhabitants of this castle. He then says, "Faith, here's an equivocator that could swear in both the scales against either scale" (2.3.8–10). While this may not resonate clearly in the 21st century, Shakespeare's audience would have heard a very specific topical reference to events that occurred just the year before.

Disappointed that the ascension of King James to England's throne in 1603 did not usher in an era of greater religious tolerance, a group of English Catholics led by Robert Catesby planned to blow up the House of Lords when the king would conduct the State Opening of Parliament on November 5, 1605. The night before the attempted assassination, the plot was discovered and one of the conspirators, Guy Fawkes, was found guarding 36 barrels of gunpowder in the cellars of the Houses of Parliament. The event has come to be known as the Gunpowder Plot, and November 5 is still celebrated as Guy Fawkes Day in the United Kingdom. One of the priests associated with the conspirators, Father Garnet, had written a treatise on equivocation, arguing that an English Catholic could be morally justified when lying to state officials if he held the truth in his heart for God. In other words, Father Garnet was arguing that lying was not a sin. At his execution for treason on May 3, 1606, it was argued that Father Garnet "could not equivocate to heaven" (2.3.11).

Thus, Shakespeare's audience at *Macbeth* in 1606 would have linked the Macbeths and their murder of King Duncan to the recent attempt to kill King James by the Catholic conspirators who were exploring the moral and religious implications of equivocation. While the porter scene in *Macbeth* renders the reference explicit, the entire play seems to swirl around ambiguity, prevarication, equivocation, and uncertainty. The play forced his audience—and it also forces your students—to question how we know what we know, why we believe what we believe, why we desire what we desire, and what forces (both internal desires and external pressures) impact our actions.

Nonetheless, *Macbeth* is far from a didactic or pedantic play. One does not leave reading or seeing *Macbeth* with a sense of certainty and security. That is part of what is so eerie, spooky, dangerous, and terrifying about "the Scottish play." For instance, while repetition can provide a sense of certainty and is often used as part of mnemonic devices, its use in *Macbeth* seems to undermine and destabilize meaning. What exactly is *fair* and *foul* in this world? Are the "weïrd sisters" fair or foul? Are the Macbeths fair or foul? Is Macduff fair or foul? Likewise, the text is deliciously unscripted in some ways. *Macbeth* regularly resists one's desire for clarity and fixity. Here's one example: How old are Duncan's sons, Malcolm and Donalbain? They flee to England and Ireland when their father is murdered, and Malcolm becomes king at the end of the play, but the play is not specific about their ages. Furthermore, the implications of the play's resolution read differently if Malcolm is a teenager rather than an adult. After all, Malcolm reveals to Macduff that he is a virgin ("I am yet / Unknown to woman" [4.3.144–45]). So how old is he? And if Malcolm is young (say, 13 years old), will he govern effectively? Will he be controlled by others? Is he a "man"? What are the implications for the future of Scotland? If Malcolm is indeed older, why does he act so childishly? And what are the implications for his reign? Is Malcolm fair or foul?

As a student studying *Macbeth*, one is allowed to explore all the nuances of these open-ended areas (does Lady Macbeth have children?). In performance, however, actors and directors have to make decisions and make some ambiguities fixed. Performance trends for *Macbeth* have varied considerably in the more than 400 years since its first performance. For example, the porter's scene (2.3), which I address above, was cut from performances for over 200 years starting in the Restoration. The scene was not performed after Shakespeare's lifetime until 1868, when the famous American actor Edwin Booth decided that he liked its inclusion. It took time for the scene's inclusion to be fully embraced in performances, and it was not until the 20th century that the porter's scene was viewed as integral to *Macbeth*, as a scene that could not be cut without altering the meaning of the play. Similarly, the witches were played as part of the comic relief of *Macbeth*, with their roles being performed by a couple of men in comic drag, for several hundred years. In addition, since William Davenant's Restoration adaptation of *Macbeth* several songs were added, making the witches' scenes musical numbers. It was not until the late 19th century that the theatrical "innovator" Henry Irving stripped out the songs, had the "weïrd sisters" played by women, and divested their performances of any humor. By the late 20th century theaters were experimenting with eliminating the witches almost entirely, arguing that their famous scenes were not quite Shakespearean enough because portions of them were written by another Early Modern playwright, Thomas Middleton. When the Oregon Shakespeare Festival attempted this in 2002—theirs was a purely Shakespearean production stripped of anything written by anyone else—audience members revolted. This was not the *Macbeth* they wanted, expected, or desired. Nonetheless, this revealed another way in which theater practitioners feel the need to create certainty, even when *Macbeth* as a text resists it.

In the mid to late 20th century, it became fashionable to stage *Macbeth* with Black casts. Some of these productions were highly successful, like the 1936 so-called "Voodoo Macbeth" directed by Orson Welles at the Lafayette Theatre in Harlem (the production was part of the Federal Theatre Project). Transporting Shakespeare's medieval Scotland to 19th-century Haiti during the reign of the slave-turned-emperor Henri Christophe, the production employed over 150 Black actors and a drumming and dancing troupe from Sierra Leone. It is guessed that over 150,000 people saw this production during its New York run alone, and it has influenced the way *Macbeth* has been envisioned as a performance piece for decades. Countless productions have subsequently cast Black actors as the "weïrd sisters," and dozens have tried to re-create the "Voodoo" setting entirely. While many of these productions have been lauded for their innovative stagings, it is worth interrogating the ways that race becomes a metaphor or sign for the exotic, the dangerous, and the demonic in these productions. Does an assumption about the exotic nature of Black cultures render *Macbeth* more understandable?

It is worth remembering, though, that the text of *Macbeth* resists the certainty and fixity that performances often strive to create. In fact, the ending of the play is one of the least hinged in Shakespeare's canon. With Macbeth killed, Malcolm takes the throne, restoring Duncan's dynastic line to power. Attempting to reassure his allies, Malcolm promises a new political establishment, converting "thanes and kinsmen" to "earls" (5.8.74, 76). And then he says, "What's more to do, / Which would be planted newly with the time," such as bringing back "exiled friends abroad," will occur "in measure, time, and place" (5.8.77–78, 79, 86). It is worth lingering on the promise of this new day and new regime, however.

First, what does it mean that the Scottish system of feudal lords (thanes) has to be changed to an English system (earls)? Why does this new age (Macduff declares that "The time is free" [5.8.66]) require an English system? Second, how new is this new leadership? How different will it be? Malcolm employs the metaphor of planting to describe the newness of his regime, but Duncan said something very similar at the beginning of the play when he promoted Macbeth to be Thane of Cawdor: "I have begun to plant thee and will labor / To make thee full of growing" (1.4.32–33). Are we meant to hear this verbal echo four acts later? How similar are father and son in their leadership styles and strategies, and what are the implications for either a continuation or a divergence?

More disturbingly, what does it mean to labor to "do" anything? Malcolm attempts to calm fears by saying that he will "do" what needs to be done "in measure, time, and place," but the play has called into question the very nature of action. After all, at the beginning of the play we hear the "weïrd sisters" chant together, "I'll do, I'll do, and I'll do," when they plot their revenge against the sailor's wife (1.3.11). Shortly thereafter, Macbeth says, "If it were done when 'tis done, then 'twere well / It were done quickly" (1.7.1–2). And later in the play, the sleepwalking and talking Lady Macbeth warns, "What's done, cannot be undone" (5.1.71). What is it to do? What does it mean to take action? Many of the characters believe that they are asserting themselves when they take action, but the play undermines any sense that agency is achieved through action and that action is ever really beneficial or good. Macbeth is a man of action, and yet toward what end? Lady Macbeth desires a "man" of action, and yet toward what end? What is self-assertion good for? What is ambition good for? What is doing good for?

Macbeth forces your students and you—along with any reader or audience member—to ponder these questions over and over again. Malcolm's ascension to the throne at the end of the play does not make the questions abate. As one of my own students astutely surmised, *Macbeth* depicts characters on the ladder of success only to reveal that the ladder leads nowhere. Who or what controls our desires? Is repetition inevitable? Is action desirable? Is newness achievable? Can time be freed? The Scottish play forces these questions upon us, and the only certainty I end with is a desire to return to *Macbeth* again and again. Repetition may not deliver certainty or clarity in *Macbeth*, but returning to *Macbeth* does deliver the pleasure of puzzling uncertainty.

PART THREE

Macbeth in *Your* Classroom With *Your* Students

The Folger Method:
You Will Never Teach Literature
the Same Way Again

Corinne Viglietta and Peggy O'Brien

Imagine a classroom where every student is so immersed in reading that they don't want to stop. A place that is buzzing with the energy of student-driven learning. Where students shout, whisper, and play with lines from Shakespeare and other authors. Where small groups discuss, with textual evidence and passion, which parts of a text are the most compelling and how to perform them effectively. Where all students bring their identities and customs, their whole selves, to fresh performances of juicy scenes. Where every student experiences firsthand that literary language is *their* language, demanding to be interpreted and reinterpreted, questioned, and yes, even resisted sometimes. Where students are doing the lion's share of the work, and the teacher, who has thoughtfully set up this zone of discovery, is observing from the side. Where joy and rigor work hand in hand. Where everyone is engaged in something that feels important and adventurous. Where every student realizes they can do hard things on their own.

This is a real place. This is *your* classroom as you try the lessons in this book. Yes, *you*.

Will it be perfect all the time? Heck no. Will it be messy, especially at first? Almost certainly. Will you have to take risks? Yes.

Does this way of teaching really work? You bet.

Don't take our word for it, though. For four decades, the Folger has been working with teachers on what has become known as the Folger Method, and here's a small sample of what teachers—mostly middle and high school teachers—have had to say:

- *"With the Folger Method, my students are reading more deeply than they ever have before. They are breaking down language and really understanding it."*

- *"I was unsure of myself and my ability to tackle Shakespeare, but this has been empowering."*

- *"Students complain when it's time to leave. I have gleefully stepped back so they can create scenes, shout words and lines, and cut speeches. They volunteer to read aloud even when reading aloud is hard for them. We dive in and focus on the words. It's working."*

37

- *"Over the course of this Folger unit, I've seen amazing things in my special education students. This one student has had an entire transformation—like, fellow teachers are asking me what happened. Before, he always had great pronunciation and sounded fluent, but he could never really understand what it was he was saying. And then all of a sudden in the middle of this play, something clicked. I think it's because he has all these strategies for understanding the words on the page now."*

- *"The Folger Method didn't just transform how I teach Shakespeare—it's changed how I teach everything."*

Great, but what *is* the Folger Method, exactly?

It is a transformative way of approaching complex texts. (And not just Shakespeare, but any complex text.) Consisting of both principles and practices, it provides a framework for everything that goes into great teaching: designing, planning, assessing, reflecting, revising, communicating, guiding, growing, listening, laughing, learning—all of it.

Behind it all is a precise, tried-and-true philosophy that we've broken down into 8 parts.

8 Foundational Principles

The more you practice this way of teaching, the more you'll see these **8 foundational principles** in action, and the clearer it all becomes. Watching your students move through the lessons in this book will give you (and them) a profound, almost visceral, understanding of these principles. They will become part of the fabric of your classroom. Teaching this way—even if it's completely new to you—will feel intuitive in no time.

1. Shakespeare's language is not a barrier but a portal. The language is what enables students to discover amazing things in the texts, the world, and themselves.

2. All students and teachers deserve the real thing—whether it's Shakespeare's original language, primary source materials, new information that expands our understanding of history, or honest conversations about tough issues that the plays present.

3. Give up Shakespeare worship. If your Shakespeare lives on a pedestal, take him down and move him to a space where he can talk to everyday people and great writers like Toni Morrison and Julia Alvarez, Frederick Douglass and Joy Harjo, F. Scott Fitzgerald and Azar Nafisi, Amy Tan and George Moses Horton, Jane Austen and Pablo Neruda, James Baldwin and Homer.

4. Throw out themes, tidy explanations, and the idea of a single right interpretation. Resist the urge to wrap up a text with a neat bow, or, as Billy Collins puts it, to tie it to a chair and "torture a confession out of it." With ambiguity comes possibility. Alongside your students, embrace the questions. How liberating!

5. The teacher is not the explainer but rather the architect. Set up the interactions through which your students and Shakespeare discover each other. This might be hard to hear (it was for Corinne at first!), but the helpful teacher is not the one who explains what the text means or who "translates" Shakespeare's words for students. The truly helpful teacher is the one who crafts opportunities for students to be successful at figuring things out for themselves. It's about getting out of the way so students can do things on their own.

6. Set students on fire with excitement about literature. When reading brings mysteries, delights, and surprises, students are motivated to read closely and cite evidence. And they gain confidence in their ability to tackle the next challenge.

7. Amplify the voice of every single student. Shakespeare has something to say to everybody, and everybody has something to say back to Shakespeare. Student voices, both literal and figurative, create the most vibrant and inclusive learning communities. The future of the humanities—and our world—depends on the insights and contributions of *all* students.

As tempting as it may be to impose our own interpretation of the text on students, or to ask students to imitate the brilliant arguments of seasoned scholars, we beg you to resist that urge. Students need to dive into a play and shape and reshape their own interpretations in order to become independent thinkers. Teaching literature is about the sparks that fly when readers of an infinite variety of perspectives engage directly and personally with the text.

8. The Folger Method is a radical engine for equity. Every student can learn this way, and every teacher can teach this way. The goal is to help all students read closely, interrogate actively, and make meaning from texts.

Now let's put these ideas into practice.

The Arc of Learning

The first step to applying these principles in class is understanding the journey, what we call **the arc of learning**, that your students will experience.

The activities in this book are not isolated, interchangeable exercises. They are a complete set of practices that work together to bring the 8 principles to life. Sequencing, scaffolding, pacing, differentiating—it's all here.

And because each of your students is unique, each journey will be unique too. If you teach AP or IB classes, this book will help each of your students navigate their own path and reach rigorous course outcomes, starting right where scholars, editors, directors, and actors start—with the words. If you teach students who have the ability and desire to dive deep—and we mean *deep*, luxuriating in the mysteries and puzzles of complex literature—the Folger Method will enable them to do just that. Alongside these students you probably also have students who need some extra support before diving deep, and these lessons are just as much for them (more on differentiation later). By its very design, this way of teaching is flexible and roomy enough to challenge and support every single learner. Use this book to meet *all* students where they are, give them space to stretch, and be amazed at what they do.

What happens over the course of a Folger unit often astonishes teachers, administrators, families, and students themselves. Remember that spirited classroom from the first paragraph? Pass by and hear students shouting lines from Macbeth's soliloquies in a cacophony. (*What in the world?*) Poke your head in and watch them mark up their scripts with notes on which words ought to be stressed or cut out entirely, which tone to use when. (*Hmmm . . . this is interesting.*) Walk into the classroom, take a seat, and observe different student performances of the same scene—and a robust whole-class discussion about the textual evidence and knowledge that led to each group's interpretive decisions. Listen to students question and teach one another. (*Whoa! Every single student just totally owned Shakespeare.*)

What at the start might appear simply as a "fun" way to meet Shakespeare's words reveals itself to be a wild and daring, deep and demanding, meaty and memorable learning experience. Behind this magic is a very deliberate design.

From day one, your students will engage directly with the language of the text(s). That's right: There's no "I do, we do, you do" teacher modeling here. Students are always doing, doing, doing. Beginning with single words and lines, your students will learn to read closely and critically and eventually tackle longer pieces of text such as speeches, scenes, text sets, and whole texts. (Real talk: Yes, scaffolding learning by increasing the length and complexity of the language means doing some prep work. It's part of being the architect. Good news: This book has already selected and chunked most of the text for you!) Like other teachers using this method, you will likely notice that pre-reading *is* reading, just in small bites. You'll also notice your students using and reusing strategies. Sometimes you'll revisit a strategy from Week One later in the unit, with a new piece of text or an added layer of complexity. For example, Choral Reading and Cutting a Scene are favorite classroom routines that teachers use multiple times not just in a Shakespeare unit but throughout the school year. Over time, as you progress through the lessons, you will observe your students doing literacy tasks that are increasingly demanding and sophisticated, and you'll all have gained a method to help you tackle any complex text.

The process of speaking lines, interrogating and editing text, negotiating meaning, deciding how language should be embodied and performed, and owning literature—and doing it all without much teacher explanation—is what matters most. Simply put, the process is more important than the product. Don't fret if the final product is not perfect (what human endeavor is "perfect," anyway?). Did the students collaborate to analyze language and create something new? Do they know what they're saying? Have they made Shakespeare's language their own? So what if a group's performance has some awkward pauses or someone mispronounces a word? If your students have been reading actively, asking and answering good questions, and reaching their own evidence-based conclusions, it's all good. The real work happens along the arc, not at the end.

9 Essential Practices

This is the moment in our live workshops when teachers typically tell us how simultaneously *excited* and *nervous* they are about trying the Folger Method.

Excited because the Principles, the Arc, the whole philosophy of turning the learning over to the students, speaks to their own deeply held conviction that all students can do much more than is often asked of them. As one high school English teacher put it, "These Principles express something I know deep down and want to act on."

Nervous because this Folger thing is really different from how most of us were taught in school. Exactly how does a teacher "act on" the 8 Foundational Principles? What happens in class? What does the teacher do and not do? What does the student do and learn? What do teachers and students have to "unlearn" or let go of in order to try this approach?

The answers to these questions lie in the nine core practices of the Folger Method— the 9 Essentials. Within the lessons that follow this chapter, you will find step-by-step instructions for these Essentials right when you need them. For now, we will provide you with a brief overview of each one.

1. Tone and Stress boosts students' confidence in speaking text aloud and explores how a text's meanings are revealed through vocal expression. Students experience firsthand how variations in tone of voice and word stress influence a listener's understanding of subtext. They see and hear that there's no single right way to interpret a text. Longtime teacher and Teaching Shakespeare Institute faculty member Mike Lo-Monico spent a lot of time and expertise developing this!

2. Tossing Words and Lines puts text into students' hands and mouths and gets them up on their feet reading, speaking, and analyzing the language together. Bonus: Students are able to make inferences about the text based on the words they encounter.

3. Two-line Scenes get all students up on their feet, creating and performing two-person mini-scenes. They discover how making collaborative decisions to enact text is exciting and reveals new understandings. They also realize they can encounter a text "cold" and make meaning from it all on their own—dispelling the myth that Shakespeare's language is too dense to understand.

4. Twenty-minute Plays involve the whole class in performing lines of text that becomes an express tour through the play. Early on, students learn and own the story and the language of the play and are motivated to keep reading. Folger Director of Education Peggy O'Brien originated this Essential and has perfected the art of finding the most fun-to-say lines in a play!

5. Choral Reading asks all students to read and reread a text aloud together. By changing what the "chorus" does in each rereading, this exercise gives students multiple opportunities to refine their understanding of the text. Students discover how the simple acts of speaking and rereading strengthen comprehension and analysis—all without any teacher explanation. In the chorus, there's an anonymity that's freeing, especially for English Learners and shy readers. Choral Reading is immersive, low-stakes, and really, really powerful.

6. 3D Lit enables a class or group of students to work together, figuring out (a) what is going on in a scene they have never before read with no explanation and very little help from you, and (b) how to informally act it out, making decisions as they go. This process enables them to refine their understanding as they transform the text from the page to a 3D "stage" in class. Michael Tolaydo, an actor, director, and faculty member of the Teaching Shakespeare Institute, created this groundbreaking Essential.

7. Cutting a Scene gets students close-reading with a purpose by challenging groups to eliminate half the lines from a piece of text while retaining its meaning. Since editors, scholars, directors, actors, and students have been cutting Shakespeare *forever*, yours are in good company. In fulfilling their mission as editors, students will naturally have to examine what the text says and implies, how the scene works, who's who, how language functions, and what's at stake. The fun part? Listening to your students debating which lines should stay or go and what the scene's "meaning" is anyway.

8. Promptbooks engage students in a process of text-based decision-making and collaborative annotation that reflects how they would stage a text. Many teachers and students call promptbooks "annotating with a real purpose." As with other Essentials, promptbooks are useful for students grappling with an unfamiliar text.

9. Group Scenes enable students to put all the pieces together. Students collaborate to select, cut, rehearse, memorize, and perform a scene for their classmates. Sometimes group scenes consist entirely of the original language of the text; other times they might include mashups or adaptations that incorporate home languages, pop culture, and/or the wide world of literature. Students make their own Shakespeares, demonstrating how they have used textual evidence and background knowledge not only to understand but also reinvent complex dramatic language.

A Note on Differentiation

You know better than anyone else that inside every single one of your students is a whole lot of talent and a whole lot of room to improve. Therefore, when we talk about "differentiation," we are not talking about "struggling readers" or "remediation." We are talking about the rich diversity of what everyone brings to—and takes from—the learning. And everyone—*everyone*—has a great deal to bring and take!

So, are we talking about students in your AP or IB classes? Neurodiverse students? Students with IEPs? Nontraditional students? English Learners? So-called "high-fliers"? Yes. All of the above. In other words, differentiation is about hearing, seeing, challenging, supporting, and inspiring each unique learner.

When teachers experience the Folger Method for themselves, they often point out how differentiation is woven right into the Essentials. Because this mode of teaching relies so heavily on student voice, it is inherently personalized.

Beyond this general fact, though, there are several specific ways in which the Folger Method accounts for the variety of learners in your classroom. Allow us to zoom in on just two of them.

Example #1: The Essential called "Two-line Scenes" provides opportunities for students of all reading abilities to be successful. Each student works with a partner to make a "mini-play" from just two lines of Shakespeare. If, in one pair, Student A knows just two words in their assigned line, they can base their performance on those two words, or they can collaborate with their scene partner, Student B, to work out the meaning of the rest of their line. And if Student B knows not only the literal but also the figurative meaning of both lines, they can share their understanding with Student A and work together to take on the additional challenge of expressing subtext with their voices and bodies. Differentiation is happening on two fronts here: first, through the "wiggle room" that allows each student to bring their own knowledge and creativity to the final product (sometimes called "variable outcomes" by learning experts); second, through peer collaboration. Throughout this book, you will see that students are supporting and stretching each other, and developing their own independent thinking skills, thanks to all kinds of grouping configurations.

Example #2: Since much of the Folger Method relies on selecting and chunking text for our students, there is a ready-made structure for matching students with passages that meet them where they are and stretch them to the next level. In this book you will find that a relentless focus on language is one of the best tools you have for differentiating learning. In other words, don't change the task, water anything down, or make it overly complicated—just chunk the text into appropriately challenging parts. (If you teach English Learners and multilingual students—who are used to attending very carefully to language, its sound, its sense, its nuance—all this will strike you as familiar. For more on the unique power of the Folger Method with English Learners, turn to Dr. Christina Porter's excellent essay in this book.)

7 Touchstone Questions

As you jump into this book and these lessons, try using the following "Touchstone Questions" as your guide to reflecting on your own teaching. Think of them as a kind of checklist for student-driven, language-focused learning. Like everything else in this book, they are grounded in the 8 Foundational Principles.

If you can answer "yes" to each Touchstone Question, there must be some serious sparks flying in your classroom!

1. Did I, the teacher, get out of the way and let students own their learning?

2. Is the language of the text(s) front and center?

3. Are the words of the text in ALL students' mouths?

4. Are students collaborating to develop their own interpretations?

5. Are students daring to grapple with complex language and issues in the text?

6. Has every voice been included and honored?

7. Am I always giving students the real thing, whether it's Shakespeare's language, or primary sources, or supporting tough conversations as prompted by the text?

You've Got This

The Folger Method is proof of what's possible when we as teachers step back and let students own their learning. When we teachers realize we don't need to have all the answers. When students are invited to question and grapple. When they approach language with curiosity and care. When they tackle the real thing. When everyone tries new challenges, takes big risks, and supports one another along the way. When all students realize they can do hard things on their own.

You have everything you need to make this happen. We believe in you and can't wait to hear how it goes.

Macbeth, Day-by-Day: The Five-Week Unit Plan

TEACHER-TO-TEACHER THOUGHTS AND THE GAME PLAN FOR THIS *MACBETH*

Elizabeth Dixon and Mark Miazga

Teacher-to-Teacher Thoughts

Fear. Treason. Guilt. Tyranny. Ambition. Grief. Revenge. Love. One of Shakespeare's most famous and commonly performed plays, as well as one of his shortest, *Macbeth* explores many big topics that can hook students. But it also has witches and blood and ghosts—even more reasons for young people to be intrigued by this 400-year-old play.

The What: For decades, *Macbeth* has been pigeonholed as a play about the dangers of too much ambition; Macbeth and his wife wanted power and were subsequently brought down by the accompanying ambition to achieve that power. Aristotle's stages of a tragedy are dutifully checked off; we can even add in a fancy word like *hamartia*, and we consequently feel we can wrap *Macbeth* up with a bow.

But we can't pigeonhole *Macbeth* as simply a play about ambition, or any other single force. *Macbeth* is a play about gender, about leadership, about what people do when they are fearful. It's about the role of fate in our lives. It's about relationships; it's about parenting; it's about the consequences of violence and fear. It's even about race. And, as teachers, it's important that we give students tools and strategies in order to let them gain access to all the big forces that are moving and developing in *Macbeth*.

The How: The Folger Method will help you put students in the driver's seat when it comes to Shakespeare. We don't want our students—or your students—to approach Shakespeare with the air of veneration that so many of us were encouraged to do, and that so many students are still doing. Our goal is to knock Shakespeare off his pedestal—not to denigrate him, but to give students the chance to play around with him, and eventually to gain ownership of his language, plays, and ideas. In doing so, students encounter Shakespeare in the way he was meant to be encountered: not as static words on a page, but through lively, energized interactivity.

You'll find the word *performance* in many of these lesson plans, and we want to be certain that you know what we mean—and what we don't mean—when we use that word. Working with lines and speeches often means putting them in motion . . . and that's what we mean by performance. If students are making choices with language—a gesture a character might make, a specific stress or tone on a word, a movement across the stage, a volume shift—then they are *interpreting* the line. They are actively reading. They are analyzing, connecting language to character, tone, conflict, and idea, just as editors, scholars, actors, and directors have been doing for centuries. Example: Lady Macbeth could be confused, angry, belittling, or hurt when she is asking her husband why he broke the enterprise with her—and which of those she might be isn't the point. Shakespeare didn't tell us. The point is that the students are digging into the language and making decisions themselves about the direction it should go. This is thoughtful analysis, and *all* students can do it.

In the use of "performance," we do *not* mean acting, acting talent, drama school prowess, or anything remotely related.

Final Projects: As if we're telling them a highly classified secret, we tell our students that the lines, scenes, choral readings, promptbooks, cut texts, and visualizations that they discuss and prepare as they go through this unit are all valuable in their own right, mainly because they provide them with active pathways through which to analyze the play and make it their own. During the fifth week in class, they put together a final project that has students cutting and producing a scene of their own, using all of the close-reading and analytical skills learned during the unit. The final performances celebrate the digging and learning that has happened along the way. These performances will not be perfect, but they will be full of learning from students who are in confident conversation with Shakespeare.

FROM LIZ DIXON

I don't remember much about studying *Macbeth* in high school, even though I know I did. I remember my teacher talking excitedly about a C-section baby and the girl next to me trying to remember how to spell *Dunsinane* while cramming for a test. I remember the "Tomorrow and tomorrow and tomorrow" soliloquy, but not how it really fit into the context of the play and that these were the words of a defeated man who had ruined the lives of the people who meant the most to him, wondering if life at all even matters. We did go on a field trip to see a performance, but never did we do anything in class out of our desks.

In college, I took a Shakespeare class from my beloved grandfather, who was a retired scholar but who still continued to teach a Shakespeare class occasionally (and I happened to take his class the last time he ever taught it). I treasured this experience, but Grandpa was pretty traditional. The syllabus was *packed*; we only spent a couple of class periods on each play, and we must have covered a dozen during the semester. We were expected to read the whole play ahead of the scheduled classes devoted to the play.

I don't remember much about the content of Grandpa's lectures, but the content I *do* remember? Every. single. line. of the 100 lines that we were required to memorize and recite during office hours. Grandpa was on to something with the importance he placed on that speaking requirement. There was magic in getting the words in our mouths, and even more magic when we got on our feet and embodied the language and characters. And there still is.

As a teacher, I didn't really know how to approach teaching a Shakespeare play beyond how I had been taught. We read the plays out loud together, and I would paraphrase when students struggled. I went to an NCTE session once about using drama techniques to teach Shakespeare and it all clicked that teaching through performance doesn't mean that you have to be an actor, or that you have to act out every line and every scene. As I continued in my journey of figuring out how to best engage students, I got my hands on the Folger's *Shakespeare Set Free* series, and I was hooked. Several years later, I was able to participate in the Folger's Teaching Shakespeare Institute, which helped me to think about how to teach *students*, not just how to teach Shakespeare. The ways that the Folger has embraced knocking Shakespeare off a pedestal, putting him in conversation with contemporary writers, and looking at his plays and their impact from a critical social justice lens are exciting pedagogies to learn for today's world and are ways that students can truly connect with words and language.

FROM MARK MIAZGA

In high school in the early 1990s, I remember very little of *Macbeth*. We sat in rows and read the play out loud, and then read scenes assigned for homework. I have vivid memories of reading dialogue from *Macbeth* and my teacher laughing after I read it, and no one else reacting; he then would explain what the lines meant and why they were funny. This remained throughout the entirety of the *Macbeth* unit: We mostly read aloud, the teacher explained, and then we answered reading questions based on his explanations.

After this experience, I avoided Shakespeare. In college, I would read online summaries—the internet was just becoming prevalent in students' lives, and professors hadn't caught up with it yet—so I was able to get by with those. And when I was tasked with teaching Shakespeare early in my career, I reverted to what I knew: desks in rows, students reading aloud or silently, the teacher—now it was me—explaining what it meant.

It wasn't until a veteran teacher handed me a copy of *Shakespeare Set*

Free—the initial set of teaching books published by the Folger Shakespeare Library in the 1990s—that a new world of instruction opened for me. I had so much fun learning the Folger methods described in that text and then integrating them into my classroom. Pursuing this further, I spent a life-changing summer at the Folger's Teaching Shakespeare Institute in Washington, DC, and have continued to use the Folger Method—now much updated from the 1990s—as the bridge between the plays and the language of Shakespeare.

What has been most profound for me over the years is how well the Folger Method works for higher-level analysis. Like many teachers, I teach in a high-stakes testing environment, in a large urban school in Baltimore, where teachers must show student growth through formal assessments. Throughout my career, I have taught in both the International Baccalaureate (IB) and the Advanced Placement (AP) programs, and in all cases, I've found that the Folger Method and the Folger Essentials help students learn at a rigorous level.

Indeed, for students to be able to write about or discuss tough language, whether it's Shakespeare, Baldwin, Morrison, Fitzgerald, or any other author, they need to be able to "live in it" for a bit. Feel it. Let it wash over them and be immersed in it. These are difficult, but important, skills to teach, whether we are teaching students literary analysis or simply to be able to read the world with an active and critical eye.

However, we can't simply assign rigorous reading like *Macbeth* and expect students to be able to grapple with it on their own, like I was expected to in high school. Assigning isn't teaching. And explaining or translating lines isn't either. And neither is using texts that "modernize" Shakespeare's language for students. This instinct that these modernized texts make things easier for EL students and other reluctant readers might be well-intentioned, but it's completely wrong. In fact, I've found that the Folger Method—students engaging in the language of Shakespeare with voices and movement—is particularly effective with English Language Learners. You'll find more specific information about the affinity between Shakespeare and ELs elsewhere in this book!

DAY-BY-DAY

Week/Act	Questions guiding exploration of the play	Lessons
1 Act 1	What creates fear and how do people respond to it? What does fear look and sound like?	**1.** "When the hurly-burly's done": Students Dive into the Language, Plot, and World of *Macbeth* **2.** "Screw your courage to the sticking place": Using Folger Essentials to Focus on the Language of Fear **3.** "What bloody man is that?": Getting an Early Scene on Its Feet **4.** Creating Our First Promptbook, and Examining an 1852 Promptbook from the Folger Collection **5.** Shakespeare in Context
2 Act 2	How does this play present gender? Duplicity? And how do those relate to real lives now? How is fear being enacted?	**6.** "Unsex me here": Lady Macbeth and Jamaica Kincaid's "Girl" in Conversation about Gender **7.** "Look like th' innocent flower / But be the serpent under't": Understanding Lady Macbeth's Duplicity in 1.6 **8.** "Tears shall drown the wind": Hearing the Voices in a Soliloquy **9.** "What cannot you and I perform . . . ?" Close-reading 1.7 (and the Macbeths' Marriage) by Cutting a Scene **10.** "Come, let me clutch thee": Taking a Dagger to Macbeth's Soliloquy and Creating a Reading
3 Act 3	What emotions are fear-adjacent? Who is Macbeth most afraid of? What were Early Modern beliefs about the order of the world?	**11.** "'Twas a rough night": Such a Range of Emotion in 2.3 **12.** "'Tis unnatural / Even like the deed that's done": Exploring the *Great Chain of Being* (1579) for Ideas about an Ordered World **13.** "Our Fears in Banquo Stick Deep": What Is Macbeth Afraid of and Why? **14.** "O treachery!": In 3.3, Learning about the Power of Movement Through a Dumb-show **15.** Daring to Look on "that which might appall the devil": Putting Banquo's Ghost in Motion

Week/Act	Questions guiding exploration of the play	Lessons
4 Act 4	How do a range of visualizations add to our understanding of *Macbeth*? How is the imagery of blackness used in *Macbeth*? What can we discern about Lady Macbeth's state of mind? What about the legacy of *Macbeth*?	**16.** Aligning Two Important Scenes—4.1 and 4.2—with Images from the Folger Collection **17.** "Black Macbeth will seem as pure as snow": *Macbeth*, Race, and Language **18.** "Dispute it as a man": Examining Gender Expectations in *Macbeth* through Another Text **19.** "Out, damned spot, out, I say!": Lady Macbeth's Conscious Lines and Her Subconscious Mind **20.** Macbeth in Act 5: Strutting and Fretting Toward His End, and . . . His Legacy Hereafter
5 Act 5	Festival! Students pull together all of their learning—the Folger Method and *Macbeth*—to demonstrate it brilliantly to themselves and others.	**21.** The Final Projects: Make Shakespeare Your Own! **22–24.** The Final Project: Making *Macbeth* Your Own **25.** The Final Project: Your Own *Macbeth*, Performed!

"When the hurly-burly's done": Students Dive into the Language, Plot, and World of *Macbeth*

Here's What We're Doing Today and Why

No time like *now* to put students right into the language, plot, and world of *Macbeth*! The Folger Essential Choral Reading focuses students on Shakespeare's language and how choices with the language create meaning; they will dive into the play this way. In addition, the 20-minute version of *Macbeth* gives students a road map of the play so that instruction can focus on language and staging rather than plot. During Shakespeare's time, most of his audience would have known the plots of his plays, at least in broad strokes. Students will learn the basic plot structure of *Macbeth* briefly and interactively and be introduced to some of its most intriguing lines at the same time.

What Will I Need?

- Copies of 1.1 for each student – **RESOURCE #1.1A**

- Separate strips with one line from *Macbeth* on each strip – **RESOURCE #1.1B**

- A copy of 20-minute *Macbeth* narration for you – **RESOURCE #1.1C**

How Should I Prepare?

- Make copies of 1.1 – **RESOURCE #1.1A**

- Make a copy of the 20-minute *Macbeth* numbered lines – **RESOURCE #1.1B**— and cut them into 29 separate strips—one line per strip

- Have your own copy of the Narration on paper

- Arrange your room so that there is a performance space somewhere

Agenda (~ 45-minute class period)

- ❏ Choral Reading of the opening scene with the three Witches (1.1) (20 minutes)
- ❏ 20-minute *Macbeth* (20 minutes)
- ❏ Whole-class reflection (5 minutes)

Here's What Students Hear (From You) and (Then What They'll) Do

Part One: Choral Reading

1. [Reading #1] We're going to read Act 1, Scene 1 of *Macbeth* – **RESOURCE #1.1A**. Let's begin by reading this out loud, all together. As you read, listen to those around you; keep pace with readers nearby. Don't race, and don't worry about pronunciation or expression right now.

2. By a show of fingers, with 1 indicating that you're still pretty unsure of what's happening here and 3 showing that you could explain this scene to someone else, how would you rate your level of understanding?

3. [Reading #2] Let's read again; this time, make a mental note of the words or phrases that are most confusing to you as well as the words or phrases that you understand best.

4. By another show of fingers, how would you rate your level of understanding? [**TEACHER NOTE:** If hands are still showing lots of "1s," read this one more time.]

5. Let's talk about what this scene tells us . . . what we understand so far:

   a. Who is speaking in this scene? What kind of people are they? How do you know?

   b. What do they seem to be speaking about? How do you know?

   c. How would you describe the mood, or the feeling, of this scene? What words give you that idea?

   d. Which words don't you know?
   [**TEACHER NOTE:** Collaboratively decide on meanings or assign a few students to perform a quick search for definitions and share their discoveries.]

6. [Reading #3] Now let's read again with what we just talked about in mind.

7. Let's talk about we understand now:

   a. What did you notice after this reading?

   b. What sounds are implied in the text of the scene?
   [**TEACHER NOTE:** Students should notice sounds such as thunder, lightning, rain, battle, Graymalkin (which a quick definition search will tell them is a cat), Paddock (a toad).]

   c. How could we create some of these sounds?

8. I'm noting these ideas on the board and let's assign individuals or small groups of students to create the various sounds.

9. Next, let's divide the class into three groups: Witch 1, Witch 2, and Witch 3. [You can multitask with sound effects plus reading one witch's lines.]

10. Let's read it again, this time with the witches' lines divided up and incorporating the sound effects. What did you notice after this reading?

Part Two: Your 20-minute *Macbeth*

1. Many in Shakespeare's own audience would have been familiar with the plots of his plays before they ever got to the theater because he based many on stories known to all. In our "20-minute *Macbeth*," you will produce a short version of the story using language and action from the play.

2. I'm going to give each of you a numbered strip with a Shakespeare line—or you can get into pairs or groups to produce your part of *Macbeth*. Some of you will probably get more than one line.

3. Recite your line to yourselves or in your groups. This line/These lines will be yours to perform in our 20-minute version of the play.

4. Now, take a few moments to move around the room, and recite your lines several times, experimenting with different volumes, speeds, gestures, and movements as you get more and more comfortable with the language.

5. Now it's time for our 20-minute *Macbeth*! I'm going to read a narrative of the plot. When I call your number, come to the performance space and share your line(s) (with gestures and emotion too, if you'd like!). You'll deliver your lines with gusto! And after you do, there will be wild applause!

Part Three: Reflection Rounds

[**TEACHER NOTE:** To conclude today's lesson, we'll do a "round" that includes all voices and helps students reflect on what they've just experienced. Teaching Shakespeare Institute faculty member Michael Tolaydo brought these to the Folger. When he starts rounds, he puts to use a range of verbs that include "observed," "discovered," "noticed," "resented," "learned," "saw," "wished," and "wondered."]

These rounds are useful to students, so you'll find them along with other modes of reflection frequently in this unit. Resist the urge to provide feedback during reflection rounds. Rounds are about students sharing their immediate reactions to what has happened in the classroom without fear of judgment.

1. We're going to wrap up by doing a Reflection Round. During rounds, everyone contributes by responding to the same prompt. One of you will begin with the prompt and your response, and then we'll continue sharing responses around the class.

2. Finish one sentence begun by the prompt. Your answers should be just one sentence—and no judgment or interruption, please.

3. Thinking about what we did in class today: Let's have everyone respond to:

    I noticed . . .

and then:

    I was surprised that . . .

Here's What Just Happened in Class

- Students spoke Shakespeare's words and gained confidence with the language in nonthreatening ways, first as a whole group and then in a smaller group or on their own with a single line.

- Students read the first scene of the play chorally several times and added sound to their performance to help incorporate tone and mood.

- Students created their own production of *Macbeth* and in doing so, experienced a skeletal 20-minute version of the story and the language. They've already learned the plot and have become familiar with key lines.

- Students discovered that Shakespeare does not seem dull or boring or too difficult.

RESOURCE #1.1A

Macbeth Act 1, Scene 1

Thunder and Lightning. Enter three Witches.

FIRST WITCH
  When shall we three meet again?
  In thunder, lightning, or in rain?

SECOND WITCH
  When the hurly-burly's done,
  When the battle's lost and won.

THIRD WITCH
  That will be ere the set of sun.   5

FIRST WITCH
  Where the place?

SECOND WITCH Upon the heath.

THIRD WITCH
  There to meet with Macbeth.

FIRST WITCH I come, Graymalkin.

SECOND WITCH Paddock calls.   10

THIRD WITCH Anon.

ALL
  Fair is foul, and foul is fair;
  Hover through the fog and filthy air.
                                        They exit.

The 20-minute *Macbeth*: List of Numbered Lines

1. WHEN SHALL WE THREE MEET AGAIN?

2. WHEN THE BATTLE'S LOST AND WON.

3. UNSEAMED HIM FROM THE NAVE TO THE CHOPS!

4. BRAVE MACBETH—WELL HE DESERVES THAT NAME!

5. HAIL! HAIL! HAIL!

6. YOU SHOULD BE WOMEN, AND YET YOUR BEARDS FORBID ME . . .

7. THIS HORRID IMAGE DOTH UNFIX MY HAIR!

8. MY DEAREST PARTNER OF GREATNESS!

9. MAKE THICK MY BLOOD!

10. LOOK LIKE THE INNOCENT FLOWER, BUT BE THE SERPENT UNDER IT.

11. YOU WOULD BE SO MUCH MORE THE MAN.

12. I HAVE DONE THE DEED!

13. KNOCK! KNOCK! KNOCK!

14. O HORROR, HORROR, HORROR!

15. 'TWAS A ROUGH NIGHT!

16. WHAT, IN OUR HOUSE?

17. LET'S AWAY!

18. O FULL OF SCORPIONS IS MY MIND, DEAR WIFE!

19. THOU ART THE BEST OF THE CUTTHROATS!

20. O TREACHERY! FLY . . . FLY, FLY! FLY!

21. HOW NOW, YOU SECRET, BLACK, AND MIDNIGHT HAGS!

22. MACBETH! MACBETH! MACBETH! BEWARE MACDUFF!

23. HE HAS KILLED ME, MOTHER!

24. OUT, DAMNED SPOT!

25. THE QUEEN, MY LORD, IS DEAD.

26. OUR POWER IS READY!

27. TURN, HELLHOUND, TURN!

28. LAY ON, MACDUFF!

29. HAIL, KING OF SCOTLAND!

The 20-minute *Macbeth*: Narration

This play begins when three witches meet in a desolate place (#1 WHEN SHALL WE THREE MEET AGAIN?). And we learn that they speak in paradoxes or riddles (#2 WHEN THE BATTLE'S LOST AND WON).

Soon after we learn of Macbeth's prowess in that battle, and how much he is praised for being a great warrior (#3 UNSEAMED HIM FROM THE NAVE TO THE CHOPS) and (#4 BRAVE MACBETH—WELL HE DESERVES THAT NAME!).

As Macbeth and Banquo head home after the battle, they stumble upon these witches who call to them (#5 HAIL! HAIL! HAIL!). Macbeth and Banquo can't figure out who they are! Banquo says: (#6 YOU SHOULD BE WOMEN, AND YET YOUR BEARDS FORBID ME . . .).

What's up with these witches? They prophesy that Macbeth will become king, and that after that, Banquo's sons will be kings. Macbeth is fascinated and horrified by the idea of being king and says to himself: (#7 THIS HORRID IMAGE DOTH UNFIX MY HAIR!). But he's also fascinated—how can he get himself on the throne sooner rather than later? He writes to his wife, Lady Macbeth, starting his letter . . . (#8 MY DEAREST PARTNER OF GREATNESS).

Lady Macbeth . . . *she* knows how to make her husband king sooner. They must kill King Duncan so that Macbeth can take over. She promises to help, and she prays for strength (#9 MAKE THICK MY BLOOD). Lady Macbeth has advice for her husband as King Duncan arrives to spend the night at their castle (#10 LOOK LIKE THE INNO-CENT FLOWER, BUT BE THE SERPENT UNDER IT), and she tries to convince him to kill Duncan by appealing to Macbeth's masculinity (#11 YOU WOULD BE SO MUCH MORE THE MAN).

So King Duncan comes to spend the night at the Macbeths' castle, but he never leaves. Macbeth says to Lady Macbeth: (#12 I HAVE DONE THE DEED!). Duncan is murdered.

The next morning, another nobleman, Macduff, arrives at the castle gate to join King Duncan (#13 KNOCK! KNOCK! KNOCK!). (We think this might be the first "Knock Knock" joke.)

Macduff finds Duncan dead, and screams: (#14 O HORROR, HORROR, HORROR). Macbeth and Lady M pretend to be surprised. Macbeth says: (#15 'TWAS A ROUGH NIGHT!). Lady Macbeth acts shocked as any good hostess might and exclaims: (#16 WHAT, IN OUR HOUSE?).

King Duncan's sons—Malcolm and Donalbain—know they need to get out of there. They say (#17 LET'S AWAY!) and head for England.

Macbeth is crowned king . . . and then he begins to get in deep (#18 O FULL OF SCORPIONS IS MY MIND, DEAR WIFE.). He's worried about the rest of the witches' prophecy that Banquo's children will become king. He hires murderers and says to them (#19 THOU ART THE BEST OF THE CUTTHROATS!). Their job is to kill Banquo AND his son Fleance (#20 O TREACHERY! FLY . . . FLY, FLY! FLY!). Fleance escapes and gets away!

Macbeth goes back to the witches for advice and reassurance (#21 HOW NOW, YOU SECRET, BLACK, AND MIDNIGHT HAGS!).

They tell him some riddles that give Macbeth false confidence, but they also warn him . . . (#22 MACBETH! MACBETH! MACBETH! BEWARE MACDUFF!).

Macbeth gets in even deeper. He has Macduff's wife and children murdered (#23 HE HAS KILLED ME, MOTHER). And still deeper: Lady Macbeth begins to fall apart, trying to wash the imaginary blood from her hands (#24 OUT, DAMNED SPOT!). And she goes from bad to worse . . . (#25 THE QUEEN, MY LORD, IS DEAD).

Meanwhile, Duncan's sons, Malcolm and Donalbain, have assembled an army and they are ready to march back in to defeat Macbeth. They surround the castle (#26 OUR POWER IS READY!). And Macbeth gets more and more desperate about his likely defeat.

. . . but it all comes down to Macbeth and Macduff one-on-one, with Macduff seeking to avenge the murder of his entire family. Macduff says: (#27 TURN, HELLHOUND, TURN). And Macbeth says: (#28 LAY ON, MACDUFF!).

They fight, fiercely. In the end, Macduff holds up Macbeth's severed head for all to see, and everyone salutes Malcolm (#29 HAIL, KING OF SCOTLAND!).

And that is our own production of *Macbeth*!

"Screw your courage to the sticking place": Using Folger Essentials to Focus on the Language of Fear

Here's What We're Doing and Why

One of the big ideas *Macbeth* explores is fear. What creates fear and how do people respond to it? What does fear look and sound like? This lesson is designed to introduce students to some of the language related to fear in the play and to get them speaking and moving with that language.

The Folger Essential practices of Tone and Stress and Tossing Lines get students up on their feet with Shakespeare's words in their mouths, allowing them to play with the language and experiment with different subtexts. While the students already know the basic plot from the 20-Minute *Macbeth* yesterday, this lesson also functions as a teaser to get the students to begin asking deeper questions about plot, characters, and mood as they begin to dig into the play.

What Will I Need?

- Selected lines about fear – **RESOURCE #1.2**, printed, and the 28 lines cut apart—so that there is one to distribute to each student (some students may get more than one line).

- Bean bag, stuffed toy, or other object for students to toss to one another.

How Should I Prepare?

- Read up on how the Folger Method describes these two Essentials:
  - Tone and Stress boosts students' confidence in speaking text aloud and explores how a text's meanings are revealed through vocal expression. Students experience firsthand how variations in tone of voice and word stress influence a listener's understanding of subtext. They see and hear that there's no single right way to interpret a text.
  - Tossing Lines puts text into students' hands and mouths and gets them up on their feet reading, speaking, and analyzing the language together. Bonus: Students are able to make inferences about the text based on the words they encounter.

- Be prepared to write on the board or project the three prompts needed for Tone and Stress work:
  - O
  - Out, out, brief candle!
  - I didn't say I killed our king.

- Arrange your room or find space so that your entire class can stand in a circle with some room in the middle.

• Either write the wrap-up reflection prompt on the board or prepare it to display at the end of the lesson.

Agenda (~ 45-minute class period)

❏ Tone and Stress (15 minutes)

❏ Distribution of lines and individual student experimentation (5 minutes)

❏ Tossing lines in a circle (10 minutes)

❏ Reflection (5 minutes)

❏ Share (10 minutes)

Here's What Students Hear (From You) and (Then What They'll) Do

Part One: Tone and Stress

1. Yesterday, we read the first scene of the play together and experimented with the way the characters might speak given the words that they said, and with sound that might accompany their words. Today, we're going to explore the relationship between words, emotions, and speech with some more lines from the play.

2. First, let's think about *tone*, the emotion we display when speaking, and the word *O*, one of the shortest words you will say in a Shakespeare play. I'm going to name a few emotions and then count down "3, 2, 1 . . . speak." After I say "speak," say "O" with that emotion.

   a. How would you say "O" when you are . . . surprised? 3, 2, 1 . . . speak!

   b. . . . scared? 3, 2, 1 . . . speak! Let's try that one more time . . .

   c. . . . exhausted? 3, 2, 1 . . .

   d. . . . sad?

   e. . . . excited? And again? . . .

   f. . . . in awe?

   g. . . . angry?

   h. . . . *really* scared? And one more time? . . .

3. Great! Notice how the sound of your voice tells us what is going on underneath the words. We call this *subtext* (think about submarines and what's above and below the water, right?). Let's try this with a longer line: "Out, out, brief candle!" [On the board or projected.]

   a. How would you say "Out, out, brief candle!" when you are . . . surprised?

   b. . . . angry?

   c. . . . afraid?

   d. . . . sad?

    e. . . . tired?

    f. . . . *really* afraid?

4. *Tone* is one way of creating subtext when we speak a line; *stress*, or the way we emphasize a word in a sentence, is another. We're going to play with stress with this sentence: "I didn't say he killed our king." [On the board or projected.]

5. After I count down from three, say this sentence and stress the first word, "I."

    a. 3, 2, 1 . . . speak!
    [**TEACHER NOTE:** Class says "*I* didn't say he killed our king."]

6. Very good! When we stress that word, what seems to be the subtext? What is the sentence suggesting? [Students might say the sentence suggests that someone else said he killed the king or that the speaker seems defensive.]

7. Let's try reading the sentence again and stressing each of its words to see how the subtext changes. [I'm going to move around the room to call on individual students to read "I didn't say he killed our king," each time stressing a different word in the sentence. And after each reading a question about what the delivery suggests.]

8. What other things can we do with our voices to change the subtext of a line?

Part Two: Tossing Lines

1. I'm going to give you each a strip of paper with a line on it. With your line in hand, stand up and walk around the room, saying the line to yourselves several times, experimenting with different tones and stressed words. Now, I'm going to give you about a minute to play with how you'll deliver your line, thinking about tone and stress. 3, 2, 1 . . . go!

2. Now, let's make a big circle.

3. I have a bean bag here. We'll now take turns saying our line and as you finish, toss the bean bag to someone else in the circle. They catch it, say their line, then toss it to someone else. Each time you receive the bean bag, say your line. If you get the bean bag a second time, say the line differently from the way you said it the first time—try some tone and stress! We'll continue tossing the bean bag until each of you has delivered your line several times in different ways.

Part Three: Reflection Two Ways

1. Let's talk a bit as a class:

    a. Did you hear any patterns in the lines we just read or heard? If you did, what were they?

    b. Thinking about what we learned about the plot of *Macbeth* yesterday, can you connect your line to any of the plot details you remember? If you can, what are the connections?

    c. When you read your line, what was the first emotion you thought about? Why?

  d. Do many of these lines seem to reflect the same emotion? Which ones do you think?

  e. Some of these lines reflect characters in *Macbeth* who experience fear. Which word in your line seems the most frightening or fearful? Why?

2. Now, have a seat and take out a piece of paper to reflect on the following question. You'll have about 5 minutes to write. Here's the question: What creates fear and how do people respond to fear?

[TEACHER NOTE: This is a broad reflection prompt, so some students might feel comfortable thinking along the lines of what specific things might create fear for them, or others might approach it from a broader angle of what circumstances or traits lead to fear.]

3. Respond using Reflection Rounds with one-word answers around the class:

  a. What creates fear?

  b. How do people respond to fear?

4. And then two more positive Reflection Rounds to conclude:

  a. I learned . . .

  b. I wonder . . .

Here's What Just Happened in Class

- Students spoke Shakespeare's words and used those words to experiment with subtext to explore the connections between language and emotion.

- Students close-read a line of Shakespeare to think about how dialogue reflects the plot of the play.

- Students used lines from *Macbeth* to explore the timeless topics of fear, its causes, and its consequences.

RESOURCE #1.2

Tossing Lines

Fair is foul, and foul is fair.

I do fear thy nature; it is too full o' the milk of human kindness.

Look like the innocent flower, but be the serpent under't.

If it were done when 'tis done, then 'twere well it were done quickly.

Screw your courage to the sticking-place, and we'll not fail.

Is this a dagger which I see before me, the handle toward my hand?

That which hath made them drunk hath made me bold.

Sleep no more! Macbeth does murder sleep!

A little water clears us of this deed.

Double, double toil and trouble; Fire burn and cauldron bubble.

By the pricking of my thumbs, something wicked this way comes.

Out, damned spot! out, I say!

We will proceed no further in this business.

Speak if you can. What are you?

Present fears are less than horrible imaginings.

The Thane of Fife had a wife: where is she now?

What's done is done.

To-morrow, and to-morrow, and to-morrow, creeps in this petty pace from day to day.

Out, out, brief candle! Life's but a walking shadow.

Knock, knock, knock! Who's there?

Why do you dress me in borrowed robes?

Stars, hide your fires; Let not light see my black and deep desires.

False face must hide what the false heart doth know.

O, full of scorpions is my mind!

My hands are of your color, but I shame to wear a heart so white.

It will have blood, they say. Blood will have blood.

And nothing is, but what is not.

All hail, Macbeth, that shalt be King hereafter!

WEEK ONE: LESSON 3

"What bloody man is that?": Getting an Early Scene on Its Feet

Here's What We're Doing and Why

This lesson uses Act 1, scene 2 (1.2) to introduce students to the conflict of the play, and to a way of getting inside the play itself without much explanation from you. The Folger Essential 3D Lit enables a class or group of students working together to figure out (a) what is going on in a scene they have never before read with no explanation and very little help from you, and (b) how to informally act it out, making decisions as they go. This process enables them to refine their understanding as they transform the text from the page to a 3D "stage" in class. Being able to collaboratively work through a difficult text independently, moving from reading to analysis, then analysis-on-its-feet—performing the scene—is an important way for students to actively read text. We want them to develop this skill so they can use it throughout the unit and beyond.

What might be new for you: You, the teacher, don't explain, don't translate, don't direct. You set up the experience and they do the work collaboratively. It may be a little chaotic, at least initially, but learning is happening!

What Will I Need?

- Copies of 1.2 (cut version, with all stage directions removed) – **RESOURCE #1.3**
- Students will need pens/pencils

How Should I Prepare?

- Arrange your classroom with desks around the perimeter in a circle and as big an open space as can be created in the center.

Agenda (~ 45-minute class period)

- ❏ 3D Lit: Part 1—Read and Own the Scene (20 minutes)
- ❏ 3D Lit: Part 2—Put the Scene on Its Feet and *Really* Own It (20 minutes)
- ❏ Reflection Rounds (5 minutes)

Here's What Students Hear (From You) and (Then What They'll) Do

Part One: Read and Own the Scene

1. You're going to dive into *Macbeth* a little deeper and together, and here we go: I'm going to hand each of you a script of Act 1, scene 2 of *Macbeth*. Everyone, sit in a circle, each with a copy of the text and a pencil.

2. For our first reading, let's read the scene aloud, together in one voice. Like we did with those witches. Read quickly and loudly; try to stay on pace with the group.

3. Let's see your level of understanding—"1, I'm not sure what's happening here" to "3, I could explain this to somebody else."

4. For our next reading, we'll read the text again, this time, one person after another in sequence, and let's read it end punctuation to end punctuation. We'll go around the circle and change readers at a period, a semicolon, a colon, a question mark, an exclamation point. (Readers do not change at a comma.)

5. Now that we've read through it that way, I have some questions for you . . . and I'll give you some time to pose answers. See what you can learn from the observations of your classmates too:

   a. "Who are these people?"

   b. "How do you know from the text?"

   c. "What is going on here?"

   d. "How do you know that from the text?"

   e. "Where are they?"

   f. "How do you know that from the text?"

6. Great observations. For our third reading, let's read aloud again, one person after another, but this time change readers at the end of each character's speech. So you each read a character's whole speech.

7. Great job, and now I have more questions for you—and I'll give you time to pose answers:

   a. "Notice anything further about these people?"

   b. "How do you know that from the text?"

   c. "Who are the people they are discussing?"

   d. "And how do you know that from the text?"

8. One last time . . . let's read again, character by character, this time marking up on your script words or ideas you don't fully understand.

9. After this reading, let's discuss your notations together and make decisions about what the unfamiliar words or phrases or ideas mean.

10. Rate your level of understanding again on a scale of 1–3 and then respond to the following questions:

    a. What do you understand now that you didn't understand before?

    b. What contributed to that understanding?

Part Two: Put the Scene on Its Feet and *Really* Own It

[**TEACHER NOTE:** For this next portion of the lesson, five students will act out the parts and the rest of the class will direct them. Our role as teachers is to facilitate the directors' work. Get out of the way as much as you can. This is not at all about a product; rather, it engages all students in the process of learning about a scene and some of the many possible variations in this scene and all of Shakespeare. The teacher should not direct. This is the work of student directors because it continues to engage them in the work. You cast the parts, though, because your sensibilities about your students are the best. Please pay no attention to gender as you cast.

Also, as you move through the next steps, remember that anytime the directors make suggestions or decisions, they should be prompted to support their decisions with evidence from the text.]

1. Now you're going to put this scene on its feet. We're going to use this center space for our stage. I'll cast the parts.

2. Actors to the stage, please. All of you who are not acting are directors. No one sits out.

3. Actors, your job is to say your character's lines and to take advice from the directors. Directors, you make decisions about the set and "build" the set with objects found in the classroom. In this scene, are there any necessary props, furniture, or features? Where are the entrances and exits? Do the lines tell us about any of this? The decisions are made by the directors—you may not agree, so I may have to negotiate which director decision we try first.

4. Decisions are made about who's onstage and why, who enters from where and why, the positions of the other actors. Everyone is clear on where the props and furniture are and why. All are ready to run the scene.

5. Actors begin running the first few lines of the scene. (Duncan's line *"O valiant cousin, worthy gentleman!"* is a good initial pausing point.)

6. Directors, share what you have noticed, what might/needs to change, and what might be missing. All your changes must be supported with evidence from the text.

7. Directors, you check on the set—do any adjustments need to be made?

8. Let's start again and keep going. If you're a director and see a change that needs to be made, put your hand up. When we can, we'll pause the scene to get your advice. All your changes must be supported with evidence from the text.

9. Repeat this "run the scene/pause for redirection/rerun the lines" process until the scene closes or your end-of-class bell nears.

Reflection Rounds

To conclude, some rounds:

a. I observed . . .

b. I wished . . .

c. I wondered . . .

d. *If responses stay focused on the language and activities, teachers should add:* What did you learn about yourself?

Here's What Just Happened in Class

- With guidance from you—as opposed to explanations and direction—students were able to work out and comprehend a scene through multiple collaborative readings.

- Students were able to cite textual evidence to inform their decisions about what's going on in this scene.

- Based on their understanding of the scene, they were able to make decisions about performance, and to stage the scene.

- Their skills and their confidence in their ability to understand this process and the play will grow as they (and you) go.

- With these tools now in their tool belts, students can now begin to feel confident in tackling other scenes in this way, and, ultimately, any challenging text.

RESOURCE #1.3

Macbeth 1.2 (edited)

DUNCAN What bloody man is that? He can report,
As seemeth by his plight, of the revolt
The newest state.

MALCOLM This is the sergeant
Who, like a good and hardy soldier, fought
'Gainst my captivity.—Hail, brave friend!

CAPTAIN Doubtful it stood,
For brave Macbeth carved out his passage
Till he unseamed him from the nave to th' chops,
And fixed his head upon our battlements.

DUNCAN O valiant cousin, worthy gentleman!

CAPTAIN Mark, King of Scotland, mark:
. . . the Norweyan lord, surveying vantage,
With furbished arms and new supplies of men,
Began a fresh assault.

DUNCAN Dismayed not this our captains, Macbeth and
Banquo?

CAPTAIN Yes . . .
So they doubly redoubled strokes upon the foe.
But I am faint. My gashes cry for help.

DUNCAN So well thy words become thee as thy wounds:
. . . —Go, get him surgeons.
Who comes here?

MALCOLM The worthy Thane of Ross.

LENNOX So should he look that seems to speak things
strange.

ROSS God save the King.

DUNCAN Whence cam'st thou, worthy thane?

ROSS From Fife, great king.
   The Thane of Cawdor began a dismal conflict,
   Point against point, rebellious arm 'gainst arm,
   . . . And to conclude,
   The victory fell on us.

DUNCAN Great happiness!
   No more that Thane of Cawdor shall deceive
   Our bosom interest. Go, pronounce his present
   Death,
   And with his former title greet Macbeth.

ROSS I'll see it done.

DUNCAN What he hath lost, noble Macbeth hath won.

Creating Our First Promptbook, and Examining an 1852 Promptbook from the Folger Collection

Here's What We're Doing and Why

In this lesson, we introduce creating a promptbook, one of the Folger Essentials. Historically and right until the present day, promptbooks—now called stage manager's books—have been used in theaters to record all the elements needed to create a scene according to the director's wishes. During rehearsals, the text is marked up with cuts, set design, notes on meaning of words, where actors should be onstage, necessary props, and reminders to the actors about how to convey meaning through the language with their voices, gestures, and movements.

Students will begin by examining the digitized pages of an 1852 promptbook from the Folger collection. Then they'll go on to work in groups creating their own short promptbooks of different scenes in Act 1 as they continue to take ownership of the language and the play. Completing our first promptbook is a logical step after 3D Lit because now students are aware that Shakespeare is indeed a three-dimensional experience rather than merely words on a page. They will continue the practice of creating promptbooks in small-scale form—and engaging in the analysis that informs their creation—throughout the unit. And creating a promptbook is an important part of their final project.

What Will I Need?

- Copies (or a projected image) of a page from the 1852 promptbook of Edwin Forrest's celebrated production of *Macbeth* – **RESOURCE #1.4A**

- Copies of the following Resources:
    - 1.3, 40–52 – **RESOURCE 1.4B**
    - 1.3, Lines 50–82 – **RESOURCE 1.4C**
    - 1.3, Lines 83–131, edited – **RESOURCE 1.4D**
    - 1.3, Lines 132–175, edited – **RESOURCE 1.4E**
    - 1.4, Lines 1–30 – **RESOURCE 1.4F**
    - 1.4, Lines 31–65 – **RESOURCE 1.4G**

How Should I Prepare?

- Review the information on promptbooks in general and on the one from the Folger collection specifically.

- Arrange your classroom so that students can work in separate groups.

Agenda (~ 45-minute period):

❑ Description of a promptbook and a close look at one from the Folger collection (8 minutes)

❑ The beginnings of the promptbook process (10 minutes)

❑ In groups, collaborate on creating your group promptbook (10 minutes)

❑ Put your promptbook into action: perform your scene (14 minutes)

❑ Reflection (3 minutes)

Here's What Students Hear (From You) and (Then What They'll) Do

1. So far, what have we been up to with *Macbeth*? Let them tell you:

   a. Chorally reading the first scene of the play—the witches!

   b. Putting the second scene on its feet and figured out what's going on in this scene.

   c. Producing our own version of *Macbeth*—learned the plot and some of the language.

2. Let's start thinking about promptbooks:

   – In theater, they're now called stage manager's books, but they have been used in theaters for centuries . . . to record all the specific elements needed in order to create a scene according to the director's wishes. During rehearsals, the text is marked up with cuts, set design, notes on meaning of words, where actors should be onstage, necessary props, and reminders to the actors about how to convey meaning through the language with their voices, gestures, and movements.

   – Let's look closely at two digitized pages from an 1852 promptbook in the Folger collection. What do you notice? Are there changes that were made in this production that surprise you?

3. Let's start the beginning of the promptbook process together . . .

   – Take a look at 1.3, 40–52 – **RESOURCE #1.4B** – Let's read the whole scene together, chorally as we've been doing.

   – What's going on in this scene? How do you know? Support your answer from the text.

   – If you were going to put this scene on its feet, where would Mac and Banquo be standing? Would they move during the scene? Where and why? What emotions might they be feeling—and how would they show that? (There is no one "right" answer . . . there are many "right" answers!)

   – Mark up *your* copy of the scene with how *you* think the scene should work onstage.

   – The notes that you have so far are the beginnings of a promptbook!

4. So let's get creating mini promptbooks in groups. I'll divide up the class into groups of 3–4 and then I'll distribute the scenes.

[**TEACHER NOTE:** Depending on your class numbers, you might have two groups working on the same piece of text. Then you'd have two different interpretations of the same scene, and that would be great.

- Gather in your groups, and start working with the scene I'm going to give you. Begin by reading it out loud together in whatever way you'd like. Talk it through and try it out live and on your feet—ways in which certain lines, movements, tones of voice, and more can give the scene deeper meaning and make it come alive.]

5. At the end of class, students can share their promptbooks by performing them— as many as time allows. One student from the group can tell the rest of the class what to look for before the performance.

Reflection Round

To conclude, go around the room and have all the students share their response to the first prompt, and then all share their response to the second.

a. I observed . . .

b. I discovered . . .

Here's What Just Happened in Class

- Students had a chance to examine an item from the Folger collection, learn about its history, draw conclusions about its use, and see its direct connection to what they are doing in class.

- Students approached the language and action in the text in a new and different way, working in groups to consider language, movement, and meaning . . . and how they work together.

- Students made collaborative decisions about language, movement, and meaning and shared those decisions actively with the rest of the class.

RESOURCE #1.4A

This promptbook describes an 1852 American production of *Macbeth* that featured the celebrated American Shakespearean actor Edwin Forrest in the title role. The Folger Library cite includes the words "With the stage business . . ." because promptbooks contain all the added notes about "stage business" particular to a specific production. The cite also makes clear that the marks in this one were made by William McFarland.

Mr. Forrest headlined a production of *Macbeth* on Broadway in the following year, 1853.

Earlier, in 1849, the rivalry and jealousy between Edwin Forrest (the American Macbeth) and William Macready (the English one) caused riots at the Astor Opera House in New York. Twenty-three people died and more than 100 were injured, many shot by the militia that was called out to quell the disturbance. They were passionately fighting about which was the better production of *Macbeth*!

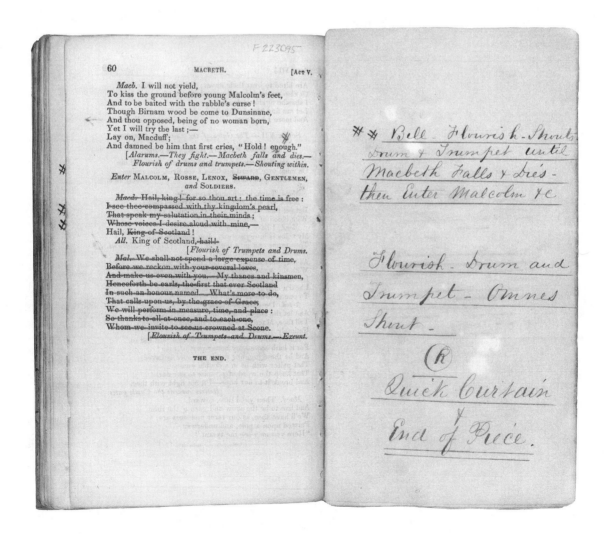

RESOURCE #1.4B

Macbeth 1.3.40–52 (edited)

MACBETH
So foul and fair a day I have not seen.

BANQUO
. . . —What are these,
So withered, and so wild in their attire,
That look not like th' inhabitants o' th' Earth
And yet are on 't?—Live you?
. . . You seem to understand me
By each at once her choppy finger laying
Upon her skinny lips. You should be women,
And yet your beards forbid me to interpret
That you are so.

MACBETH Speak if you can. What are you?

RESOURCE #1.4C

Macbeth 1.3.50–82 (edited)

FIRST WITCH

All hail, Macbeth! Hail to thee, Thane of Glamis!

SECOND WITCH

All hail, Macbeth! Hail to thee, Thane of Cawdor!

THIRD WITCH

All hail, Macbeth, that shalt be king hereafter!

BANQUO

Good sir, why do you start and seem to fear
Things that do sound so fair? . . .
. . . My noble partner
You greet with present grace and great prediction
Of noble having and of royal hope . . .
. . . To me you speak not.
. . .
Speak, then, to me, who neither beg nor fear
Your favors nor your hate.

FIRST WITCH Hail!

SECOND WITCH Hail!

THIRD WITCH Hail!

FIRST WITCH

Lesser than Macbeth and greater.

SECOND WITCH

Not so happy, yet much happier.

THIRD WITCH

Thou shalt get kings, though thou be none.
So all hail, Macbeth and Banquo!

FIRST WITCH

Banquo and Macbeth, all hail!

MACBETH

> Stay, you imperfect speakers. Tell me more.
> . . . To be king
> Stands not within the prospect of belief.
> . . . Say from whence
> You owe this strange intelligence or why
> Upon this blasted heath you stop our way
> With such prophetic greeting. Speak, I charge you.
>
> *Witches vanish.*

RESOURCE #1.4D

Macbeth 1.3.83–131 (edited)

BANQUO
Whither are they vanished?

MACBETH
Into the air, and what seemed corporal melted,
As breath into the wind. Would they had stayed!

BANQUO
Were such things here as we do speak about?
Or have we eaten on the insane root?

MACBETH
Your children shall be kings.

BANQUO You shall be king.

MACBETH
And Thane of Cawdor too. Went it not so?

BANQUO
To th' selfsame tune and words.—Who's here?
                              Enter Ross and Angus.

ROSS
The King hath happily received, Macbeth,
The news of thy success.
Every one did bear
Thy praises in his kingdom's great defense,
And poured them down before him.

ANGUS We are sent
To give thee from our royal master thanks,
And [to] herald thee into his sight.

ROSS
He bade me call thee Thane of Cawdor,
In which addition, hail, most worthy thane,
For it is thine.

BANQUO
What, can the devil speak true?

MACBETH
The Thane of Cawdor lives. Why do you dress me
In borrowed robes?

ANGUS Who was the Thane lives yet,
. . .
But treasons capital, confessed and proved,
Have overthrown him.

MACBETH, [aside] Glamis and Thane of Cawdor!
The greatest is behind. [To Ross and Angus.] Thanks
for your pains.
[Aside to Banquo.] Do you not hope your children
shall be kings,
When those that gave the Thane of Cawdor to me
Promised no less to them?

RESOURCE #1.4E

Macbeth 1.3.132–175 (edited)

BANQUO
That, trusted home,
Might yet enkindle you unto the crown,
Besides the Thane of Cawdor. But 'tis strange.
And oftentimes . . .
The instruments of darkness tell us truths . . .
Cousins, a word, I pray you.   *They step aside.*

MACBETH
[Aside] This supernatural soliciting
Cannot be ill, cannot be good. If ill,
. . . I am Thane of Cawdor.
If good, why do I yield to that suggestion
Whose horrid image doth unfix my hair
And make my seated heart knock at my ribs
Against the use of nature?

BANQUO Look how our partner's rapt.

MACBETH, [aside]
If chance will have me king, why, chance may
crown me
Without my stir.

BANQUO New honors come upon him.

MACBETH, [aside] Come what come may,
Time and the hour runs through the roughest day.

BANQUO
Worthy Macbeth, we stay upon your leisure.

MACBETH
Give me your favor.
. . . Let us toward the King.
[Aside to Banquo.] Think upon what hath chanced,
and at more time . . . let us speak
Our free hearts each to other.

BANQUO Very gladly.

MACBETH
Till then, enough.—Come, friends.
                                        They exit.

Macbeth 1.4.1–30 (edited)

Flourish. Enter King Duncan, Lennox, Malcolm,
Donalbain, and Attendants.

DUNCAN

    Is execution done on Cawdor? Are not
    Those in commission yet returned?

MALCOLM My liege,

    They are not yet come back. But I have spoke
    With one that saw [Cawdor] die, who did report
    That very frankly he confessed his treasons,
    Implored your Highness' pardon, and set forth
    A deep repentance. Nothing in his life
    Became him like the leaving it.

DUNCAN There's no art

    To find the mind's construction in the face.
    He was a gentleman on whom I built
    An absolute trust.

                 Enter Macbeth, Banquo, Ross, and Angus.

    O worthiest cousin,
    The sin of my ingratitude even now
    Was heavy on me.
    Only I have left to say,
    More is thy due than more than all can pay.

MACBETH

    The service and the loyalty I owe
    In doing it pays itself . . . Our duties
    Are to your throne and state, children and servants,
    Which do but what they should by doing everything
    Safe toward your love and honor.

RESOURCE #1.4G

Macbeth 1.4.31–65 (edited)

DUNCAN Welcome hither.
   I . . . will labor
   To make thee full of growing.—Noble Banquo,
   That hast no less deserved nor must be known
   No less to have done so, let me enfold thee
   And hold thee to my heart.

BANQUO There, if I grow,
   The harvest is your own.

DUNCAN
   Sons, kinsmen, thanes,
   And you whose places are the nearest, know
   We will establish our estate upon
   Our eldest, Malcolm, whom we name hereafter
   The Prince of Cumberland.

MACBETH
   The rest is labor which is not used for you.
   I'll . . . make joyful
   The hearing of my wife with your approach.
   So humbly take my leave.

DUNCAN My worthy Cawdor.

MACBETH, [aside]
   The Prince of Cumberland! That is a step
   On which I must fall down or else o'erleap,
   For in my way it lies. Stars, hide your fires;
   Let not light see my black and deep desires.
                         He exits.

DUNCAN
   True, worthy Banquo. He is full so valiant,
   And in his commendations I am fed:
   It is a banquet to me.—Let's after him,
   Whose care is gone before to bid us welcome.
   It is a peerless kinsman.
                    Flourish. They exit.

Shakespeare in Context

Here's What We're Doing and Why

Today we'll take a minute to allow students to discover that the universe of Shakespeare is bigger, more diverse, and more interesting than your students may realize. This lesson is all about giving everyone a glimpse into some of the most expansive, exciting, and surprising aspects of studying Shakespeare, his words, and his world. It zooms out beyond *Macbeth* for a moment!

By the end of this lesson, students will have examined their own ideas about Shakespeare's world. They will have enlarged their sense of history by studying 5 primary source documents spanning the 1600s to the 1900s. They will have reflected on the wide world of Shakespeare and their place in it.

What Will I Need?

- Portrait of Abd el-Ouahed ben Messaoud ben Mohammed Anoun, Moroccan Ambassador to Queen Elizabeth I, ca. 1600 – **RESOURCE #1.5A**

- John Smith's Map of Virginia and the Chesapeake, a 1631 copy of the 1612 original – **RESOURCE #1.5B**

- Portraits by Wenceslaus Hollar, 1645 – **RESOURCE #1.5C**

- Ira Aldridge's First Appearance at Covent Garden as Othello, 1833 – **RESOURCE #1.5D**

- *Romeo y Julieta*, "Prologo," Pablo Neruda, written in 1964, published in 2001 – **RESOURCE #1.5E**

- 6 Mind-blowing Facts about Shakespeare and History – **RESOURCE #1.5F**

- Large paper, markers, and/or Post-it Notes for the gallery walk we're calling "Document Speed Dating"

How Should I Prepare?

- Set up your classroom for "Document Speed Dating": Post the 5 documents at various stations around the room, and make sure that (1) the images are big and clear enough for everyone to see details and (2) there's enough space around each document for students to respond in writing. You can use whiteboards, butcher paper, or Post-it Notes—just make sure that there's room for everyone to "talk back" to each image.

- Organize your students into 5 groups, each one starting at a different station.

Agenda (~ 45-minute class period)

❏ Prior Knowledge Free Write: 7 minutes

❏ Speed Dating Instructions: 3 minutes

❏ Speed Dating Exercise: 21 minutes

❏ The List: 6 minutes

❏ Reflection Round: 8 minutes

Here's What Students Hear (From You) and (Then What They'll) Do

Part One: Prior Knowledge Free Write

1. Write: Jot down your thoughts on any of the following questions. When you imagine the world of Shakespeare, what do you see? What images **come** to your mind? Who are the people? What do they look and sound like? What are the places and objects? What's the vibe?

2. Talk: Turn to a classmate and discuss what each of you wrote.

3. Share: As a class, we'll share the images and ideas that arose in the paired conversations.

[**TEACHER NOTE:** Record student responses on the board in a broad way—no need to be exhaustive here. The point is to capture things like "people in ruffs and crowns" or "outdoor theaters" or "white Europeans" or "candlelight and quills" or "street fighting" or "plague" or "boring" or "lively" or "smelly clothes" or "harp music"—whatever comes to your students' minds. Welcome all responses without editorializing.]

Part Two: Document Speed Dating

1. Now you are going to meet actual historical documents from the world of Shakespeare. Your job is to look very closely at what you see and write down your observations right alongside the document. Keeping in mind your earlier impressions of Shakespeare's world, what in each image jumps out at you? What do you wonder about?

[**TEACHER NOTE:** You can keep the "What in the image jumps out **at you**?" prompt posted for students to see throughout this exercise.]

2. Get into your groups and begin at your assigned station. Each group should be at a different station.

3. You will have roughly 3 minutes at each station. As a group, move to the next station when you hear "Next!" Continue until every group has studied and written observations about all 5 documents.

4. Now that everyone has gone on a "speed date" with each document, return to your seat and find a partner. With this partner, discuss the main things that jumped out at you in these documents. Did anything surprise you? Did you learn anything new about the world of Shakespeare? We'll share more as a whole class in a few moments . . .

Part Three: The List

1. Let's look at the list of "6 Mind-blowing Facts about Shakespeare and History." (**RESOURCE #1.5F**)

[**TEACHER NOTE:** Call for 6 volunteers to read each fact aloud. Save discussion for the reflection round below.]

Part Four: Reflection Rounds

1. Now it's time for each of you to share your reflections on today's learning. We'll do 2 rounds. Remember, just one sentence and not more at this point. We want to hear from EVERY voice!

2. First, finish the sentence, "Something that changed my original mental picture of Shakespeare's world was . . ."

3. Second, finish the sentence, "I am still wondering . . ."

[**TEACHER NOTE:** As closure, ask students to summarize the main ways these primary source documents have enlarged or transformed their collective understanding of the universe of Shakespeare.]

Here's What Just Happened in Class

- Students have identified and interrogated their prior knowledge—and assumptions—of Shakespeare's world.

- Students have examined 5 different primary source documents spanning 4 centuries in order to enlarge their understanding of Shakespeare and history. They have seen for themselves that Shakespeare's Britain was multicultural and very much connected to the Americas.

- Students know important and surprising facts about the wide world of Shakespeare.

RESOURCE #1.5A

Abd el-Ouahed ben Messaoud ben Mohammed Anoun, Ambassador from Morocco to the court of Queen Elizabeth I, beginning in 1600

John Smith's Map of Virginia and the Chesapeake, a 1631 copy of the 1612 original

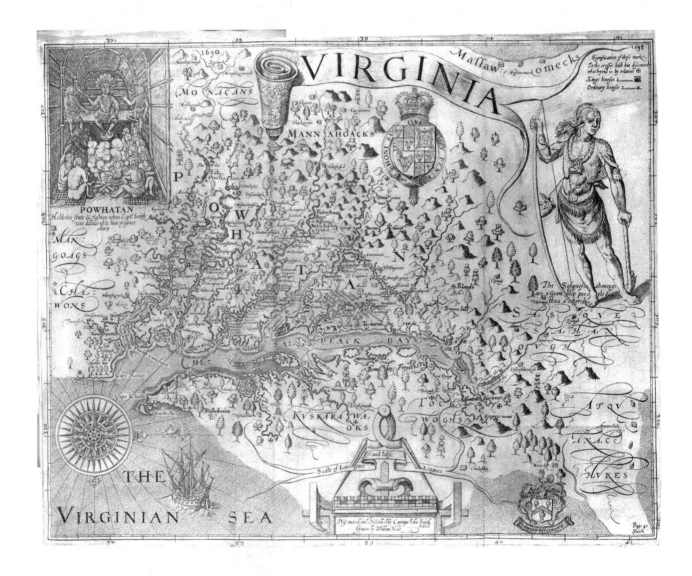

RESOURCE #1.5C

Portraits by Wenceslaus Hollar, made in and around 1645

 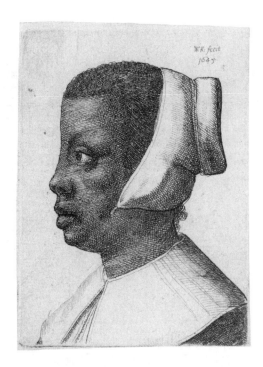

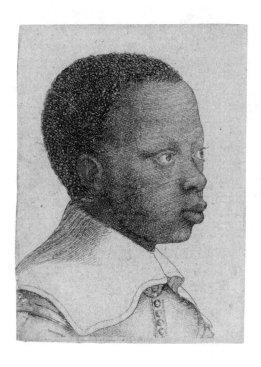

Ira Aldridge's First Appearance at Covent Garden as Othello

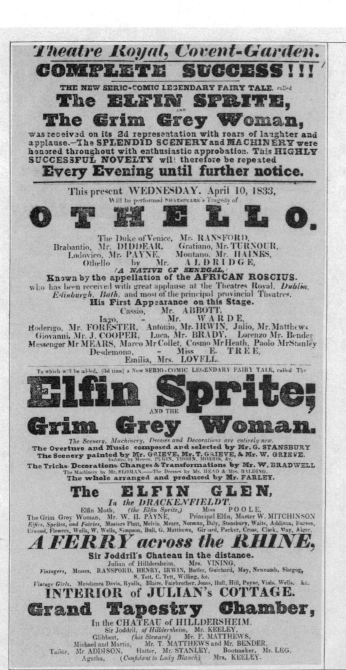

RESOURCE #1.5E

Romeo y Julieta, "Prologo," Pablo Neruda, written 1964, published 2001

PRÓLOGO

ENTRA EL CORO

CORO
    En la bella Verona esto sucede:
    dos casas ambas en nobleza iguales
    con odio antiguo hacen discordia nueva.
    La sangre tiñe sus civiles manos.

Dos horas durará en nuestro escenario esta historia: escuchadla con paciencia, suplirá nuestro esfuerzo lo que falte.

6 Mind-blowing Facts about Shakespeare and History

1. There were many people of different ethnicities and religions in Shakespeare's Britain. An important facet of this history: Africans participated in life at many social levels. Many were baptized—Protestant parishes retain the records. Black citizens included merchants, silk weavers, seamstresses, shoemakers, a circumnavigator who sailed with Sir Francis Drake, and a royal musician.

2. During her coronation festivities in 1600, Queen Elizabeth I entertained a large delegation of Muslim African officials, including Moroccan ambassador Abd el-Ouahed ben Messaoud ben Mohammed Anoun. He returned to court often and served as her advisor. Some think that Shakespeare might have seen him and African diplomats at court and drawn inspiration from them.

3. William Shakespeare was writing plays as English settlers colonized Jamestown, Virginia, in 1607. He is even thought to have based his play *The Tempest* on accounts of the wreck of a ship called the *Sea Venture*, which was on its way to Jamestown.

4. Ira Aldridge was the first African American actor to play the role of Othello at a professional theater: the Theatre Royal, Covent Garden, London, in 1833. Born in New York City, Aldridge performed all over Europe and was one of the first international stars of the Shakespeare stage. Paul Robeson was the first African American actor to play Othello in the United States—more than 100 years later, in 1943.

5. It was not until 1660 that the first female performed Shakespeare onstage. Until then, men and boys had played all the parts. After this point, though, women took on not just female characters but also male characters.

6. Shakespeare's works have been adapted and performed around the globe for centuries, and they have been translated into over 100 languages.

WEEK TWO: LESSON 1

"Unsex me here": Lady Macbeth and Jamaica Kincaid's "Girl" in Conversation about Gender

Here's What We're Doing and Why

In this lesson, students dive into the character of Lady Macbeth. Macbeth has sent her a letter, confiding in her about his meeting with the three weïrd sisters and their predictions. Lady Macbeth hears this news and begins to hatch a plan. Her soliloquies in this scene—in comparison with a contemporary paired text—give students an opportunity to think critically about historical notions of femininity. We pair up Shakespeare with contemporary Antiguan American author Jamaica Kincaid, allowing students to make connections between two different women—one in *Macbeth* and another in Kincaid's short story "Girl"—and between two very different pieces of literature.

Pairing texts and text mashups put two authors from different centuries, genders, cultures, and belief sets in conversation with each other. Examining these texts together illuminates each one in new and energizing ways and allows students to get a sense of the differences and/or similarities. Pairing texts gets Shakespeare off the pedestal, and at the Folger we are always interested in doing that! You can read more about paired texts and get further suggestions about texts to pair with *Macbeth* in Donna Denizé's chapter on page 235 in this book.

What Will I Need?

- Copies of excerpts from Lady Macbeth's soliloquy in 1.5 to distribute and/or project – **RESOURCE #2.1A**

- Copies of "Girl" by Jamaica Kincaid to distribute and/or project – **RESOURCE #2.1B**

- Group Discussion Prompt (included below) for the board or to project

- Micro Mashup instructions (included below) for the board or to project

- Copies of Macro Mashup – **RESOURCE #2.1C**

- Journal reflection prompt (below) for the board or to project

- Highlighters and pens/pencils for students

How Should I Prepare?

- Be familiar with Here's What Students Hear (From You) and (Then What They'll) Do

- Start with students in groups of 3–4, and be ready to group and regroup!

Agenda (~ 45-minute class period)

- Quick small group discussion (3 minutes)

- Discussions on Lady Macbeth's soliloquies and "Girl" (25 minutes total)
- Micro Mashups and share (9 minutes)
- All-class Choral Reading of the Macro Mashup (3 minutes)
- Reflection (5 minutes)

Here's What Students Hear (From You) and (Then What They'll) Do

Part One: Pairing Up Lady Macbeth with "Girl" by Jamaica Kincaid

1. In our first groups, discuss the following: *What are some ideas that various cultures have about masculinity and femininity?*

[TEACHER NOTE: While the groups discuss the prompt, hand out **RESOURCE #2.1A**.]

2. Now we'll move to look at these ideas in another way. Have a look at Lady Macbeth in **RESOURCE #2.1A**. With your group, read through her soliloquies together, either chorally or with each person reading a line or a sentence. Highlight words, phrases, lines, and/or sentences that relate to gender: masculinity, femininity, roles, expectations, conflicts. Use the margins to make notes on each place you've highlighted. Think about connections between what you're noticing now and what you already know about the world of the play. You will have about 8–10 minutes to do this.

3. Now, regroup into new groups. Now that you're in your new groups, share your annotations with each other and add more to your own annotations based on discussion in your new group. (5 minutes)

4. Now, we'll proceed to the next text—Jamaica Kincaid's short story "Girl."

   IMPORTANT: Before we begin that, though, it's essential to note that this short story contains demeaning language in some places. We're not removing that language because the author felt it was important to include it. It's part of her story. However, because I don't want anyone in here to feel demeaned for any reason, we're each going to read "Girl" silently rather than aloud.

5. You're going to annotate "Girl" in the same way you did with Lady Macbeth's speeches—highlight words, phrases, lines, and/or sentences that relate to gender: masculinity, femininity, roles, expectations. Use the margins to annotate each highlighted place with a note about your thinking. (10 minutes)

6. Now back in your original groups, share these annotations with each other and add more to your own based on discussion with your new-ish group. (5 minutes)

Part Two: Welcome to Mashups!

1. We're now going to create "Micro Mashups." You'll have 5 minutes to do this!

[**TEACHER NOTE:** You can talk them through these directions or post them on the board or screen, or both:]

Micro Mashup Instructions:

- As a group, select one word, phrase, line, or sentence that focuses on gender from Lady Macbeth and another word, phrase, line, or sentence that focuses on gender from "Girl."

- Your two selections should relate to each other in some way (which you will explain).

- Prepare a QUICK choral reading of your two-line mashup, with some in your group assigned to Shakespeare's words and others assigned to Kincaid's. You may mix these two different lines together as creatively as you'd like.

- All members of your group must participate in the choral reading.

- Designate a member of your group to briefly explain your choices—of lines and in the reading.

2. Share your micro mashups and your insights about them with us all!

3. Now we're going to divide the class in half and everyone will participate in exploring a macro mashup of these two texts. A macro mashup remixes multiple lines in different ways, and gives you different ways to explore two texts. We're still exploring how these passages relate to each other in terms of gender.

4. Let's look at **RESOURCE #2.1C**. Half of the class will read Lady Macbeth's lines and the other half the lines from "Girl."

Reflection Round on the Macro Mashup

One after another around the room, reflect individually and orally on the first prompt:

1. I observed . . .

   And then the second:

2. I sense fear . . .

   And the third:

3. I wonder . . .

Here's What Just Happened in Class

- Students read two disparate texts—*Macbeth* and Kincaid's short story "Girl"—closely and collaboratively. Pairing up texts allows students to get a stronger sense of them, both individually and as a pair.

- Students considered each text and then the pair together; they focused on gender and difference from two vastly different sources, how they were alike and different. This allows students to make contemporary connections to Shakespeare.

- Students continued thinking about fear, how it drives the action through *Macbeth* and where it is evident in "Girl."

- Students actively demonstrated their analysis by creating micro mashups, and were introduced to another analysis by actively participating in the macro mashup that identified more connections between the two texts.

- Students are now familiar with the rich potential of pairing texts and of text mashups—analytical, creative, and collaborative—to illuminate all kinds of texts in new and energizing ways.

RESOURCE #2.1A

Two Soliloquies From Lady M

1.5.15–33

LADY MACBETH

> Glamis thou art, and Cawdor, and shalt be   15
> What thou art promised. Yet do I fear thy nature;
> It is too full o' th' milk of human kindness
> To catch the nearest way. Thou wouldst be great,
> Art not without ambition, but without
> The illness should attend it. What thou wouldst   20
>   highly,
> That wouldst thou holily; wouldst not play false
> And yet wouldst wrongly win. Thou 'dst have, great
>   Glamis,
> That which cries "Thus thou must do," if thou have   25
>   it,
> And that which rather thou dost fear to do,
> Than wishest should be undone. Hie thee hither,
> That I may pour my spirits in thine ear
> And chastise with the valor of my tongue   30
> All that impedes thee from the golden round,
> Which fate and metaphysical aid doth seem
> To have thee crowned withal.

1.5.45–61

LADY MACBETH

> The raven himself is hoarse   45
> That croaks the fatal entrance of Duncan
> Under my battlements. Come, you spirits
> That tend on mortal thoughts, unsex me here,
> And fill me from the crown to the toe top-full
> Of direst cruelty. Make thick my blood.   50
> Stop up th' access and passage to remorse,
> That no compunctious visitings of nature
> Shake my fell purpose, nor keep peace between
> Th' effect and it. Come to my woman's breasts
> And take my milk for gall, you murd'ring ministers,   55
> Wherever in your sightless substances
> You wait on nature's mischief. Come, thick night,
> And pall thee in the dunnest smoke of hell,
> That my keen knife see not the wound it makes,
> Nor heaven peep through the blanket of the dark   60
> To cry "Hold, hold!"

RESOURCE #2.1B

"Girl" by Jamaica Kincaid

The New Yorker, June 26, 1978

Wash the white clothes on Monday and put them on the stone heap; wash the color clothes on Tuesday and put them on the clothesline to dry; don't walk bare-head in the hot sun; cook pumpkin fritters in very hot sweet oil; soak your little cloths right after you take them off; when buying cotton to make yourself a nice blouse, be sure that it doesn't have gum in it, because that way it won't hold up well after a wash; soak salt fish overnight before you cook it; is it true that you sing benna in Sunday school?; always eat your food in such a way that it won't turn someone else's stomach; on Sundays try to walk like a lady and not like the slut you are so bent on becoming; don't sing benna in Sunday school; you mustn't speak to wharf-rat boys, not even to give directions; don't eat fruits on the street—flies will follow you; but I don't sing benna on Sundays at all and never in Sunday school; this is how to sew on a button; this is how to make a buttonhole for the button you have just sewed on; this is how to hem a dress when you see the hem coming down and so to prevent yourself from looking like the slut I know you are so bent on becoming; this is how you iron your father's khaki shirt so that it doesn't have a crease; this is how you iron your father's khaki pants so that they don't have a crease; this is how you grow okra—far from the house, because okra tree harbors red ants; when you are growing dasheen, make sure it gets plenty of water or else it makes your throat itch when you are eating it; this is how you sweep a corner; this is how you sweep a whole house; this is how you sweep a yard; this is how you smile to someone you don't like too much; this is how you smile to someone you don't like at all; this is how you smile to someone you like completely; this is how you set a table for tea; this is how you set a table for dinner; this is how you set a table for dinner with an important guest; this is how you set a table for lunch; this is how you set a table for breakfast; this is how to behave in the presence of men who don't know you very well, and this way they won't recognize immediately the slut I have warned you against becoming; be sure to wash every day, even if it is with your own spit; don't squat down to play marbles—you are not a boy, you know; don't pick people's flowers—you might catch something; don't throw stones at blackbirds, because it might not be a blackbird at all; this is how to make a bread pudding; this is how to make doukona; this is how to make pepper pot; this is how to make a good medicine for a cold; this is how to make a good medicine to throw away a child before it even becomes a child; this is how to catch a fish; this is how to throw back a fish you don't like, and that way something bad won't fall on you; this is how to bully a man; this is how a man bullies you; this is how to love a man, and if this doesn't work there are other ways, and if they don't work don't feel too bad about giving up; this is how to spit up in the air if you feel like it, and this is how to move quick so that it doesn't fall on you; this is how to make ends meet; always squeeze bread to make sure it's fresh; but what if the baker won't let me feel the bread?; you mean to say that after all you are really going to be the kind of woman who the baker won't let near the bread?

RESOURCE #2.1C

"Girl" and Lady Macbeth Macro Mashup

MOTHER/DAUGHTER VOICES IN "GIRL"	LADY MACBETH
wash the white clothes on Monday	
wash the color clothes on Tuesday	
make yourself a nice blouse,	
you are not a boy, you know	
	The raven himself is hoarse
don't	
don't	
don't	
you mustn't	
be sure to	
	The raven himself is hoarse
this is how to sew on a button	
this is how to hem a dress	
this is how you iron your father's khaki shirt	
This is how	
This is how	
	hoarse
	hoarse
this is how you grow okra	
this is how you sweep	
this is how you set a table for an important guest	
	The raven himself is hoarse
	That croaks the fatal entrance of Duncan
an important guest	
	under my battlements
this is how to behave in the presence of men	
try to walk like a lady	
you are not a boy, you know	
	Unsex me
	Unsex me here
this is how you smile to someone you don't like too much	
this is how you smile to someone you don't like at all	
	And fill me from the crown to the toe top-full
	Of direst cruelty.
this is how to make a bread pudding	
this is how to make pepper pot	
this is how to make	
this is how to make	
	Make thick my blood

or else
that way something bad won't fall on you;
something bad

> Come, you spirits
> you murd'ring ministers

You are not a boy, you know

> Unsex me here,
> And fill me from the crown to the toe top-full
> Of direst cruelty.

this is how to love a man,
and if this doesn't work there are other ways
and if they don't work don't feel too bad about giving up
don't feel too bad

> Remorse
> Stop up th' access and passage to remorse,
> That no compunctious visitings of nature
> Shake my fell purpose,

this is how to make a good medicine to throw
away a child before it even becomes a child;

> Come to my woman's breasts
> And take my milk for gall,
> Milk for gall

this is how to bully a man;

> Hie thee hither,
> That I may pour my spirits in thine ear
> And chastise with the valor of my tongue

this is how to make ends meet;

> Glamis thou art, and Cawdor, and shalt be
> What thou art promised.

"Look like th' innocent flower / But be the serpent under't": Understanding Lady Macbeth's Duplicity in 1.6

Here's What We're Doing and Why

In the previous lesson, students explored the cultural, historical, and societal subtext of Lady Macbeth's soliloquies and Jamaica Kincaid's "Girl." Now, they will use their understanding of soliloquy and subtext to explore a new piece of the play and the effects of *dramatic irony*, when the audience knows something that some of the characters don't. Macbeth and Lady Macbeth start down their path of duplicity by saying things that the reader or the audience or the student in this class knows are lies. Because we know they are lying, we can see how the fear of being caught affects their behavior. Students will work in groups to consider the Macbeths' words and what drives them . . . and they can begin to think about how these lies and the Macbeths' fear work together.

What Will I Need?

- Copies of 1.5.62–86 and all of 1.6 to distribute to each student – **RESOURCE #2.2A**

- Copies of a specially emended version of 1.6 to distribute to each student for Choral Reading – **RESOURCE #2.2B**

How Should I Prepare?

- Prepare spaces for students to work in different parts of the room and a performance space in the center

Agenda (~ 45-minute class period)

❑ Whole class reads the scene together (7 minutes)

❑ Groups work on a Choral Reading of a few lines and an original 2–3-line soliloquy (15 minutes)

❑ All-class Choral Reading of 1.6 with their additions (18 minutes)

❑ Reflection (5 minutes)

Here's What Students Hear (From You) and (Then What They'll) Do

1. Before we begin reading today's scenes—they are about Duncan's visit to the Macbeths' castle—let's think about one of Lady Macbeth's lines: "Look like th' innocent flower, / But be the serpent under't." Given her words, what can you predict about the Macbeths' behavior when the king arrives?

2. Now, let's read 1.6 together. We'll read this end punctuation to end punctuation, changing readers each time we encounter any punctuation mark other than a comma.

3. Now, let's create groups by counting off by 6.

[**TEACHER NOTE:** If your class is smaller, you can count off by 4.]

Then I'll give each group a number. Those groups with an even number will work with lines 1.6.18–24:

> *All our service,*
> *In every point twice done and then done double,*
> *Were poor and single business to contend*
> *Against those honors deep and broad wherewith*
> *Your Majesty loads our house. For those of old,*
> *And the late dignities heaped up to them,*
> *We rest your hermits.*

and groups with an odd number will work with 1.6.32–35:

> *Your servants ever*
> *Have theirs, themselves, and what is theirs in compt*
> *To make their audit at your Highness' pleasure,*
> *Still to return your own.*

4. In your group, take your assigned few lines and do these things in the next 15 minutes:

   - Prepare an all-together choral reading of these lines, using what you learned the previous week about tone and stress and various ways to say lines.

   - Next, write an original, 2–3-line speech (also known as a soliloquy, a speech that shares a character's thoughts out loud when they think they are alone) for Lady M that explores what she might be *really* thinking in contrast to the words she's speaking.

5. Then you'll read 1.6 together, made more exciting by your work. First, you'll read 1.6 as noted in **RESOURCE #2.2B**. Then you'll give us your original soliloquies on what Lady M was *really* thinking.

6. These readings and comments have been great! Here are a few quick questions to consider as we conclude:

   a. How are Lady Macbeth's words here different from her thoughts?

   b. What has Lady Macbeth already said that led you to write the soliloquy you shared?

   c. How do you feel, knowing what Lady Macbeth might really be thinking, when Duncan and Banquo do not?

Reflection Rounds

Let's go around the class as each of you finishes the sentence, thinking about what we've done in class today:

> First: I observed . . .
>
> Then: I wondered . . .
>
> Finally: I think fear is . . .

Here's What Just Happened in Class

- Everyone read some of Shakespeare's text aloud, in different ways to learn different things.

- Students close-read Shakespeare's text to consider subtext.

- Students worked together to write a brief soliloquy grounded in what they already know about Macbeth and Lady Macbeth and supported their writing choices with textual evidence.

- Students considered the effects of dramatic irony and how that can shape the audience's experience of a play.

RESOURCE #2.2A

1.5.62–86 (end of scene)

Enter Macbeth.

LADY MACBETH
    Great Glamis, worthy Cawdor,
    Greater than both by the all-hail hereafter!
    Thy letters have transported me beyond
    This ignorant present, and I feel now   65
    The future in the instant.

MACBETH My dearest love,
    Duncan comes here tonight.

LADY MACBETH And when goes hence?

MACBETH
    Tomorrow, as he purposes.   70

LADY MACBETH O, never
    Shall sun that morrow see!
    Your face, my thane, is as a book where men
    May read strange matters. To beguile the time,
    Look like the time. Bear welcome in your eye,   75
    Your hand, your tongue. Look like th' innocent
      flower,
    But be the serpent under't. He that's coming
    Must be provided for; and you shall put
    This night's great business into my dispatch,   80
    Which shall to all our nights and days to come
    Give solely sovereign sway and masterdom.

MACBETH
    We will speak further.

LADY MACBETH Only look up clear.
    To alter favor ever is to fear.   85
    Leave all the rest to me.
                  They exit.

1.6.1–39 (entire scene)

Hautboys and Torches. Enter King Duncan, Malcolm,
Donalbain, Banquo, Lennox, Macduff, Ross, Angus,
and Attendants.

DUNCAN

This castle hath a pleasant seat. The air
Nimbly and sweetly recommends itself
Unto our gentle senses.

BANQUO This guest of summer,
   The temple-haunting martlet, does approve,   5
   By his loved mansionry, that the heaven's breath
   Smells wooingly here. No jutty, frieze,
   Buttress, nor coign of vantage, but this bird
   Hath made his pendant bed and procreant cradle.
   Where they most breed and haunt, I have   10
     observed,
   The air is delicate.

                       Enter Lady Macbeth.

DUNCAN See, see our honored hostess!—
   The love that follows us sometime is our trouble,
   Which still we thank as love. Herein I teach you   15
   How you shall bid God 'ild us for your pains
   And thank us for your trouble.

LADY MACBETH All our service,
   In every point twice done and then done double,
   Were poor and single business to contend   20
   Against those honors deep and broad wherewith
   Your Majesty loads our house. For those of old,
   And the late dignities heaped up to them,
   We rest your hermits.

DUNCAN Where's the Thane of Cawdor?   25
   We coursed him at the heels and had a purpose
   To be his purveyor; but he rides well,
   And his great love, sharp as his spur, hath helped
    him
   To his home before us. Fair and noble hostess,   30
   We are your guest tonight.

LADY MACBETH Your servants ever
    Have theirs, themselves, and what is theirs in compt
    To make their audit at your Highness' pleasure,
    Still to return your own.   35

DUNCAN Give me your hand.
                            Taking her hand.
    Conduct me to mine host. We love him highly
    And shall continue our graces towards him.
    By your leave, hostess.
                            They exit.

RESOURCE #2.2B

Macbeth 1.6, emended

Hautboys and Torches. Enter King Duncan, Malcolm, Donalbain,
Banquo, Lennox, Macduff, Ross, Angus, and Attendants.

DUNCAN
    This castle hath a pleasant seat. The air
    Nimbly and sweetly recommends itself
    Unto our gentle senses.

BANQUO This guest of summer,
    The temple-haunting martlet, does approve,   5
    By his loved mansionry, that the heaven's breath
    Smells wooingly here. No jutty, frieze,
    Buttress, nor coign of vantage, but this bird
    Hath made his pendant bed and procreant cradle.
    Where they most breed and haunt, I have   10
       observed,
    The air is delicate.
                      Enter Lady Macbeth.

DUNCAN See, see our honored hostess!—
    The love that follows us sometime is our trouble,
    Which still we thank as love. Herein I teach you   15
    How you shall bid God 'ild us for your pains
    And thank us for your trouble.

LADY MACBETH
    [Performed by half of the class] All our service,
    In every point twice done and then done double,
    Were poor and single business to contend   20
    Against those honors deep and broad wherewith
    Your Majesty loads our house. For those of old,
    And the late dignities heaped up to them,
    We rest your hermits.
    [Response from the rest of the class: "Thou liest!"]

DUNCAN Where's the Thane of Cawdor?   25
    We coursed him at the heels and had a purpose
    To be his purveyor; but he rides well,
    And his great love, sharp as his spur, hath helped
       him
    To his home before us. Fair and noble hostess,   30
    We are your guest tonight.

LADY MACBETH

[Performed by the other half of the class]

Your servants ever
Have theirs, themselves, and what is theirs in compt
To make their audit at your Highness' pleasure,
Still to return your own.   35

[Response from the rest of the class: "Thou liest!"]

DUNCAN Give me your hand.

Taking her hand.

Conduct me to mine host. We love him highly
And shall continue our graces towards him.
By your leave, hostess.   40

They exit.

"Tears shall drown the wind": Hearing the Voices in a Soliloquy

Here's What We're Doing and Why

Today, you're going to feel like one of the weïrd sisters because we're going to go more deeply into Choral Reading, which, like so much of the Folger Method, works like magic. A speech that might feel dense and unfamiliar at first becomes clearer and more exciting with repeated reading, and the steps of Choral Reading, which eventually lead to a reading performed in two voices, lend themselves naturally to exposing the internal conflicts that soliloquies express. While students have read in unison before, today we'll use all of the steps of the Folger Essential of Choral Reading to prompt student discovery and creativity surrounding one of Macbeth's most famous soliloquies.

What Will I Need?

- Copies of Macbeth's soliloquy in 1.7 in one voice – **RESOURCE #2.3A**—and in two voices – **RESOURCE #2.3B**

How Should I Prepare?

- Familiarize yourself with Macbeth's 1.7 soliloquy so that you recognize how and where Macbeth expresses internal conflict (this will be helpful as you listen and respond to students' suggestions—they should be the ones making the discoveries and drawing conclusions today).

Agenda (~ 45-minute class period)

- ❏ Choral Reading (30 minutes)
- ❏ Discussion (10 minutes)
- ❏ Reflection (5 minutes)

Here's What Students Hear (From You) and (Then What They'll) Do

Part One: Choral Reading

Here, we follow the steps for Choral Reading, a Folger Essential.

1. Read the speech – **RESOURCE #2.3A** – as loud and fast as you can while still staying together with the rest of the class.

2. Read the speech again, loud and fast. Think about how you feel when you are trying to make a difficult decision. Read it that way.

3. By a show of fingers (1=I'm lost, 3=I've got this!), indicate your understanding of the speech.

4. Now, read person to person, end punctuation to end punctuation.

5. By a show of fingers, indicate your understanding.

6. What do you notice about this speech? What do you hear?

7. Next, I'll ask two volunteers (Reader 1 and Reader 2) to read the speech by alternating lines.

8. After listening to our two volunteers read, what do you think Macbeth is thinking about or feeling? How do you know?

9. Next, form two lines that face each other. Let's go to **RESOURCE #2.3B** to use the script broken into sides 1 and 2.

10. Now, let's take turns reading the passage—the whole class in unison—alternating sides, speaking the passage back and forth.

11. By a show of fingers, indicate your understanding.

[**TEACHER NOTE:** If more students are holding up two fingers, ask, "What more did you notice about the speech in this reading?" and perhaps read it one more time. Remind students to point out words or lines in the speech that help them to develop their answers.]

12. Read the speech again; this time Side 1 will start reading very quietly, Side 2 will read a little louder, and then your sides will get louder and louder with each subsequent line (a *crescendo*, of sorts, if you're a musical person). If there's time, we'll read again, starting loud and then speaking and getting softer and softer as we go.

13. What new understanding do you have of the speech? Did you think the dynamics were appropriate for what your side read? Why or why not?

Part Two: Hearing Voices

1. Now, let's take a seat and talk some more about this speech as a whole class.

    a. We've broken this speech into two sides, or two "voices." If you had to name those voices, what would you call them? Why?

    b. Do you feel like there should be more than two voices delivering this speech? Why or why not?

    c. Which words in this speech feel most important to you? Why?

    d. What emotions do you hear or read in this speech? Where?

Part Three: Reflection Rounds

1. Today, I noticed . . .

2. Today, I learned . . .

3. Today, I wondered . . .

Here's What Just Happened in Class

- All students spoke Shakespeare's words—repeatedly!

- Students close-read a complex Shakespeare soliloquy with little input from you.

- Students identified the sources and "sides" of Macbeth's internal conflict.

- Students have learned a tool to use when analyzing other soliloquies too.

- Students used Shakespeare's language to guide their decisions about meaning and about performance, including tone and dynamics.

Choral Reading of Soliloquy in 1.7

Script in One Voice

If it were done when 'tis done, then 'twere well
It were done quickly. If th' assassination
Could trammel up the consequence and catch
With his surcease success, that but this blow
Might be the be-all and the end-all here,   5
But here, upon this bank and shoal of time,
We'd jump the life to come. But in these cases
We still have judgment here, that we but teach
Bloody instructions, which, being taught, return
To plague th' inventor. This even-handed justice   10
Commends th' ingredient of our poisoned chalice
To our own lips. He's here in double trust:
First, as I am his kinsman and his subject,
Strong both against the deed; then, as his host,
Who should against his murderer shut the door,   15
Not bear the knife myself. Besides, this Duncan
Hath borne his faculties so meek, hath been
So clear in his great office, that his virtues
Will plead like angels, trumpet-tongued, against
The deep damnation of his taking-off;   20
And pity, like a naked newborn babe
Striding the blast, or heaven's cherubin horsed
Upon the sightless couriers of the air,
Shall blow the horrid deed in every eye,
That tears shall drown the wind. I have no spur   25
To prick the sides of my intent, but only
Vaulting ambition, which o'erleaps itself
And falls on th' other—

RESOURCE #2.3B

Choral Reading of Soliloquy in 1.7

Script in Two Voices

SIDE 1: If it were done when 'tis done, then 'twere well it were done quickly.

SIDE 2: If th' assassination could trammel up the consequence and catch with his surcease success, that but this blow might be the be-all and the end-all here,

SIDE 1: But here, upon this bank and shoal of time, we'd jump the life to come.

SIDE 2: But in these cases we still have judgment here,

SIDE 1: that we but teach bloody instructions, which, being taught, return to plague th' inventor.

SIDE 2: This even-handed justice commends th' ingredience of our poisoned chalice to our own lips.

SIDE 1: He's here in double trust:

SIDE 2: First, as I am his kinsman and his subject, strong both against the deed;

SIDE 1: Then, as his host, who should against his murderer shut the door, not bear the knife myself.

SIDE 2: Besides, this Duncan hath borne his faculties so meek,

SIDE 1: hath been so clear in his great office,

SIDE 2: that his virtues will plead like angels, trumpet-tongued, against the deep damnation of his taking-off;

SIDE 1: And pity, like a naked newborn babe striding the blast,

SIDE 2: or heaven's cherubin horsed upon the sightless couriers of the air,

SIDE 1: shall blow the horrid deed in every eye, that tears shall drown the wind.

SIDE 2: I have no spur to prick the sides of my intent

SIDE 1: but only vaulting ambition, which o'erleaps itself

SIDE 2: And falls on th' other—

"What cannot you and I perform . . . ?": Close-Reading 1.7 (and the Macbeths' Marriage) by Cutting a Scene

Here's What We're Doing and Why

Cutting a Text is one of the easiest Folger Essentials to practice. It gets students collaborating, playfully arguing, and—most importantly—speaking and close-reading Shakespeare's words as they slash scenes or speeches to their essence. The magic of this method is in the madness of so many small groups at work at once: Learning is happening while students suggest, defend, and change their cuts to create their own versions of the scene. Your vision for or understanding of the scene doesn't matter here. Don't skip the step that requires students to justify their choices; this is where they connect Shakespeare's language to their own reasoning and demonstrate what they have understood best. When you begin this lesson, remind students that cutting a scene is part of working with Shakespeare: Editors, scholars, teachers, directors, and actors have been cutting Shakespeare forever. (We think Shakespeare probably cut his own plays to make them a better length for performance.) Cutting is part of any Shakespeare production, as it will be a part of theirs!

What Will I Need?

- Copies of 1.7.29–95 – **RESOURCE #2.4A**. You may wish to provide electronic versions so that students can edit the text easily.
- Copies of Cutting *Macbeth* – **RESOURCE #2.4B** (perhaps stapled to the script)

How Should I Prepare?

- Prepare your classroom for collaborative work
- Organize students in small groups of 4–5

Agenda (~ 45-minute class period)

- ❏ Whole-class reading of the scene (5 minutes)
- ❏ Time to cut the scene (20 minutes)
- ❏ Perform cut scenes (10 minutes)
- ❏ Discussion of the cuts (10 minutes)

Here's What Students Hear (From You) and (Then What They'll) Do

Part One: Read the Scene

1. Let's look at this scene – **RESOURCE #2.4A**. Yesterday, we read Macbeth's soliloquy following Duncan's arrival to his castle. What was Macbeth conflicted about during that speech?

[**TEACHER NOTE:** Students will share that Macbeth wondered whether killing the king would come back to haunt him ("Bloody instructions . . . return to plague th' inventor"), recognized the king's "double trust" in him as nobleman and host, and worried that the public outcry over a popular king's death would undo anyone who succeeded him.]

2. Now, we're going to study the conversation that follows Macbeth's soliloquy. After he delivers that speech, Lady Macbeth enters, and they talk with each other about their plans for the king's visit. Let's read this out loud together. We'll read end punctuation to end punctuation, changing readers at any punctuation mark other than a comma.

3. By a show of fingers (1=I'm pretty lost, 3=I've got this!), how well do you understand this scene? What are Macbeth and Lady Macbeth discussing? Do they seem conflicted about anything?

[**TEACHER NOTE:** If many are lost, read the scene one more time. Students should recognize that the Macbeths are arguing about murdering Duncan.]

Part Two: Cut the Scene

1. Now, you're going to do what most directors do before rehearsing a Shakespeare play; you're going to cut this scene. Currently, there are 66 lines. Your task today is to cut the scene from 66 lines ultimately to 8 LINES! In your small groups, first cut the scene in half—to 33 lines. Then cut from 33 to 16 lines. Finally, in half one more time to 8 lines—all of this by striking through lines in the script. Make sure that you can explain why you are cutting the lines. The 8 lines that remain should represent what you understand as the "heart" of this scene: What do you most want an audience to see or understand about this scene?

2. Once you've arrived at your 8 remaining lines, write them down on your handout and share your rationale, your reasons, for keeping those lines or cutting others. If you felt like some lines were unnecessary, make sure that you explain why.

Part Three: Read the New Scenes

1. Now, we will share our cut versions of the scene with one another. Appoint two group members to read as Macbeth and Lady Macbeth. We'll go around the room to listen to each group's dialogue.

Part Four: Discussing Your Cuts

1. Now that we've heard all of your cuttings, let's discuss this scene a bit further:

   a. As you cut lines or listened to others' cut scenes, did you notice any patterns in language? Any words or ideas that were repeated?

[**TEACHER NOTE:** Students might notice the repetition of words like *man* and ideas about what manhood is and what courage is. They may also have noticed how many questions are posed; if so, ask a follow-up about the effect of having characters respond to someone's question with another question.]

   b. What else did you notice about the Macbeths' words in this conversation?

[**TEACHER NOTE:** Here might be a great moment to address Lady Macbeth's line about "dashing out the brains" of the babe that milks her . . . students will want to talk about it!]

   c. I noticed that many of you kept this line: [Insert a line that appears in many groups' scripts]; why do you think that is?

   d. How would you describe the Macbeths' emotions in this scene? Why? What does the language tell us?

   e. What do you think this conversation shows us about what the Macbeths expect of each other? What does the language tell us?

   f. What do you think this conversation shows us about what the Macbeths' society expects of noblemen and noblewomen (or simply, men and women)? How do you know?

   g. Does our society expect some of the same things? Which expectations are the same? Which are different?

Here's What Just Happened in Class

- You got out of the way after you charged students with drastically cutting a scene, calling on all of the knowledge they have acquired in the unit this far.

- In cutting, students collaborated to make big decisions about who Lord and Lady Macbeth are and what the important elements and big ideas of this scene are.

- Students identified patterns and repetition in Shakespeare's language and analyzed their effects.

- Students made connections between *Macbeth*, its cultural context, and their own lives and society (and these connections began with the language of the text).

- Students thought critically about gender roles and expectations in the past and present.

RESOURCE #2.4A

Cutting *Macbeth*, 1.7.29–95

Directions:

1. Read the scene aloud.

2. Read the scene aloud again.

3. Cut the scene from 66 lines to 33 lines.

4. Cut the scene from 33 lines to 16 lines.

5. Cut the scene from 16 lines to 8 lines.

6. Write your 8 remaining lines and a rationale for your cuts (or keeps) on the attached handout.

Enter Lady Macbeth.

MACBETH How now, what news?

LADY MACBETH
He has almost supped. Why have you left the   30
    chamber?

MACBETH
Hath he asked for me?

LADY MACBETH Know you not he has?

MACBETH
We will proceed no further in this business.
He hath honored me of late, and I have bought   35
Golden opinions from all sorts of people,
Which would be worn now in their newest gloss,
Not cast aside so soon.

LADY MACBETH Was the hope drunk
Wherein you dressed yourself? Hath it slept since?   40
And wakes it now, to look so green and pale
At what it did so freely? From this time
Such I account thy love. Art thou afeard
To be the same in thine own act and valor
As thou art in desire? Wouldst thou have that   45
Which thou esteem'st the ornament of life
And live a coward in thine own esteem,
Letting "I dare not" wait upon "I would,"
Like the poor cat i' th' adage?

MACBETH Prithee, peace.   50
   I dare do all that may become a man.
   Who dares do more is none.

LADY MACBETH What beast was 't,
     then,
   That made you break this enterprise to me?   55
   When you durst do it, then you were a man;
   And to be more than what you were, you would
   Be so much more the man. Nor time nor place
   Did then adhere, and yet you would make both.
   They have made themselves, and that their fitness   60
     now
   Does unmake you. I have given suck, and know
   How tender 'tis to love the babe that milks me.
   I would, while it was smiling in my face,
   Have plucked my nipple from his boneless gums   65
   And dashed the brains out, had I so sworn as you
   Have done to this.

MACBETH If we should fail—

LADY MACBETH We fail?
   But screw your courage to the sticking place   70
   And we'll not fail. When Duncan is asleep
   (Whereto the rather shall his day's hard journey
   Soundly invite him), his two chamberlains
   Will I with wine and wassail so convince
   That memory, the warder of the brain,   75
   Shall be a fume, and the receipt of reason
   A limbeck only. When in swinish sleep
   Their drenchèd natures lies as in a death,
   What cannot you and I perform upon
   Th' unguarded Duncan? What not put upon   80
   His spongy officers, who shall bear the guilt
   Of our great quell?

MACBETH Bring forth men-children only,
   For thy undaunted mettle should compose
   Nothing but males. Will it not be received,   85
   When we have marked with blood those sleepy two
   Of his own chamber and used their very daggers,
   That they have done 't?

LADY MACBETH Who dares receive it other,
    As we shall make our griefs and clamor roar   90
    Upon his death?

MACBETH I am settled and bend up
    Each corporal agent to this terrible feat.
    Away, and mock the time with fairest show.
    False face must hide what the false heart doth   95
      know.
                                They exit.

Cut Scene and Rationale

Rewrite your 8 lines below (in order):

_____

_____

_____

_____

_____

_____

_____

_____

Explain why you kept the lines above (or cut those that have been left out) below:

WEEK TWO: LESSON 5

"Come, let me clutch thee": Taking a Dagger to Macbeth's Soliloquy and Creating a Reading

Here's What We're Doing and Why

Earlier this week, students performed a choral reading in two voices and considered whether that soliloquy could have even more than two "consciences" at work. Then, students cut a scene between the Macbeths and explored what their dialogue revealed about their characters and their relationship. Now, they will put their skills and knowledge from the past few lessons together to cut and create a dramatic reading of Macbeth's "Is this a dagger" speech in 2.1. Everything that students practice today will be useful for their final project in Week Five. In order to put a scene on its feet, any acting company must make decisions about how to cut a scene (or a speech), what "voices" the audience ought to hear, and how Shakespeare's words should be delivered.

What Will I Need?

- Copies of Macbeth's 2.1 soliloquy – **RESOURCE #2.5A**

How Should I Prepare?

- Space for students to work in small groups of 4–5 and all together in a large open space
- Organize students into small groups of 4–5

Agenda (~ 45-minute class period)

- ❏ Quick full-class Choral Reading (5 minutes)
- ❏ Cut the text, create your 16-line scripted reading, and rehearse (25 minutes)
- ❏ Scripted reading performances (10 minutes)
- ❏ Reflection (5 minutes)

Here's What Students Hear (From You) and (Then What They'll) Do

Part One: Read the Speech

Distribute the soliloquies to students – **RESOURCE #2.5A**

1. Earlier this week, you performed a choral reading of a soliloquy and listened for the different "voices" or perspectives that were battling in Macbeth's mind. Today, you will also perform a soliloquy, but this time you will create a multiple-voiced scripted reading, dividing up the soliloquy in a creative way. To begin, let's read this soliloquy once, all together.

Part Two: Cut the Speech, Create the Scripted Reading, and Perform It

1. Now, assemble in your small groups. First, read the speech again in your group.

2. Then, work together to cut this speech IN HALF. Your script should reduce from 33 lines to 16 lines.

3. Next, divide the remaining 16 lines into two or more voices. The voices can read complete sentences or partial lines—it's all up to you. Then, decide what sort of volume, speed, or emotion the speakers responsible for each voice should use.

4. Practice your scripted reading and then let's have all groups perform theirs for the class.

Reflection Round

- I learned . . .

- I observed . . .

- I wish . . .

Here's What Just Happened in Class

- Students close-read a soliloquy in order to cut the text.

- Students identified the "voices" in a soliloquy.

- Students worked together to make decisions about a Shakespeare text with little input from you. This involves significant analysis, meaning-making, and decision-making.

- Students performed a soliloquy *from an original script that they created*. This skill of breaking up a text allows students to focus on meaning and key lines and phrases from a complex text.

RESOURCE #2.5A

Macbeth's Dagger Soliloquy, 2.1

MACBETH

Is this a dagger which I see before me,
The handle toward my hand? Come, let me clutch 45
   thee.
I have thee not, and yet I see thee still.
Art thou not, fatal vision, sensible
To feeling as to sight? Or art thou but
A dagger of the mind, a false creation 50
Proceeding from the heat-oppressèd brain?
I see thee yet, in form as palpable
As this which now I draw.
                       He draws his dagger.
Thou marshal'st me the way that I was going,
And such an instrument I was to use. 55
Mine eyes are made the fools o' th' other senses
Or else worth all the rest. I see thee still,
And, on thy blade and dudgeon, gouts of blood,
Which was not so before. There's no such thing.
It is the bloody business which informs 60
Thus to mine eyes. Now o'er the one-half world
Nature seems dead, and wicked dreams abuse
The curtained sleep. Witchcraft celebrates
Pale Hecate's off'rings, and withered murder,
Alarumed by his sentinel, the wolf, 65
Whose howl's his watch, thus with his stealthy pace,
With Tarquin's ravishing strides, towards his
   design
Moves like a ghost. Thou sure and firm-set earth,
Hear not my steps, which way they walk, for fear 70
Thy very stones prate of my whereabouts
And take the present horror from the time,
Which now suits with it. Whiles I threat, he lives.
Words to the heat of deeds too cold breath gives.
                            A bell rings.
I go, and it is done. The bell invites me. 75
Hear it not, Duncan, for it is a knell
That summons thee to heaven or to hell.

"'Twas a rough night": Such a Range of Emotion in 2.3

Here's What We're Doing and Why

There's a lot going on in 2.3—lots of emotion and several emotional shifts, from the humor of the Porter, to the horrific discovery of Duncan's body, to Macbeth and Lady Macbeth's attempts at distraction. Students will study the scene closely by first identifying and then depicting the key emotional moments. In doing this, they'll examine the emotional shifts and how they work.

What Will I Need?

- Copies of 2.3 – **RESOURCE #3.1A**

- Copies of – **RESOURCE #3.1B**

- Space for groups to create and present their "moments"

How Should I Prepare?

- Be ready to assign students in groups of 4–8 (depending on the size of your class)

- Familiarize yourself with the assignment

Agenda (~ 45-minute class period)

- ❏ Students in groups reading through 2.3 together (10 minutes)

- ❏ Explanation of "freeze-framing" task (5 minutes)

- ❏ In groups, choose 4 lines and plan your 4 moments (15 minutes)

- ❏ Speedy presentation of all moments to class (15 minutes)

Here's What Students Hear (From You) and (Then What They'll) Do

1. We've worked a good bit with stress and tone. Today, we are building off the use of our voices by adding a little movement to our analytical choices and by "freezing" these moments.

2. In 2.3, we see comic relief, horror, fear, attempted distraction (even a fake fainting!), and dramatic irony—all in a short scene of only 172 lines. Today, your goal is to capture the wide range of emotion and action in the scene by creating 4 "moments" that you will share with the rest of the class.

3. You'll work in groups of 4–8 students. First, get with **RESOURCE #3.1A** and do a first read-through, using the techniques we've been using almost daily. Get a sense of all that's happening in this scene before we dig deeper.

4. Now that you've read the scene, let's go through the guidelines for creating your frames – **RESOURCE #3.1B**.

   – Choose 4 lines that you think represent important moments of either a dominant emotion or a shift in emotion.

   – One of these 4 lines must be a line from the Porter.

   – As a group, figure out the "moment" you will capture that depicts the emotion by showing the character frozen at the exact moment the line is delivered—their frozen movement, reaction, facial expression, sense of action.

   – In performing your "moments" live in class, every member of your group must participate. As you do, how about photographs of these moments?!

   – As part of your presentation, one member of your group should share how you arrived at your choices.

5. We'll have *rapid* presentations to the class, and discussion afterwards!

Here's What Just Happened in Class

- Students dug into Shakespeare's language—and a key scene in *Macbeth*—by approaching it through analysis and visualization.

- Students collaborated on discussing the emotional moments in the scene, the shifts from one moment to another, and the creation of depictions of those moments.

- Students mined the language of the play for deeper insight, and considered the relationships and power dynamics between the characters and their environments.

- Students presented their insights in static "moments," distilling the language of the play and what they know thus far into concrete statements in body language.

- Students' understanding of language and of character grows stronger.

RESOURCE #3.1A

2.3.1–172 (entire scene)

Knocking within. Enter a Porter.

PORTER Here's a knocking indeed! If a man were
porter of hell gate, he should have old turning the
key. (*Knock.*) Knock, knock, knock! Who's there, i'
th' name of Beelzebub? Here's a farmer that hanged
himself on th' expectation of plenty. Come in time!   5
Have napkins enough about you; here you'll sweat
for 't. (*Knock.*) Knock, knock! Who's there, in th'
other devil's name? Faith, here's an equivocator
that could swear in both the scales against either
scale, who committed treason enough for God's   10
sake yet could not equivocate to heaven. O, come in,
equivocator. (*Knock.*) Knock, knock, knock! Who's
there? Faith, here's an English tailor come hither for
stealing out of a French hose. Come in, tailor. Here
you may roast your goose. (*Knock.*) Knock, knock!   15
Never at quiet.—What are you?—But this place is
too cold for hell. I'll devil-porter it no further. I had
thought to have let in some of all professions that go
the primrose way to th' everlasting bonfire. (*Knock.*)
Anon, anon!   20

> *The Porter opens the door to*
> *Macduff and Lennox.*

I pray you, remember the porter.

MACDUFF
Was it so late, friend, ere you went to bed
That you do lie so late?

PORTER Faith, sir, we were carousing till the second
cock, and drink, sir, is a great provoker of three   25
  things.

MACDUFF What three things does drink especially
  provoke?

PORTER Marry, sir, nose-painting, sleep, and urine.
Lechery, sir, it provokes and unprovokes. It provokes   30
the desire, but it takes away the performance.
Therefore much drink may be said to be an
equivocator with lechery. It makes him, and it

mars him; it sets him on, and it takes him off; it
persuades him and disheartens him; makes him   35
stand to and not stand to; in conclusion, equivocates
him in a sleep and, giving him the lie, leaves
    him.

MACDUFF I believe drink gave thee the lie last night.

PORTER That it did, sir, i' th' very throat on me; but I   40
    requited him for his lie, and, I think, being too
    strong for him, though he took up my legs sometime,
    yet I made a shift to cast him.

MACDUFF Is thy master stirring?

                    Enter Macbeth.
    Our knocking has awaked him. Here he comes.   45
                    Porter exits.

LENNOX
    Good morrow, noble sir.

MACBETH Good morrow, both.

MACDUFF
    Is the King stirring, worthy thane?

MACBETH Not yet.

MACDUFF
    He did command me to call timely on him.   50
    I have almost slipped the hour.

MACBETH I'll bring you to him.

MACDUFF
    I know this is a joyful trouble to you,
    But yet 'tis one.

MACBETH
    The labor we delight in physics pain.   55
    This is the door.

MACDUFF I'll make so bold to call,
    For 'tis my limited service.
                    Macduff exits.

LENNOX Goes the King hence today?

MACBETH He does. He did appoint so.   60

LENNOX
  The night has been unruly. Where we lay,
  Our chimneys were blown down and, as they say,
  Lamentings heard i' th' air, strange screams of
      death,
  And prophesying, with accents terrible,   65
  Of dire combustion and confused events
  New hatched to th' woeful time. The obscure bird
  Clamored the livelong night. Some say the Earth
  Was feverous and did shake.

MACBETH 'Twas a rough night.   70

LENNOX
  My young remembrance cannot parallel
  A fellow to it.
                                              Enter Macduff.

MACDUFF O horror, horror, horror!
  Tongue nor heart cannot conceive nor name thee!

MACBETH AND LENNOX What's the matter?   75

MACDUFF
  Confusion now hath made his masterpiece.
  Most sacrilegious murder hath broke ope
  The Lord's anointed temple and stole thence
  The life o' th' building.

MACBETH What is 't you say? The life?   80

LENNOX Mean you his Majesty?

MACDUFF
  Approach the chamber and destroy your sight
  With a new Gorgon. Do not bid me speak.
  See and then speak yourselves.
                                    Macbeth and Lennox exit.
  Awake, awake!   85
  Ring the alarum bell.—Murder and treason!
  Banquo and Donalbain, Malcolm, awake!
  Shake off this downy sleep, death's counterfeit,
  And look on death itself. Up, up, and see
  The great doom's image. Malcolm, Banquo,   90
  As from your graves rise up and walk like sprites

To countenance this horror.—Ring the bell.
                              Bell rings.
                              Enter Lady Macbeth.

LADY MACBETH What's the business,
    That such a hideous trumpet calls to parley
    The sleepers of the house? Speak, speak!   95

MACDUFF O gentle lady,
    'Tis not for you to hear what I can speak.
    The repetition in a woman's ear
    Would murder as it fell.
                              Enter Banquo.
    O Banquo, Banquo,   100
    Our royal master's murdered.

LADY MACBETH Woe, alas!
    What, in our house?

BANQUO Too cruel anywhere.—
    Dear Duff, I prithee, contradict thyself   105
    And say it is not so.
                              Enter Macbeth, Lennox, and Ross.

MACBETH
    Had I but died an hour before this chance,
    I had lived a blessèd time; for from this instant
    There's nothing serious in mortality.
    All is but toys. Renown and grace is dead.   110
    The wine of life is drawn, and the mere lees
    Is left this vault to brag of.
                              Enter Malcolm and Donalbain.

DONALBAIN What is amiss?

MACBETH You are, and do not know 't.
    The spring, the head, the fountain of your blood   115
    Is stopped; the very source of it is stopped.

MACDUFF
    Your royal father's murdered.

MALCOLM O, by whom?

LENNOX
    Those of his chamber, as it seemed, had done 't.
    Their hands and faces were all badged with blood.   120

So were their daggers, which unwiped we found
Upon their pillows. They stared and were distracted.
No man's life was to be trusted with them.

MACBETH
    O, yet I do repent me of my fury,
    That I did kill them.   125

MACDUFF Wherefore did you so?

MACBETH
    Who can be wise, amazed, temp'rate, and furious,
    Loyal, and neutral, in a moment? No man.
    Th' expedition of my violent love
    Outrun the pauser, reason. Here lay Duncan,   130
    His silver skin laced with his golden blood,
    And his gashed stabs looked like a breach in nature
    For ruin's wasteful entrance; there the murderers,
    Steeped in the colors of their trade, their daggers
    Unmannerly breeched with gore. Who could refrain   135
    That had a heart to love, and in that heart
    Courage to make 's love known?

LADY MACBETH Help me hence, ho!

MACDUFF
    Look to the lady.

MALCOLM, *aside to Donalbain* Why do we hold our   140
        tongues,
    That most may claim this argument for ours?

DONALBAIN, *aside to Malcolm*
    What should be spoken here, where our fate,
    Hid in an auger hole, may rush and seize us?
    Let's away. Our tears are not yet brewed.   145

MALCOLM, *aside to Donalbain*
    Nor our strong sorrow upon the foot of motion.

BANQUO Look to the lady.
                        Lady Macbeth is assisted to leave.
    And when we have our naked frailties hid,
    That suffer in exposure, let us meet
    And question this most bloody piece of work   150
    To know it further. Fears and scruples shake us.

In the great hand of God I stand, and thence
Against the undivulged pretense I fight
Of treasonous malice.

MACDUFF And so do I.   155

ALL So all.

MACBETH
Let's briefly put on manly readiness
And meet i' th' hall together.

ALL Well contented.
All but Malcolm and Donalbain exit.

MALCOLM
What will you do? Let's not consort with them.   160
To show an unfelt sorrow is an office
Which the false man does easy. I'll to England.

DONALBAIN
To Ireland I. Our separated fortune
Shall keep us both the safer. Where we are,
There's daggers in men's smiles. The near in blood,   165
The nearer bloody.

MALCOLM This murderous shaft that's shot
Hath not yet lighted, and our safest way
Is to avoid the aim. Therefore to horse,
And let us not be dainty of leave-taking   170
But shift away. There's warrant in that theft
Which steals itself when there's no mercy left.
They exit.

Determining Key Emotions in 2.3

Guidelines for you:

1. Read the scene and choose 4 lines that you think represent important moments of either a dominant emotion or a shift in emotion.

2. One of these 4 lines must be a line from the Porter.

3. Slot the 4 lines in the spaces below.

4. As a group, figure out how you will capture a "moment" depicting the emotion by showing the character frozen at the exact moment the line is delivered—their frozen movement, reaction, facial expression, sense of action.

5. Depending on the line, consider where the character is in relation to their environment or their relationships. Where would Duncan's bedroom be, for example? Where's the door that the Porter answers? From which direction would the Macbeths enter? How will you show relationships and power dynamics by your placement of each character?

6. As you perform your "moments" live in class, every member of your group must participate.

EMOTION or SHIFT	LINE
#1	
#2	
#3	
#4	

"'Tis unnatural / Even like the deed that's done": Exploring the *Great Chain of Being* (1579) for Ideas about an Ordered World

Here's What We're Doing and Why

This lesson focuses on *Macbeth* 2.4 and the idea of natural order. The imagery in this scene describes the fear and chaos of a disrupted world, presumably caused by the Macbeths' deeds. They have disturbed the natural order: strange natural occurrences are haunting Scotland as Macbeth prepares to become king and Macduff departs for his own castle.

We'll start by doing some quick thinking about familiar ecosystems or entities and how they are organized, and compare them to an image of the ordered world popular in Shakespeare's time. Students will examine an image of a primary source—the Elizabethan *Great Chain of Being* (1579)—that offers insight into perceptions of the world's natural order and hierarchy that people held at that time.

Briefly: The philosophy of the "Great Chain of Being" derives from Aristotle, Plato, and other ancient philosophers, and it was adapted by various Western groups through the Middle Ages and during the Early Modern period when Shakespeare was writing. Though there were many iterations of this philosophy, what remained foundational was the idea that the universe has a natural order and hierarchy. Though this notion died out in the 19th century, it was commonly known during Shakespeare's lifetime. The image included here (**RESOURCE #3.2A**) illustrates the Eurocentric view of the ordered world in 1579. It was included in *Rhetorica Christiana*, a book written by Diego de Valadés, a Spaniard and a Franciscan friar who was a missionary to indigenous groups in Mexico.

What Will I Need?

- Image of the *Great Chain of Being* to distribute or project – **RESOURCE #3.2A**
- Copies of 2.4 – **RESOURCE #3.2B**

How Should I Prepare?

- Secure board space or chart paper to create organizational diagrams
- Decide whether you'll work this class as a whole or in groups

Agenda (~ 45-minute class period)

- ❑ Quick discussion about organizations and order (12 minutes)
- ❑ Create a visual organizational map of the order in *Macbeth* from the beginning of the play to *just before* Duncan's murder (8 minutes)

❏ Take a close look at a primary source, the *Great Chain of Being* (10 minutes)

❏ Read 2.4 looking for post-murder mayhem (8 minutes)

❏ Revise the world order in *Macbeth* (7 minutes)

Here's What Students Hear (From You) and (Then What They'll) Do

1. Let's pick two familiar "ecosystems" or entities from the list below, and quickly describe what we know about how they're organized. What are the different roles or functions within each one? Are there hierarchical structures present? What else?

   - A school
   - U.S. Government
   - Life in the ocean
   - The insect world
   - A grocery store
   - Another idea suggested by students

2. Now that you are deep into the world of *Macbeth*, think about its organization. What was the established social order of Scotland before the murder? What are the roles of the thanes? What seems to be the thane/king relationship? How do servants fit in? What about roles within families and between spouses? Is there a hierarchical structure?

3. Focus on the play *after* the opening battle, but *before* Duncan's murder. Either in in groups or as a class with a volunteer at the board drawing, create a visual map or diagram showing the social hierarchy that exists among the characters in the Scottish kingdom as *Macbeth* tells us about them. As far as we can tell, who fits where?

   - Duncan
   - Thanes (including Macbeth, Lennox, Ross, Macduff, Banquo)
   - Lady Macbeth
   - Duncan's guards
   - Malcolm
   - Donalbain
   - Former Thane of Cawdor, now dead
   - Macdonwald

4. Now, let's look at an image from the late 1500s in order to see what people might have thought then about how the world is organized.

[TEACHER NOTE: Give them a little background on the philosophy and the image—see above.]

   - What do you notice about the imagery in the drawing?
     [TEACHER NOTE: Allow students to study the image closely without pointing things out to them. Let them discover and make inferences. De-

pending on what your students notice, you might ask some guiding questions such as . . .]

   – Who/What are on each level?

   – Are there any divisions within levels?

   – What do you see in the margin area?

   – Who's at the top? How do you know?

   – What's going vertically down the center of the drawing? Why might the artist have put in this detail?

   – What else do you notice?

- What might this Chain of Being image reveal to you about how people saw the world in the late 1500s, right around the time that Shakespeare wrote *Macbeth*?

5. Now let's see what the play tells us in 2.4 – **RESOURCE #3.2B**.

[**TEACHER NOTE:** Since this is a short scene, you can divide the class into thirds, and each group can chorally read the lines of Old Man, Ross, and Macduff.]

- What does this scene tell you about the organization and state of the natural world in this part of *Macbeth*? How do you know? Which words or phrases from the text give you this idea?

- Does the Chain of Being image offer insight into what is happening in Scotland now that Duncan has been murdered?

6. Finally, let's return to your original diagram about the social order in Scotland before Duncan's murder. Now that the murder has already occurred, how has order been disrupted? Which characters are now out of order, either by their own choices or as a result of others' choices? What is the feeling of 2.4 as a result of the disorder in Scotland? Where can you sense the fear playing in this scene?

[**TEACHER NOTE:** You might want to nudge students toward thinking about Macduff's choice to go to his home at Fife instead of heading to Scone, where Macbeth will be crowned king.]

Here's What Just Happened in Class

- Students accessed prior knowledge and understanding about organized "ecosystems" in their own world.

- Students used this knowledge about organization of systems to visually show their understanding of the social order of the characters at one point in the play.

- Students expanded their knowledge by (a) examining a 1579 image of the Chain of Being and made inferences about what the image is depicting, and by (b) analyzing 2.4 for clues of disorder and chaos, and by (c) visually representing the social order in *Macbeth* at a different time in the play.

- Students were able to examine structures of social power and status in *Macbeth*, in a historical primary source, and in their day-to-day lives.

RESOURCE #3.2A

1579 drawing of the Great Chain of Being from
Diego de Valadés, Rhetorica Christiana

RESOURCE #3.2B

2.4 (entire scene)

Enter Ross with an Old Man.

OLD MAN

    Threescore and ten I can remember well,
    Within the volume of which time I have seen
    Hours dreadful and things strange, but this sore night
    Hath trifled former knowings.   5

ROSS Ha, good father,

    Thou seest the heavens, as troubled with man's act,
    Threatens his bloody stage. By th' clock 'tis day,
    And yet dark night strangles the traveling lamp.
    Is 't night's predominance or the day's shame   10
    That darkness does the face of earth entomb
    When living light should kiss it?

OLD MAN 'Tis unnatural,

    Even like the deed that's done. On Tuesday last
    A falcon, tow'ring in her pride of place,   15
    Was by a mousing owl hawked at and killed.

ROSS

    And Duncan's horses (a thing most strange and
    certain),
    Beauteous and swift, the minions of their race,
    Turned wild in nature, broke their stalls, flung out,   20
    Contending 'gainst obedience, as they would
    Make war with mankind.

OLD MAN 'Tis said they eat each
    other.

ROSS

    They did so, to th' amazement of mine eyes   25
    That looked upon 't.

                      Enter Macduff.

    Here comes the good
      Macduff.—
    How goes the world, sir, now?

MACDUFF Why, see you not?   30

ROSS
Is 't known who did this more than bloody deed?

MACDUFF
Those that Macbeth hath slain.

ROSS Alas the day,
What good could they pretend?

MACDUFF They were suborned.   35
Malcolm and Donalbain, the King's two sons,
Are stol'n away and fled, which puts upon them
Suspicion of the deed.

ROSS 'Gainst nature still!
Thriftless ambition, that will ravin up   40
Thine own lives' means. Then 'tis most like
The sovereignty will fall upon Macbeth.

MACDUFF
He is already named and gone to Scone
To be invested.

ROSS Where is Duncan's body?   45

MACDUFF Carried to Colmekill,
The sacred storehouse of his predecessors
And guardian of their bones.

ROSS Will you to Scone?

MACDUFF
No, cousin, I'll to Fife.   50

ROSS Well, I will thither.

MACDUFF
Well, may you see things well done there. Adieu,
Lest our old robes sit easier than our new.

ROSS Farewell, father.

OLD MAN
God's benison go with you and with those   55
That would make good of bad and friends of foes.
                        All exit.

"Our Fears in Banquo Stick Deep": What Is Macbeth Afraid of and Why?

Here's What We're Doing and Why

This lesson is designed to help students get a deeper sense of Macbeth's character, and how he is grappling with his new status as king. Students' attention is drawn to word associations, especially royalty and lineage, or crowns and (family) trees in 3.2. Since this is a character study lesson, it helps students to clarify the threat Macbeth feels from Banquo, whom he decides to kill. This soliloquy is where Macbeth works through this decision to commit yet another heinous act. We will then look at how the threat of Banquo's children—as perceived by Macbeth—informs Macbeth's choices in later interactions. Students will differentiate between the influence of royalty and the influence of lineage—the family tree—on Macbeth's fears of Banquo, and they will predict how these will influence Macbeth's future decisions.

What Will I Need?

- Copies of Macbeth's soliloquy (3.1.52–77) – **RESOURCE #3.3A**

- Copies of Crown and Tree Questions, distributed or projected – **RESOURCE #3.3B**

How Should I Prepare?

- Be ready for students to work in groups of 3–4, assigned or in easy partnerships

Agenda (~ 45-minute class period)

- ❏ All-class Choral Reading of 3.1.52–77 (5 minutes)
- ❏ Individual rereading, marking up, and taking a shot at the questions (10 minutes)
- ❏ Small group discussion on students' notes and thoughts (15 minutes)
- ❏ All-class discussion of Macbeth's emotions (10 minutes)
- ❏ Reflection Round (5 minutes)

Here's What Students Hear (From You) and (Then What They'll) Do

1. Let's read the soliloquy out loud, everyone together, just to get the words in our mouths.

2. Next, each of you read the soliloquy independently and draw a crown over words associated with royalty and a tree over words associated with lineage. By yourselves, take a shot at answering the questions posed in **RESOURCE #3.3B**:

- Which words did you mark up? Discuss and debate contested words.
- Which of the royalty words are connected to Banquo or Duncan? Which are connected to Macbeth himself? From these observations, can you draw any conclusions about Macbeth's internal conflict?
- Notice places in the soliloquy where the words related to royalty seem to be set up against the words associated with lineage or family succession. Could this placement help us to understand Macbeth's position at this point in the play?
- Are there any other ways in which visually noting how the royal and lineal words connect answers to the question of how fear affects one's actions?

3. Now gather in your groups and share out/discuss your answers/notes with each other. Discuss where your notes overlap and diverge—and how your group experience with this speech expands the understanding that you found individually.

4. Now let's discuss as a class how you think Macbeth—who sees Banquo as a threat—might be feeling as he heads into the following conversations that are coming up for him:
   - Banquo's conversation with Macbeth;
   - Macbeth's conversation with murderers;
   - Macbeth's conversation with Lady Macbeth.

   Can you make some predictions? Does fear feature here? How might that fear show itself?

Reflection Round

- I observed . . .
- For the first time, I thought . . .
- I wonder . . .

Here's What Just Happened in Class

- Students engaged in a close-reading of a soliloquy—both collaboratively and independently.
- Students annotated the text and explored it through choral reading.
- Students used both of these experiences to analyze the speech and Macbeth's state of mind, giving close attention to connotations of the words.
- Students used close-reading to examine character motivation.
- Students tested and discussed their analyses with their classmates, and learned from those discussions.
- Students are poised to put this analysis to use as they move into Act 4.

RESOURCE #3.3A

3.1.52–77

MACBETH

> To be thus is nothing,
> But to be safely thus. Our fears in Banquo
> Stick deep, and in his royalty of nature
> Reigns that which would be feared. 'Tis much he   55
>   dares,
> And to that dauntless temper of his mind
> He hath a wisdom that doth guide his valor
> To act in safety. There is none but he
> Whose being I do fear; and under him   60
> My genius is rebuked, as it is said
> Mark Antony's was by Caesar. He chid the sisters
> When first they put the name of king upon me
> And bade them speak to him. Then, prophet-like,
> They hailed him father to a line of kings.   65
> Upon my head they placed a fruitless crown
> And put a barren scepter in my grip,
> Thence to be wrenched with an unlineal hand,
> No son of mine succeeding. If 't be so,
> For Banquo's issue have I filed my mind;   70
> For them the gracious Duncan have I murdered,
> Put rancors in the vessel of my peace
> Only for them, and mine eternal jewel
> Given to the common enemy of man
> To make them kings, the seeds of Banquo kings.   75
> Rather than so, come fate into the list,
> And champion me to th' utterance.

Crown and Tree Follow-up Questions

- Which words did you mark up? Discuss and debate contested words.

- Which of the royalty words are connected to Banquo or Duncan? Which are connected to Macbeth himself? From these observations, can you draw any conclusions about Macbeth's internal conflict?

- Notice places in the soliloquy where the words related to royalty seem to be set up against the words associated with lineage or family succession. Could this placement help us to understand Macbeth's position at this point in the play?

- Are there any other ways in which visually noting how the royal and lineal words connect answers the question of how fear affects one's actions?

"O treachery!": In 3.3, Learning about the Power of Movement through a Dumb-Show

Here's What We're Doing and Why

Today's lesson has students exploring the power of movement—how movement allows them to understand the language more deeply, and really take ownership of the text. It also introduces students to the historical theater convention of a dumb-show.

Early medieval plays would often be performed without actors speaking, and this tradition continued into the Early Modern period when Shakespeare was writing. They were called dumb-shows, short plays performed without words and often inserted into a longer play with spoken parts. Characters in the play mimed what was about to happen so audiences would be ready for the action when it took place. "The Murder of Gonzago" dumb-show is a key element of *Hamlet*.

It is important for students to know that in Shakespeare's time, the word *dumb* had only one meaning: "without words" or "silent." We don't use that definition for *dumb* anymore; if we could go backwards in history, we would call what happens in a dumb-show a *mime* or *pantomime*.

In this lesson, while actually paying very close attention to language, students will create and then perform two versions of their dumb-show. They'll have to focus on language in order to strip away language and voice, as they convey the meaning of words only through movement, facial expressions, and gestures. Assessing how these kinds of choices convey different shades of meaning is a skill that deepens understanding of language.

What Will I Need?

- Copies of text of Banquo's Murder, 3.3 – **RESOURCE #3.4A**

- Copies of Creative Enhancements for Dumb-Show of Banquo's Murder – **RESOURCE #3.4B**

How Should I Prepare?

- Divide the class into groups of 5–6. The *Macbeth* scene has 5 parts, but if you have more than 5, students can alternate (or be scenery!) to incorporate more people.

- Be ready to explain verbally the idea of a dumb-show and the directions.

Agenda (~ 45-minute class period)

- ❏ Intro to dumb-show and today's project (5 minutes)

- ❏ Group creation and rehearsal of 3.3 dumb-shows (12 minutes)

- ❏ Performance of 2 dumb-shows (5 minutes)

- ❏ Further group work to create second version (8 minutes)

❏ Performance of 2 dumb-shows (5 minutes)

❏ Reflection (10 minutes)

Here's What Students Hear (From You) and (Then What They'll) Do

1. Today, we're going to learn a little about something that often appeared in medieval and Early Modern plays—and that's a dumb-show. Shakespeare's *Hamlet* even has a dumb-show written right into the play. We're going to create and share dumb-shows at this point because they will help us focus on the importance of language and how it is enhanced by movement.

   - Medieval plays were often performed with silent actors, and this tradition continued into the Early Modern period when Shakespeare was writing. They were called dumb-shows, short plays performed without words and inserted into a longer play with spoken parts. Characters in the play mimed what was about to happen so audiences would be ready for the action when it took place.

   - In Shakespeare's time, the word *dumb* had only one meaning: "without words" or "silent." We don't use that definition for *dumb* anymore; if we could go backwards in history, we would call what happens in a dumb-show a *mime* or *pantomime*.

2. Today, in groups, you will start with 3.3, the spoken scene. You will read and get a sense of the language, and then you'll create a dumb-show that depicts the murder of Banquo (*Macbeth* 3.3). In dumb-shows, there is NO SPEAKING, so you'll be using ONLY body movements, facial expressions, and gestures to tell the story. You will still pay extremely close attention to the words, though, because you'll need to use movement accurately. NO SPEAKING, but you may improvise with furniture and props available in the classroom. You'll have 12 minutes to create your dumb-shows and rehearse them a bit. Then as time allows, let's see some of them!

3. Next—after you create your original "dumb-show"—you'll have a chance to think about interpreting it further in an *enhanced version*. **RESOURCE #3.4B** will give you a few suggestions for how you might go beyond what's on the page to imagine the story and visually show your creative interpretations. Then we'll see a couple of those too.

Reflection Round

Discuss in the last lively few minutes:

- How did removing most of the language from the scene change the way we approached performance?

- Were we successful in conveying a creative interpretation? Why or why not?

- Who might the third murderer be? Might it be Macbeth? Macduff? Some random extra? Why do you say so?

- How is fear being explored in this scene?

Here's What Just Happened in Class

- Students had to leave speaking behind for this class, and were made to embody Shakespeare's language through making text-based visual choices.

- Students, because they could not speak, had to go beyond the words to make some creative visual choices that more strongly conveyed the action and/or emotion.

- Students created two versions of a dumb-show—these are scene analyses, really—and observed the creations of other groups as well. The absence of language allowed them to envision the murder of Banquo and escape of Fleance in a number of different ways.

RESOURCE #3.4A

Text of Banquo's Murder

3.3.1–33 (entire scene)

Enter three Murderers.

FIRST MURDERER
But who did bid thee join with us?

THIRD MURDERER Macbeth.

SECOND MURDERER, *to the First Murderer*
He needs not our mistrust, since he delivers
Our offices and what we have to do
To the direction just.   5

FIRST MURDERER Then stand with us.—
The west yet glimmers with some streaks of day.
Now spurs the lated traveler apace
To gain the timely inn, and near approaches
The subject of our watch.   10

THIRD MURDERER Hark, I hear horses.

BANQUO, *within* Give us a light there, ho!

SECOND MURDERER Then 'tis he. The rest
That are within the note of expectation
Already are i' th' court.   15

FIRST MURDERER His horses go about.

THIRD MURDERER
Almost a mile; but he does usually
(So all men do) from hence to th' palace gate
Make it their walk.
                              Enter Banquo and Fleance, with a torch.

SECOND MURDERER A light, a light!   20

THIRD MURDERER 'Tis he.

FIRST MURDERER Stand to 't.

BANQUO, *to Fleance* It will be rain tonight.

FIRST MURDERER Let it come down!

The three Murderers attack.

BANQUO
O treachery! Fly, good Fleance, fly, fly, fly!   25
Thou mayst revenge—O slave!

He dies. Fleance exits.

THIRD MURDERER
Who did strike out the light?

FIRST MURDERER Was 't not the way?

THIRD MURDERER There's but one down. The son is
fled.   30

SECOND MURDERER We have lost best half of our
affair.

FIRST MURDERER
Well, let's away and say how much is done.

They exit.

Possible Creative Enhancements: Dumb-Show of Banquo's Murder

In your *enhanced* version, try one or more of the following enhancements:

1. LANGUAGE: In your dumb-show, emphasize the use of words that connect to LIGHT.

2. CHARACTER CHOICE: Banquo or the Murderers

   Emphasize Banquo's excellence, his warriorship, and his long struggle to survive the attack.

   OR

   Emphasize the excellence of the murderers, the surprise of the attack, the murderers' stealth, and Banquo's quick death.

3. RELATIONSHIPS: Banquo and Fleance

   Emphasize Fleance's quick-thinking and fast escape.

   OR

   Emphasize Banquo's sacrificing himself for his son.

Daring to Look on "that which might appall the devil": Putting Banquo's Ghost in Motion

Here's What We're Doing and Why

We're moving toward preparation and performance of final scenes, so now is a good time to revisit the cold-reading and collaborative staging that takes place in 3D Lit. Earlier in this unit, your students put a scene on its feet with just a little guidance from you; now, it's time to revisit the strategy so that they can get busy and you can get out of the way.

Today, students will engage in a speedy version of 3D Lit, and then perform 3.4 in relay. We've broken this long scene into 4 smaller parts. Each small group will perform their part of the scene, and then "pass the relay baton" from one Macbeth, Lady Macbeth, Lennox, and Ross (and maybe Banquo's ghost?) to the next. The "batons" can be a prop or costume piece, an everyday item, or even a just a name tag. This relay engages everyone in the whole scene and keeps those skills in practice as we get closer to the final projects.

What Will I Need?

- Copies of *Macbeth* 3.4 "Relay" scripts (each group member needs to have a copy of their part) – **RESOURCE #3.5A, RESOURCE #3.5B, RESOURCE #3.5C, RESOURCE #3.5D**

- Your relay "batons": costume pieces or props such as a tiara for Lady Macbeth, a sword for Macbeth, a sash for Ross or Lennox, and a cloak for the ghost. Or construction-paper-on-string name placards. Or everyday items used creatively!

How Should I Prepare?

- Organize your class into groups of 4 or 5

- Figure out how the relay will work in the space you've got

Agenda (~ 45-minute class period)

- ❑ 3D Lit (30 minutes)
- ❑ Performance (15 minutes)

Here's What Students Will Hear (From You) and (Then What They'll) Do

Part One: Speedy 3D Lit

1. In the last class, you gave us great versions of Banquo's murder. Today we'll dive into what happens next. We've broken scene 3.4 into 4 parts and you'll perform it in relay. Just like in a relay race, when your "leg" of the scene is complete, you

will pass a "baton" to the person playing your character in the next part of the scene.

2. Get into small groups and I'll pass out your relay text to each group. Use the techniques we've been using all along:

   - Work together to determine what's going on and what's being expressed. (For groups performing parts 2 and 3: Can the audience see Banquo's ghost?)
   - Work together to cut the number of lines in half.
   - Cast the parts. Make decisions about how to move, based on the words on the page. Pull all of this together into a promptbook on your copies of the script.
   - Rehearse.

Part Two: Perform the Scene Relay

1. Perform the parts of the scene in order, passing props between groups to help the audience understand who's who.

2. As each group finishes, applaud wildly!

Reflection Round

- As you leave class, finish "I discovered . . ."

Here's What Just Happened in Class

- Students collaborated to cut their scene and stage it.
- Students used their bodies and movement to express understanding of Shakespeare's language.
- Students demonstrated understanding of the characters, dialogue, and conflict through performance.
- Students considered the dramatic impact of what is seen (and not seen) on a stage.
- Students staged a play . . . and you stayed out of the way!

RESOURCE #3.5A

3.4 Part 1 (1–41): The Murderer Reports
(four or more actors)

Banquet prepared. Enter Macbeth, Lady Macbeth, Ross, Lennox, Lords, and Attendants.

MACBETH

You know your own degrees; sit down. At first
And last, the hearty welcome.

They sit.

LORDS Thanks to your Majesty.

MACBETH

Ourself will mingle with society
And play the humble host.   5
Our hostess keeps her state, but in best time
We will require her welcome.

LADY MACBETH

Pronounce it for me, sir, to all our friends,
For my heart speaks they are welcome.

Enter First Murderer to the door.

MACBETH

See, they encounter thee with their hearts' thanks.   10
Both sides are even. Here I'll sit i' th' midst.
Be large in mirth. Anon we'll drink a measure
The table round.   *He approaches the Murderer.*
There's blood upon thy face.

MURDERER 'Tis Banquo's then.   15

MACBETH

'Tis better thee without than he within.
Is he dispatched?

MURDERER

My lord, his throat is cut. That I did for him.

MACBETH

Thou art the best o' th' cutthroats,
Yet he's good that did the like for Fleance.   20
If thou didst it, thou art the nonpareil.

MURDERER

Most royal sir, Fleance is 'scaped.

MACBETH, *aside*

Then comes my fit again. I had else been perfect,
Whole as the marble, founded as the rock,
As broad and general as the casing air.   25
But now I am cabined, cribbed, confined, bound in
To saucy doubts and fears.—But Banquo's safe?

MURDERER

Ay, my good lord. Safe in a ditch he bides,
With twenty trenchèd gashes on his head,
The least a death to nature.   30

MACBETH Thanks for that.

There the grown serpent lies. The worm that's fled
Hath nature that in time will venom breed,
No teeth for th' present. Get thee gone. Tomorrow
We'll hear ourselves again.   35

Murderer exits.

LADY MACBETH My royal lord,

You do not give the cheer. The feast is sold
That is not often vouched, while 'tis a-making,
'Tis given with welcome. To feed were best at home;
From thence, the sauce to meat is ceremony;   40
Meeting were bare without it.

RESOURCE #3.5B

3.4, Part 2 (42–87): Macbeth Sees Banquo's Ghost
(four to five actors)

What happened in lines 1–41: The Macbeths entered the banquet. One of the murderers reported to Macbeth that Banquo was killed but Fleance escaped.

Enter the Ghost of Banquo, and sits in Macbeth's place.

MACBETH, *to Lady Macbeth* Sweet remembrancer!—
   Now, good digestion wait on appetite
   And health on both!

LENNOX May 't please your Highness sit.   45

MACBETH
   Here had we now our country's honor roofed,
   Were the graced person of our Banquo present,
   Who may I rather challenge for unkindness
   Than pity for mischance.

ROSS His absence, sir,   50
   Lays blame upon his promise. Please 't your
      Highness
   To grace us with your royal company?

MACBETH
   The table's full.

LENNOX Here is a place reserved, sir.   55

MACBETH Where?

LENNOX
   Here, my good lord. What is 't that moves your
      Highness?

MACBETH
   Which of you have done this?

LORDS What, my good lord?   60

MACBETH, *to the Ghost*
   Thou canst not say I did it. Never shake
   Thy gory locks at me.

ROSS
Gentlemen, rise. His Highness is not well.

LADY MACBETH
Sit, worthy friends. My lord is often thus
And hath been from his youth. Pray you, keep seat.   65
The fit is momentary; upon a thought
He will again be well. If much you note him
You shall offend him and extend his passion.
Feed and regard him not.
                                                   Drawing Macbeth aside.
Are you a man?   70

MACBETH
Ay, and a bold one, that dare look on that
Which might appall the devil.

LADY MACBETH O, proper stuff!
This is the very painting of your fear.
This is the air-drawn dagger which you said   75
Led you to Duncan. O, these flaws and starts,
Impostors to true fear, would well become
A woman's story at a winter's fire,
Authorized by her grandam. Shame itself!
Why do you make such faces? When all's done,   80
You look but on a stool.

MACBETH
Prithee, see there. Behold, look! *To the Ghost.* Lo,
    how say you?
Why, what care I? If thou canst nod, speak too.—
If charnel houses and our graves must send   85
Those that we bury back, our monuments
Shall be the maws of kites.
                                                   Ghost exits.

RESOURCE #3.5C

3.4, Part 3 (88–129): The Ghost Returns (three to four actors)

What happened in lines 42–87: As Macbeth was about to sit down at the banquet, he saw the ghost of Banquo in his chair. He spoke to and about the ghost, leaving the rest of the guests puzzled, since they couldn't see it. Lady Macbeth excused Macbeth's behavior, telling everyone that Macbeth has suffered from fits since childhood, and then she chided her husband for his behavior. Then, the ghost exited.

LADY MACBETH What, quite unmanned in folly?

MACBETH
  If I stand here, I saw him.

LADY MACBETH Fie, for shame!   90

MACBETH
  Blood hath been shed ere now, i' th' olden time,
  Ere humane statute purged the gentle weal;
  Ay, and since too, murders have been performed
  Too terrible for the ear. The time has been
  That, when the brains were out, the man would die,   95
  And there an end. But now they rise again
  With twenty mortal murders on their crowns
  And push us from our stools. This is more strange
  Than such a murder is.

LADY MACBETH My worthy lord,   100
  Your noble friends do lack you.

MACBETH I do forget.—
  Do not muse at me, my most worthy friends.
  I have a strange infirmity, which is nothing
  To those that know me. Come, love and health to   105
    all.
  Then I'll sit down.—Give me some wine. Fill full.
                                          Enter Ghost.
  I drink to th' general joy o' th' whole table
  And to our dear friend Banquo, whom we miss.
  Would he were here! To all, and him we thirst,   110
  And all to all.

LORDS Our duties, and the pledge.

                    They raise their drinking cups.

MACBETH, *to the Ghost*
    Avaunt, and quit my sight! Let the earth hide thee.
    Thy bones are marrowless; thy blood is cold;
    Thou hast no speculation in those eyes   115
    Which thou dost glare with.

LADY MACBETH Think of this, good
  peers,
    But as a thing of custom. 'Tis no other;
    Only it spoils the pleasure of the time.   120

MACBETH, *to the Ghost* What man dare, I dare.
    Approach thou like the rugged Russian bear,
    The armed rhinoceros, or th' Hyrcan tiger;
    Take any shape but that, and my firm nerves
    Shall never tremble. Or be alive again   125
    And dare me to the desert with thy sword.
    If trembling I inhabit then, protest me
    The baby of a girl. Hence, horrible shadow!
    Unreal mock'ry, hence!
                                Ghost exits.

RESOURCE #3.5D

3.4, Part 4 (130–176, end): The Aftermath of Banquo's Visit (four actors)

What happened in lines 88–129: Banquo's ghost appeared at the banquet for a second time, seen only by Macbeth. Macbeth spoke to the ghost and scared his guests. The ghost exited.

MACBETH
    Why so, being gone,   130
    I am a man again.—Pray you sit still.

LADY MACBETH
    You have displaced the mirth, broke the good
       meeting
    With most admired disorder.

MACBETH Can such things be   135
    And overcome us like a summer's cloud,
    Without our special wonder? You make me strange
    Even to the disposition that I owe
    When now I think you can behold such sights
    And keep the natural ruby of your cheeks   140
    When mine is blanched with fear.

ROSS What sights, my
    lord?

LADY MACBETH
    I pray you, speak not. He grows worse and worse.
    Question enrages him. At once, good night.   145
    Stand not upon the order of your going,
    But go at once.

LENNOX Good night, and better health
    Attend his Majesty.

LADY MACBETH A kind good night to all.   150
          Lords and all but Macbeth and Lady Macbeth exit.

MACBETH
    It will have blood, they say; blood will have blood.
    Stones have been known to move, and trees to
       speak.

Augurs and understood relations have

By maggot pies and choughs and rooks brought 155
    forth

The secret'st man of blood.—What is the night?

LADY MACBETH

Almost at odds with morning, which is which.

MACBETH

How say'st thou that Macduff denies his person

At our great bidding? 160

LADY MACBETH Did you send to him, sir?

MACBETH

I hear it by the way; but I will send.

There's not a one of them but in his house

I keep a servant fee'd. I will tomorrow

(And betimes I will) to the Weïrd Sisters. 165

More shall they speak, for now I am bent to know

By the worst means the worst. For mine own good,

All causes shall give way. I am in blood

Stepped in so far that, should I wade no more,

Returning were as tedious as go o'er. 170

Strange things I have in head that will to hand,

Which must be acted ere they may be scanned.

LADY MACBETH

You lack the season of all natures, sleep.

MACBETH

Come, we'll to sleep. My strange and self-abuse

Is the initiate fear that wants hard use. 175

We are yet but young in deed.
                              They exit.

WEEK FOUR: LESSON 1

Aligning Two Important Scenes—4.1 and 4.2— with Images from the Folger Collection

Here's What We're Doing and Why

Macbeth 4.1 is an important scene because it guides Macbeth's actions for the rest of the play, and 4.2 shows us just how low Macbeth has sunk . . . as if we didn't think he was already at rock-bottom. These are both great scenes for students to dig into! Today students will collaborate, closely reading and debating the text of the two scenes. They will examine primary source images from the Folger collection and take on creating their own illustrations. These actions help students to think about a scene visually, to make decisions about which distinct moments are important, and to think about how one moment in a scene looks different from the next. Together, these activities strengthen both creative and analytical skills.

Note: In considering 4.1 today, we're skipping over the witches' lines 1–38 (their "hell-broth" spell) because we'll focus on it specifically later this week.

What Will I Need?

- One packet per group: Folger Collection Images A through F – **RESOURCE #4.1A**
- Copies of excerpts from 4.1 and 4.2 – **RESOURCE #4.1B**
- One per group: Our Decisions Recorded – **RESOURCE #4.1C**
- Copies of Death at the Macduffs' – **RESOURCE #4.1D**
- Illustration materials such as markers, colored pencils, and/or crayons for each group

How Should I Prepare?

- Put students in collaborative groups of 4–5

Agenda (~ 45-minute class period)

- ❑ Part One: Language, Imagery, and Action in 4.1 (30 minutes)
- ❑ Part Two: A DIY Image in 4.2 (10 minutes)
- ❑ Speedy Reflection (5 minutes)

Here's What Students Hear (From You) and (Then What They'll) Do

Part One: Macbeth, the Witches, and the Apparitions

1. Today you'll look carefully at 4.1 and 4.2 from two different perspectives. First you'll examine 6 images from the Folger collection—6 artistic representations that

depict various moments and elements found in *Macbeth* 4.1. (Each was created in a different time period by a different artist, and each could represent a different moment in the play.)

2. In your groups, you will receive a packet of these 6 images – **RESOURCE #4.1A**. First browse through the scrambled collection of images labeled A–F in order to get an initial idea of 6 moments from 4.1 that these images might illustrate.

3. Then read through the text with your group (**RESOURCE #4.1B**), either chorally, by assigning parts, or by taking turns reading one sentence apiece.

4. After you are finished reading, go back to the collection of images, look at them very carefully, and put them in the proper order of occurrence, supported by the text. If group members disagree, argue your perspectives by pointing out evidence from the text and the images. Look for your Our Decisions Recorded sheet (**RESOURCE #4.1C**) so you can do just that. In the right column of the chart below, write a quotation from 4.1 that your group thinks would best serve as a caption for each image. Your "captions" should be lines spoken directly by the characters (not stage directions!).

[**TEACHER NOTE:** Make sure that students read the whole excerpt together (chorally, by assigning parts, or taking turns reading a sentence apiece). Let them grapple with the task and debate their choices. For your reference, the order of the images should be B, D, A, E, C, F.]

5. Let's reflect briefly as a class:
   - What is the chronological order of the images?
   - Which details in the illustrations helped you decide on the order?
   - Which details in the illustrations did you perhaps overlook?
   - Which details are creative choices?
   - What nuances or other details did you notice in the illustrations?

Part Two: The Murder of Macduff's Family

1. We'll do a quick, home-grown version of what we just did with the last scene. Together, read the scene (**RESOURCE #4.1D**). As you read, make note of a quote or image—or both—that captures a key moment in this scene.

2. In your group, select 2 line-and-image combinations that represent 2 powerful moments in the scene. Quickly create the images (stick figures are fine!).

3. As a class, let's reflect on that scene by sharing your groups' line-and-image combinations along with your rationale for choosing them.

Quick Reflection

- How did today's activity with visual illustrations, both from the artists in the Folger images and from your classmates, help you to see what is important in a scene?

- What are the components from the illustrations you looked at and created today that could transfer to a live performance and help an audience interpret a scene?

- How did you choose to convey fear?

Here's What Just Happened in Class

- Students participated in a close-reading of both Shakespeare scenes.

- Students analyzed and evaluated the visual cues in illustrations that helped them to identify corresponding text.

- Students shared, celebrated, and critiqued their work with another group.

- Students made connections between visual illustrations and live performance.

Folger Collection Images—A through F

Image A

Image C

Image B

Image D

Image E

Image F

RESOURCE #4.1B

4.1.48–148 (edited)

MACBETH
   How now, you secret, black, and midnight hags?
   What is 't you do?

ALL A deed without a name.

MACBETH
   I conjure you by that which you profess
   . . .
   Though castles topple on their warders' heads,
   Though palaces and pyramids do slope
   Their heads to their foundations, though the treasure
   Of nature's germens tumble all together
   Even till destruction sicken, answer me
   To what I ask you.

FIRST WITCH Speak.

SECOND WITCH Demand.

THIRD WITCH We'll answer.

FIRST WITCH
   Say if th' hadst rather hear it from our mouths
   Or from our masters'.

MACBETH Call 'em. Let me see 'em.
   . . .

ALL Come high or low;
   Thyself and office deftly show.

Thunder. First Apparition, an Armed Head.

MACBETH
   Tell me, thou unknown power—
   . . .

FIRST APPARITION
   Macbeth! Macbeth! Macbeth! Beware Macduff!
   Beware the Thane of Fife! Dismiss me. Enough.
   He descends.

MACBETH

    Whate'er thou art, for thy good caution, thanks.
    Thou hast harped my fear aright. But one word
    more—

FIRST WITCH

    He will not be commanded. Here's another
    More potent than the first.

Thunder. Second Apparition, a Bloody Child.

SECOND APPARITION Macbeth! Macbeth! Macbeth!—

    . . .

    Be bloody, bold, and resolute. Laugh to scorn
    The power of man, for none of woman born
    Shall harm Macbeth. He descends.

MACBETH

    Then live, Macduff; what need I fear of thee?
    But yet . . .
      Thou shalt not live,
    That I may tell pale-hearted fear it lies,
    And sleep in spite of thunder.

Thunder. Third Apparition, a Child Crowned,
with a tree in his hand.

    What is this
    That rises like the issue of a king
    And wears upon his baby brow the round
    And top of sovereignty?

ALL Listen but speak not to 't.

THIRD APPARITION

    Macbeth shall never vanquished be until
    Great Birnam Wood to high Dunsinane Hill
    Shall come against him. He descends.

MACBETH That will never be.

    Who can impress the forest, bid the tree
    Unfix his earthbound root? . . .
    Yet my heart
    Throbs to know one thing. Tell me, if your art
    Can tell so much: shall Banquo's issue ever
    Reign in this kingdom?

ALL Seek to know no more.

MACBETH
I will be satisfied. . . .

FIRST WITCH Show.

SECOND WITCH Show.

THIRD WITCH Show.

ALL
Show his eyes and grieve his heart.
Come like shadows; so depart.
A show of eight kings, the eighth king with a glass in
his hand, and Banquo last.

MACBETH
Thou art too like the spirit of Banquo. Down!
Thy crown does sear mine eyeballs. And thy hair,
Thou other gold-bound brow, is like the first.
. . . And yet the eighth appears who bears a glass
Which shows me many more.
Horrible sight! Now I see 'tis true,
For the blood-boltered Banquo smiles upon me
And points at them for his.
What, is this so?

FIRST WITCH
Ay, sir, all this is so. But why
Stands Macbeth thus amazedly?
Come, sisters, cheer we up his sprites
And show the best of our delights.
I'll charm the air to give a sound
While you perform your antic round,
That this great king may kindly say
Our duties did his welcome pay.

Music. The Witches dance and vanish.

RESOURCE #4.1C

Our Decisions Recorded

Order of occurrence in the scene	Image Letter	Caption for the image (a quotation spoken by a character)
1st		
2nd		
3rd		
4th		
5th		
6th		

RESOURCE #4.1D

Death at the Macduffs'

4.2.35–97 (edited)

LADY MACDUFF Sirrah, your father's dead.
  And what will you do now? How will you live?

SON
  As birds do, mother.

LADY MACDUFF What, with worms and flies?

SON
  With what I get, I mean; and so do they.

LADY MACDUFF
  Poor bird, thou 'dst never fear the net nor lime,
  The pitfall nor the gin.

SON
  Why should I, mother? Poor birds they are not set for.
  My father is not dead, for all your saying.

LADY MACDUFF
  Yes, he is dead. How wilt thou do for a father?

SON Nay, how will you do for a husband?

LADY MACDUFF
  Why, I can buy me twenty at any market.

SON Then you'll buy 'em to sell again.

LADY MACDUFF Thou speak'st with all thy wit,
  And yet, i' faith, with wit enough for thee.

SON Was my father a traitor, mother?

LADY MACDUFF Ay, that he was.

SON What is a traitor?

LADY MACDUFF Why, one that swears and lies.

SON And be all traitors that do so?

LADY MACDUFF Every one that does so is a traitor
and must be hanged.

SON And must they all be hanged that swear and lie?

LADY MACDUFF Every one.

SON Who must hang them?

LADY MACDUFF Why, the honest men.

SON Then the liars and swearers are fools, for there
are liars and swearers enough to beat the honest
men and hang up them.

LADY MACDUFF Now God help thee, poor monkey! But
how wilt thou do for a father?

SON If he were dead, you'd weep for him. If you would
not, it were a good sign that I should quickly have a
new father.

LADY MACDUFF Poor prattler, how thou talk'st!

Enter a Messenger.

MESSENGER
. . . If you will take a homely man's advice,
Be not found here. Hence with your little ones!
To fright you thus methinks I am too savage;
To do worse to you were fell cruelty,
Which is too nigh your person. Heaven preserve you!
I dare abide no longer.

Messenger exits.

LADY MACDUFF Whither should I fly?
I have done no harm. But I remember now
I am in this earthly world, where to do harm
Is often laudable, to do good sometime
Accounted dangerous folly. Why then, alas,
Do I put up that womanly defense
To say I have done no harm?

Enter Murderers.

What are these faces?

MURDERER Where is your husband?

LADY MACDUFF
I hope in no place so unsanctified
Where such as thou mayst find him.

MURDERER He's a traitor.

SON
Thou liest, thou shag-eared villain!

MURDERER What, you egg?

Stabbing him.

Young fry of treachery!

SON He has killed
me, mother.
Run away, I pray you.

Lady Macduff exits, crying "Murder!" followed by the Murderers bearing the Son's body.

"Black Macbeth will seem as pure as snow": *Macbeth*, Race, and Language; Act 4–5

Here's What We're Doing and Why

Throughout this unit, we have explored what fear causes people to do: to murder, to tyrannize, to flee, to resist. Today, we will examine how the word *black* has developed over the centuries to also be a source of or a catalyst for fear—a connection that predates Shakespeare and *Macbeth*, but that is evident in *Macbeth*, as it is in many Shakespeare plays.

Is *Macbeth* a play about race? It might not seem like it, but with lines like "How now, you secret, black, and midnight hags" and "Black Macbeth will seem as pure as snow" we can see that the play surely doesn't ignore it. In fact, many of Shakespeare's plays use images of blackness to suggest evil. They also use whiteness—and words like *fair* and *snowy*—to suggest beauty and virtue. Today's lesson examines how these constructions show up in *Macbeth*.

We believe that to slide over these conventions and not to talk about them with students is simply not good teaching. We hope that your own self-awareness and sense of comfort along with the spirit of safety and collaboration that has been building with your students through this unit will spark some meaningful class conversations—about whiteness and blackness, how they are presented in the play, and where reverberations of race still show up today. Your intuition will guide you, as will your wisdom about your students and the dynamics in your class.

As always, we start with a deep dive into Shakespeare's language—first through the whole play, then with a focus on the witches (4.1.1–38). And lastly, as a final bonus, we offer a fresh way to look at blackness from Pulitzer Prize and Presidential Medal of Honor winner Maya Angelou.

What Will I Need?

- Copies of Examining Black and White in *Macbeth* – **RESOURCE #4.2A**

- Copies of Investigating the Witches' Use of Language in 4.1.1–38 – **RESOURCE #4.2B**

- Copies of the bonus from Ms. Angelou – **RESOURCE #4.2.C**

How Should I Prepare?

- Students should have laptops or phones so they can search folger.edu /shakespeares-works using the API (application programming interface) that both teachers and students find so useful. Easy searching, character finding, all of that.

- Display Malcolm's 3 lines (4.3.62–64 and below) on board or screen

- Review discussion questions below

Agenda (~ 45-minute period)

❑ Quick discussion on black and white (5 minutes)

❑ Deep dive into black and white in *Macbeth* (12 minutes)

❑ All-class discussion on your research (8 minutes)

❑ Deep dive into 4.1 witches' spell (5 minutes)

❑ All-class discussion on 4.1 (10 minutes)

❑ Reflection (5 minutes)

Here's What Students Hear (From You) and (Then What They'll) Do

1. Let's look at these three lines from Malcolm—we already know he hates Macbeth and why:

   > All the particulars of vice so grafted
   > That, when they shall be opened, black Macbeth
   > Will seem as pure as snow . . . (4.3.62–64).

Questions:

- Why is Macbeth referred to as *black*?

- Why is snow described as *pure*?

- What do you think these words are trying to convey? Have you noticed any other examples? In this play or elsewhere?

2. We're going to look more deeply into how Shakespeare uses these words in *Macbeth*:

   - In groups, you'll dive into Folger Shakespeare online—folger.edu/shake speares-works—and **RESOURCE 4.2A**. Get familiar with the resources and search the word *black*, which is used eight times in the play. Jot down the line in which it appears, what you think the subtext and the effect of repetition might be. You also might want to look up associated words such as *dark* and *midnight*.

   - Also in your groups, do similar research focused on the word *white* and derivations of it such as *pure*, *light*, and *clean*.

[**TEACHER NOTE:** You lead the all-class discussion on this student research:

   - How Shakespeare uses the words *black* and *white* . . . Groups share what they have found.

   - What inferences can you make about how and why Shakespeare uses the word *black* in the play? And what about *white*? Why do you think they would be used in these ways? Is there a parallel in how they are used in our world today? Can you give an example?]

3. Next, stay in your groups, and take a look at the witches' spell in 4.1 – **RESOURCE #4.2B**. Can you identify the human parts listed in the spell? Make a list in your group.

[**TEACHER NOTE:** You lead the all-class discussion on what groups have found:

- What did you find or learn? Did you need to look up *Turk*, or *Tartar*, or *Ottoman Empire*? What did you find?

- What does the witches' use of this language suggest about the feelings toward certain groups during this time period? Your thoughts about that? Can comparisons be made today in terms of how some groups/cultures feel about other ones?

- Overall, are there some conclusions you could draw from both of these investigations? What are they or might they be? How might that relate to the lesson early in this unit about the world in which Shakespeare wrote?]

Reflection Round

Going around the room, students complete each sentence verbally:

- I wondered . . .

- I felt . . .

- I wished . . .

As you leave class: Collect your bonus—a different way to look at blackness from Pulitzer Prize and Presidential Medal of Honor winner Maya Angelou – **RESOURCE #4.2C**.

Here's What Just Happened in Class

- Students collaborated in researching and reading closely.

- Students searched the text, found relevant lines, and considered words and their context.

- Students discovered a new lens—the lens of race—through which to consider *Macbeth*, and other Shakespeare plays too.

- Students can begin to consider the relationship between "then" and "now" . . . opinions about various races and cultures held in Shakespeare's time, and those evident in our "now."

Examining Black and White in *Macbeth*

Part 1: BLACK	
Use of word *black* examples: Write the line(s), choosing the most interesting six examples.	
What inferences can you make about the word's use in *Macbeth*? What's the subtext here?	
Part 2: WHITE	
Use of word *white* (or *pure, light, or clean*) examples: Write the line(s), choosing the most interesting six examples.	
What inferences can you make about the word's use in *Macbeth*? Is there a subtext here?	

RESOURCE #4.2B

Investigating the Witches' Use of Language in 4.1.1–38

Thunder. Enter the three Witches.

FIRST WITCH

Thrice the brinded cat hath mewed.

SECOND WITCH

Thrice, and once the hedge-pig whined.

THIRD WITCH

Harpier cries "'Tis time, 'tis time!"

FIRST WITCH

Round about the cauldron go;
In the poisoned entrails throw.   5
Toad, that under cold stone
Days and nights has thirty-one
Sweltered venom sleeping got,
Boil thou first i' th' charmèd pot.

The Witches circle the cauldron.

ALL

Double, double toil and trouble;   10
Fire burn, and cauldron bubble.

SECOND WITCH

Fillet of a fenny snake
In the cauldron boil and bake.
Eye of newt and toe of frog,
Wool of bat and tongue of dog,   15
Adder's fork and blindworm's sting,
Lizard's leg and howlet's wing,
For a charm of powerful trouble,
Like a hell-broth boil and bubble.

ALL

Double, double toil and trouble;   20
Fire burn, and cauldron bubble.

THIRD WITCH

Scale of dragon, tooth of wolf,

Witch's mummy, maw and gulf
Of the ravined salt-sea shark,
Root of hemlock digged i' th' dark, 25
Liver of blaspheming Jew,
Gall of goat and slips of yew
Slivered in the moon's eclipse,
Nose of Turk and Tartar's lips,
Finger of birth-strangled babe 30
Ditch-delivered by a drab,
Make the gruel thick and slab.
Add thereto a tiger's chaudron
For th' ingredience of our cauldron.

ALL
Double, double toil and trouble; 35
Fire burn, and cauldron bubble.

SECOND WITCH
Cool it with a baboon's blood.
Then the charm is firm and good.

RESOURCE #4.3C

Ain't That Bad

Dancin' the funky chicken
Eatin' ribs and tips
Diggin' all the latest sounds
And drinkin' gin in sips

Puttin' down that do-rag
Tighten' up my 'fro
Wrappin' up in Blackness
Don't I shine and glow?

Hearin' Stevie Wonder
Cookin' beans and rice
Goin' to the opera
Checkin' out Leontyne Price.

Get down, Jesse Jackson
Dance on, Alvin Ailey
Talk, Miss Barbara Jordan
Groove, Miss Pearlie Bailey.

Now ain't they bad?
An' ain't they Black?
An' ain't they Black?
An' ain't they Bad?
An' ain't they bad?
An' ain't they Black?
An' ain't they fine?

Black like the hour of the night
When your love turns and wriggles close to your side
Black as the earth which has given birth
To nations, and when all else is gone will abide.

Bad as the storm that leaps raging from the heavens
Bringing the welcome rain

Bad as the sun burning orange hot at midday
Lifting the waters again.

Arthur Ashe on the tennis court
Mohammed Ali in the ring
Andre Watts and Andrew Young
Black men doing their thing.

Dressing in purples and pinks and greens
Exotic as rum and Cokes
Living our lives with flash and style
Ain't we colorful folks?

Now ain't we bad?
An' ain't we Black?
An' ain't we Black?
An' ain't we bad?
An' ain't we bad?
An' ain't we Black?
An' ain't we fine?

—Maya Angelou, 2016

"Dispute it as a man": Examining Gender Expectations in *Macbeth* through Another Text

Here's What We're Doing and Why

We've found that students are intrigued by the gender roles in *Macbeth*, and they will certainly relate them to their own ideas about masculinity and femininity. Many have heard statements about gender conformity during their lives: "act like a man," "boys don't cry," "be more ladylike." In one classroom, there are bound to be many different opinions on gender roles—just like there are around *Macbeth*.

Students will examine different presentations of masculinity in *Macbeth*, as well as an edited selection from Nigerian writer Chimamanda Ngozi Adichie's 2012 talk entitled "We Should All Be Feminists." Students explore, consider, and analyze from several angles how masculinity and femininity are presented in *Macbeth*.

Macbeth presents masculinity and femininity in different ways, from different characters, and from different angles. Review for you:

- Throughout the play, Lady Macbeth repeatedly attacks her husband's masculinity in order to convince him to do what she wants.

- Macbeth's fear of violating his society's gender norms and values, which align with his wife's orders, helps lead him on to his path of murder.

- In 4.3, when we see Malcolm attempt a similar call to masculinity in order to prompt Macduff to avenge the deaths of his family, Macduff resists:

  Malcolm: "Dispute it like a man."

  Macduff: "I shall do so, / But I must also feel it as a man" (4.3.259–261).

- Macduff soon reverts to the traditional gender role, though, saying a few lines later that he could "play the woman with mine eyes / And braggart with my tongue!" (4.3.270–271).

- Early in the play, we see Lady Macbeth attempting to cast off her traditional femininity to ascend to power with her husband. Later we meet Lady Macduff, a wife and mother who yearns to live with her husband and children in domesticity.

We pair *Macbeth* with an edited selection from "We Should All Be Feminists," Adichie's very popular TED Talk, so that students can examine the characters' adherence—or lack of adherence—to traditional gender norms. To use Adichie's metaphor, what does the language tell us about which characters in *Macbeth* are most "caged" by gender norms?

Finally, as part of their analysis, students will create a short exchange between Adichie and characters in *Macbeth*.

What Will I Need?

- Copies of the selection from Adichie's "We Should All Be Feminists" – **RESOURCE #4.3A**

- Copies of focus scenes for all students:
    - Lady Macduff's conversation with her son (4.2.35–70) – **RESOURCE #4.3B**
    - Malcolm and Macduff's conversation (4.3.240–281) – **RESOURCE #4.3C**
    - Lady Macbeth pre-murder (and a little Macbeth too) (1.7.39–88) – **RESOURCE #4.3D**

How Should I Prepare?

- Read the Adichie selection and the scenes students will be working with

- Be ready to put students into mixed-gender (if possible) groups of 4–5

Agenda (~ 45-minute class period)

- ❏ Students read the selection from Adichie's "We Should All Be Feminists" (8 minutes)
- ❏ Quick Discussion #1 in groups: What have you noticed about gender in *Macbeth* so far? (7 minutes)
- ❏ Quick Discussion #2 in same groups: Where do elements of gender appear in these specific scenes in *Macbeth*? (10 minutes)
- ❏ Write Adichie–*Macbeth* dialogues (15 minutes)
- ❏ Reflection Round (5 minutes)
- ❏ Find extra time somewhere and perform those dialogues!

Here's What Students Will Hear (From You) and (Then What They'll) Do

1. Today we're going to explore gender roles in *Macbeth*, starting with something that is far from that play. Or is it? First, we'll read an excerpt from "We Should All Be Feminists" by award-winning Nigerian writer Chimamanda Ngozi Adichie. We'll invite Ms. Adichie to introduce the subject of gender. Afterward, in groups, you'll quickly discuss gender in *Macbeth* thus far. What have you noticed? After you discuss, let's have someone from each group share one thing that you talked about.

2. Next, each group will receive a scene from *Macbeth* and in your groups, you'll discuss your scene very specifically in terms of gender. Each group reports out on the *Macbeth* conversation, and we'll have a short all-class discussion about what you see in the language. Where does gender appear? And why? Does it connect to fear? Does it connect to anything else?

3. Finally, you'll work within your groups to create a short dialogue or scene between Adichie and a character in your *Macbeth* scene. Have fun and be creative! Suggestions:

   - a direct conversation between Adichie and the character
   - Adichie and the character are both guests on a talk show, and the topic is gender
   - Adichie is a guest on a talk show, and the character is the host, asking how she liked *Macbeth*

4. **Reflection Round.** Students share their response to the following prompts:

   - I observed . . .
   - This made me think about . . .

5. Close out class by performing as many dialogues as time allows!

Here's What Just Happened in Class

- Students dove into Shakespeare's language and the language of a modern writer to investigate elements of gender.

- In order to do this, students made connections (or pointed out the lack of connections) between Shakespeare and Adichie.

- Students discussed elements of gender and how they affect the action in *Macbeth*.

- Students learned that Lady Macbeth and Lady Macduff, and Macbeth and Macduff, are different presentations of gender role conformity.

- Using what they've discovered, students collaborated on a written piece in which Adichie and characters in *Macbeth* talk to each other.

- Students may have discovered a new writer, Chimamanda Ngozi Adichie.

- Students may have discovered how gender roles and expectations play a part in their own personal worlds.

RESOURCE #4.3A

Edited selection from "We Should All Be Feminists" by Chimamanda Ngozi Adichie

TEDxEuston, November 2012

We do a great disservice to boys in how we raise them. We stifle the humanity of boys. We define masculinity in a very narrow way. Masculinity is a hard, small cage, and we put boys inside this cage.

We teach boys to be afraid of fear, of weakness, of vulnerability. We teach them to mask their true selves, because they have to be, in Nigerian-speak—a hard man.

In secondary school, a boy and a girl go out, both of them teenagers with meager pocket money. Yet the boy is expected to pay the bills, always, to prove his masculinity. (And we wonder why boys are more likely to steal money from their parents.)

What if both boys and girls were raised not to link masculinity and money? What if their attitude was not "the boy has to pay," but rather, "whoever has more should pay"? Of course, because of their historical advantage, it is mostly men who will have more today. But if we start raising children differently, then in fifty years, in a hundred years, boys will no longer have the pressure of proving their masculinity by material means.

But by far the worst thing we do to males—by making them feel they have to be hard—is that we leave them with very fragile egos. The harder a man feels compelled to be, the weaker his ego is.

And then we do a much greater disservice to girls, because we raise them to cater to the fragile egos of males. We teach girls to shrink themselves, to make themselves smaller. We say to girls: You can have ambition, but not too much. You should aim to be successful but not too successful, otherwise you will threaten the man.

If you are the breadwinner in your relationship with a man, pretend that you are not, especially in public, otherwise you will emasculate him.

But what if we question the premise itself: Why should a woman's success be a threat to a man? What if we decide to simply dispose of that word—and I don't know if there is an English word I dislike more than this—emasculation.

A Nigerian acquaintance once asked me if I was worried that men would be intimidated by me.

I was not worried at all—it had not even occurred to me to be worried, because a man who will be intimidated by me is exactly the kind of man I would have no interest in. Still, I was struck by this. Because I am female, I'm expected to aspire to marriage. I am expected to make my life choices always keeping in mind that marriage is the most important. Marriage can be a good thing, a source of joy, love, and mutual support. But why do we teach girls to aspire to marriage, but we don't teach boys to do the same?

. . .

The problem with gender is that it prescribes how we should be rather than recognizing how we are. Imagine how much happier we would be, how much freer to be our true individual selves, if we didn't have the weight of gender expectations.

RESOURCE #4.3B

Macbeth, 4.2.35–70

LADY MACDUFF Sirrah, your father's dead.   35
    And what will you do now? How will you live?

SON
    As birds do, mother.

LADY MACDUFF What, with worms and flies?

SON
    With what I get, I mean; and so do they.

LADY MACDUFF
    Poor bird, thou 'dst never fear the net nor lime,   40
    The pitfall nor the gin.

SON
    Why should I, mother? Poor birds they are not set
        for.
    My father is not dead, for all your saying.

LADY MACDUFF
    Yes, he is dead. How wilt thou do for a father?   45

SON Nay, how will you do for a husband?

LADY MACDUFF
    Why, I can buy me twenty at any market.

SON Then you'll buy 'em to sell again.

LADY MACDUFF Thou speak'st with all thy wit,
    And yet, i' faith, with wit enough for thee.   50

SON Was my father a traitor, mother?

LADY MACDUFF Ay, that he was.

SON What is a traitor?

LADY MACDUFF Why, one that swears and lies.

SON And be all traitors that do so?   55

LADY MACDUFF Every one that does so is a traitor
    and must be hanged.

SON And must they all be hanged that swear and lie?

LADY MACDUFF Every one.

SON Who must hang them?   60

LADY MACDUFF Why, the honest men.

SON Then the liars and swearers are fools, for there
    are liars and swearers enough to beat the honest
    men and hang up them.

LADY MACDUFF Now God help thee, poor monkey! But   65
    how wilt thou do for a father?

SON If he were dead, you'd weep for him. If you would
    not, it were a good sign that I should quickly have a
    new father.

LADY MACDUFF Poor prattler, how thou talk'st!   70

RESOURCE #4.3C

Macbeth, 4.3.240–281

ROSS
Your castle is surprised, your wife and babes   240
Savagely slaughtered. To relate the manner
Were on the quarry of these murdered deer
To add the death of you.

MALCOLM Merciful heaven!—
What, man, ne'er pull your hat upon your brows.   245
Give sorrow words. The grief that does not speak
Whispers the o'erfraught heart and bids it break.

MACDUFF My children too?

ROSS
Wife, children, servants, all that could be found.

MACDUFF
And I must be from thence? My wife killed too?   250

ROSS I have said.

MALCOLM Be comforted.
Let's make us med'cines of our great revenge
To cure this deadly grief.

MACDUFF
He has no children. All my pretty ones?   255
Did you say "all"? O hell-kite! All?
What, all my pretty chickens and their dam
At one fell swoop?

MALCOLM Dispute it like a man.

MACDUFF I shall do so,   260
But I must also feel it as a man.
I cannot but remember such things were
That were most precious to me. Did heaven look on
And would not take their part? Sinful Macduff,
They were all struck for thee! Naught that I am,   265
Not for their own demerits, but for mine,
Fell slaughter on their souls. Heaven rest them now.

MALCOLM

    Be this the whetstone of your sword. Let grief
    Convert to anger. Blunt not the heart; enrage it.

MACDUFF

    O, I could play the woman with mine eyes   270
    And braggart with my tongue! But, gentle heavens,
    Cut short all intermission! Front to front
    Bring thou this fiend of Scotland and myself.
    Within my sword's length set him. If he 'scape,
    Heaven forgive him too.   275

MALCOLM This tune goes manly.

    Come, go we to the King. Our power is ready;
    Our lack is nothing but our leave. Macbeth
    Is ripe for shaking, and the powers above
    Put on their instruments. Receive what cheer you   280
      may.
    The night is long that never finds the day.

They exit.

RESOURCE #4.3D

Macbeth, 1.7, 39–88
Lady Mac (and a tiny bit of Mac)

LADY MACBETH Was the hope drunk

    Wherein you dressed yourself? Hath it slept since?   40
    And wakes it now, to look so green and pale
    At what it did so freely? From this time
    Such I account thy love. Art thou afeard
    To be the same in thine own act and valor
    As thou art in desire? Wouldst thou have that   45
    Which thou esteem'st the ornament of life
    And live a coward in thine own esteem,
    Letting "I dare not" wait upon "I would,"
    Like the poor cat i' th' adage?

MACBETH Prithee, peace.   50

    I dare do all that may become a man.
    Who dares do more is none.

LADY MACBETH What beast was 't,

      then,
    That made you break this enterprise to me?   55
    When you durst do it, then you were a man;
    And to be more than what you were, you would
    Be so much more the man. Nor time nor place
    Did then adhere, and yet you would make both.
    They have made themselves, and that their fitness   60
      now
    Does unmake you. I have given suck, and know
    How tender 'tis to love the babe that milks me.
    I would, while it was smiling in my face,
    Have plucked my nipple from his boneless gums   65
    And dashed the brains out, had I so sworn as you
    Have done to this.

MACBETH If we should fail—

LADY MACBETH We fail?

    But screw your courage to the sticking place   70
    And we'll not fail. When Duncan is asleep
    (Whereto the rather shall his day's hard journey
    Soundly invite him), his two chamberlains

Will I with wine and wassail so convince
That memory, the warder of the brain, 75
Shall be a fume, and the receipt of reason
A limbeck only. When in swinish sleep
Their drenchèd natures lies as in a death,
What cannot you and I perform upon
Th' unguarded Duncan? What not put upon 80
His spongy officers, who shall bear the guilt
Of our great quell?

MACBETH Bring forth men-children only,
For thy undaunted mettle should compose
Nothing but males. Will it not be received, 85
When we have marked with blood those sleepy two
Of his own chamber and used their very daggers,
That they have done 't?

"Out, damned spot, out, I say!": Lady Macbeth's Conscious Lines and Her Subconscious Mind

Here's What We're Doing and Why

In the haunting 5.1 sleepwalking scene, we get a snapshot of how the previous events of the play are affecting Lady Macbeth's mental state. Students can see this clearly when they dig into lines from her sleepwalking scene and compare them with her lines from earlier in the play. This lesson asks students to examine and then organize those lines in ways that illuminate something new about Lady Macbeth's mental state, and then create a performance piece with their paired lines. Once again, we see the fearful effects of the Macbeths' lies.

Pairing up lines from different parts of the play requires the kind of attention to language, hard thinking, and careful decision-making that we've been reinforcing throughout this unit.

What Will I Need?

- Copies of "Information on Sleepwalking" from the Mayo Clinic – **RESOURCE #4.4A**

- Copies of Lady Macbeth's sleepwalking scene—5.1 – **RESOURCE #4.4B**

- Copies of Line Sets: Lady Macbeth Waking and Sleeping – **RESOURCE #4.4C**

How Should I Prepare?

- Review the assignment. Be familiar with what you're asking students to do with the lines—both parts

- Be ready for students to work in small groups of 3–4

Agenda (~ 45-minute class period)

- ❏ Quick discussion about sleepwalking, including information from the Mayo Clinic (12 minutes)

- ❏ Read 5.1 (13 minutes)

- ❏ Reorganizing Lady Macbeth's lines (15 minutes)

- ❏ Reflect (5 minutes)

Here's What Students Hear (From You) and (Then What They'll) Do

[**TEACHER NOTE:** If you have a family sleepwalking story to tell, you can start there. If you feel comfortable, you could ask your students if they might have a family sleepwalking or sleeptalking story to share.]

1. What do we really know about sleepwalking? Take some time to read what scientists and doctors say about sleepwalking. Take a look at this article from the Mayo Clinic about sleepwalking (**RESOURCE #4.4A**).

   - Let's share as a whole class: What was interesting or surprising? What do you wonder about?

   - The article mentions that stress can lead to sleepwalking. What are some stressors for Lady Macbeth at this point in the play?

   - Can you predict which symptoms from the Mayo Clinic article Lady Macbeth might exhibit?

2. Now, you'll read 5.1 in small groups of 3 (**RESOURCE #4.4B**). You may read chorally, assign parts, or each read sequentially, one sentence at a time.

3. Now we'll use these lines and more to look more deeply into Lady Macbeth. Let's look at **RESOURCE #4.4C**.

   - **Part 1:** First, each of you will match up pairs of lines, one line from Set A (lines said by Lady M *before 5.1*) and one line from Set B (lines said by Lady M *in 5.1*). Put lines together that you think offer insight into the way that Lady Macbeth is mentally processing her choices—and her husband's choices—all the way from her role in Duncan's murder to her husband's current tyranny. Pair lines that speak to each other in some way and that take on new life and meaning when they are put together.

   - **Part 2:** Next, in your group, you'll choose a favorite pairing to perform for the class. (Note: You may be asked to perform your second or third choice in case multiple groups chose to pair the same lines.)

   - After you choose your pair, focus on your Set A line, and find where it appears in the text of *Macbeth*, either in your book or the Folger Shakespeare online at folger.edu/shakespeares-works.

   - Everyone in the group must participate in your performance. Divide the two lines within your group; discuss performance choices and rehearse. Your goal is to show the difference between Lady Macbeth's conscious and unconscious minds. Some tools already in your toolbox: words to stress, tone, gesture, pose, movements.

   - Designate one group member to explain why you paired these lines and how your performance choices offer insight into Lady Macbeth's processing of the events of the play.

Reflection Round

About these pairings and performances,

   - I observed . . .

   - I wonder . . .

   - I never thought before that . . .

   Whole-class question: How does this scene answer our essential questions about what causes fear and how people respond to it?

Here's What Just Happened in Class

- Students read closely and carefully one character's lines from two different parts of the play. This helped to show a clear transformation in character development throughout the whole text.

- Students analyzed collaboratively the pairings, and decided which pair showed the most obvious difference between Lady Macbeth early and late in the play.

- Students worked collaboratively on how to put this analysis on its feet; they did so and provided an explanation of what caused them to make the performance choices they did.

- Students are reinforcing their confidence with the text and their ability to work with it; all of this will be helpful when they get to their final projects next week.

RESOURCE #4.4A

Excerpts from *Information on Sleepwalking*
Mayo Clinic

Mayo Foundation for Medical Education and Research

March 2022

Sleepwalking—also known as somnambulism—involves getting up and walking around while in a state of sleep. More common in children than adults, sleepwalking is usually outgrown by the teen years. Isolated incidents of sleepwalking often don't signal any serious problems or require treatment. However, recurrent sleepwalking may suggest an underlying sleep disorder.

Sleepwalking in adults has a higher chance of being confused with or coexisting with other sleep disorders as well as medical conditions.

Symptoms

Sleepwalking usually occurs early in the night—often one to two hours after falling asleep. It's unlikely to occur during naps. A sleepwalking episode can occur rarely or often, and an episode generally lasts several minutes, but can last longer.

Someone who is sleepwalking may:

- Get out of bed and walk around

- Sit up in bed and open his or her eyes

- Have a glazed, glassy-eyed expression

- Not respond or communicate with others

- Be difficult to wake up during an episode

- Be disoriented or confused for a short time after being awakened

- Not remember the episode in the morning

- Have problems functioning during the day because of disturbed sleep

- Have sleep terrors in addition to sleepwalking

Sometimes, a person who is sleepwalking will:

- Do routine activities, such as getting dressed, talking, or eating

- Leave the house

- Drive a car

- Engage in unusual behavior, such as urinating in a closet

- Get injured, for example, by falling down the stairs or jumping out a window

- Become violent during the period of brief confusion immediately after waking or, occasionally, during sleepwalking

When to see a doctor

Occasional episodes of sleepwalking aren't usually a cause for concern and typically resolve on their own. You can simply mention the sleepwalking at a routine physical or well-child exam.

However, consult your doctor if the sleepwalking episodes:

- Occur often—for example, more than one to two times a week or several times a night

- Lead to dangerous behavior or injury to the person who sleepwalks or to others

- Cause significant sleep disruption to household members or the person who sleepwalks

- Result in daytime symptoms of excessive sleepiness or problems functioning

- Start for the first time as an adult

- Continue into your child's teen years

Causes

Sleepwalking is classified as a parasomnia—an undesirable behavior or experience during sleep. Sleepwalking is a disorder of arousal, meaning it occurs during N3 sleep, the deepest stage of non-rapid eye movement (NREM) sleep. Another NREM disorder is sleep terrors, which can occur together with sleepwalking.

Many factors can contribute to sleepwalking, including:

- Sleep deprivation

- Stress

- Fever

- Sleep schedule disruptions, travel or sleep interruptions

Complications

Sleepwalking itself isn't necessarily a concern, but a person who sleepwalks can:

- Hurt themselves—especially if they walk near furniture or stairs, wander outdoors, drive a car, or eat something inappropriate during a sleepwalking episode

- Experience prolonged sleep disruption, which can lead to excessive daytime sleepiness and possible school or behavior issues

- Be embarrassed or experience problems with social relationships

- Disturb others' sleep

- Rarely, injure someone else nearby

RESOURCE #4.4B

5.1

Enter a Doctor of Physic and a Waiting-Gentlewoman.

DOCTOR I have two nights watched with you but can
perceive no truth in your report. When was it she
last walked?

GENTLEWOMAN Since his Majesty went into the field, I
have seen her rise from her bed, throw her nightgown   5
upon her, unlock her closet, take forth paper,
fold it, write upon 't, read it, afterwards seal it, and
again return to bed; yet all this while in a most fast
sleep.

DOCTOR A great perturbation in nature, to receive at   10
once the benefit of sleep and do the effects of
watching. In this slumb'ry agitation, besides her
walking and other actual performances, what at any
time have you heard her say?

GENTLEWOMAN That, sir, which I will not report after   15
her.

DOCTOR You may to me, and 'tis most meet you
should.

GENTLEWOMAN Neither to you nor anyone, having no
witness to confirm my speech.   20
                              Enter Lady Macbeth with a taper.
Lo you, here she comes. This is her very guise and,
upon my life, fast asleep. Observe her; stand close.

DOCTOR How came she by that light?

GENTLEWOMAN Why, it stood by her. She has light by
her continually. 'Tis her command.   25

DOCTOR You see her eyes are open.

GENTLEWOMAN Ay, but their sense are shut.

DOCTOR What is it she does now? Look how she rubs
her hands.

GENTLEWOMAN It is an accustomed action with her to   30
seem thus washing her hands. I have known her
continue in this a quarter of an hour.

LADY MACBETH Yet here's a spot.

DOCTOR Hark, she speaks. I will set down what comes
from her, to satisfy my remembrance the more   35
strongly.

LADY MACBETH Out, damned spot, out, I say! One. Two.
Why then, 'tis time to do 't. Hell is murky. Fie, my
lord, fie, a soldier and afeard? What need we fear
who knows it, when none can call our power to   40
account? Yet who would have thought the old man
to have had so much blood in him?

DOCTOR Do you mark that?

LADY MACBETH The Thane of Fife had a wife. Where is
she now? What, will these hands ne'er be clean? No   45
more o' that, my lord, no more o' that. You mar all
with this starting.

DOCTOR Go to, go to. You have known what you should
not.

GENTLEWOMAN She has spoke what she should not,   50
I am sure of that. Heaven knows what she has
known.

LADY MACBETH Here's the smell of the blood still. All
the perfumes of Arabia will not sweeten this little
hand. O, O, O!   55

DOCTOR What a sigh is there! The heart is sorely
charged.

GENTLEWOMAN I would not have such a heart in my
bosom for the dignity of the whole body.

DOCTOR Well, well, well.   60

GENTLEWOMAN Pray God it be, sir.

DOCTOR This disease is beyond my practice. Yet I have
known those which have walked in their sleep,
who have died holily in their beds.

LADY MACBETH Wash your hands. Put on your nightgown.   65
　　Look not so pale. I tell you yet again, Banquo's
　　buried; he cannot come out on 's grave.

DOCTOR Even so?

LADY MACBETH To bed, to bed. There's knocking at the
　　gate. Come, come, come, come. Give me your   70
　　hand. What's done cannot be undone. To bed, to
　　bed, to bed.

Lady Macbeth exits.

DOCTOR Will she go now to bed?

GENTLEWOMAN Directly.

DOCTOR
　　Foul whisp'rings are abroad. Unnatural deeds   75
　　Do breed unnatural troubles. Infected minds
　　To their deaf pillows will discharge their secrets.
　　More needs she the divine than the physician.
　　God, God forgive us all. Look after her.
　　Remove from her the means of all annoyance   80
　　And still keep eyes upon her. So, good night.
　　My mind she has mated, and amazed my sight.
　　I think but dare not speak.

GENTLEWOMAN Good night, good doctor.

They exit.

RESOURCE #4.4C

Line Sets: Lady Macbeth Waking and Sleeping

Set A: Lines spoken by Lady M. *before* her Sleepwalking Scene (5.1)

- "Come, thick night, / And pall thee in the dunnest smoke of hell" (1.5.57–8).

- "Give me the daggers. The sleeping and the dead / Are but as pictures . . . / If he do bleed, / I'll gild the faces of the grooms withal" (2.2.69–70, 71–2).

- "My hands are of your color, but I shame / To wear a heart so white" (2.2.82–3).

- "I hear a knocking / At the south entry. Retire we to our chamber" (2.2.84–5).

- "A little water clears us of this deed. / How easy is it, then!" (2.2.86–7).

- "Get on your nightgown, lest occasion call us / And show us to be watchers" (2.2.90–1).

- "What's done is done" (3.2.14).

- "Why do you make such faces? When all's done, / You look but on a stool" (3.4.80–1).

- "What, quite unmanned in folly? . . . Fie, for shame!" (3.4.88, 90).

Set B: Lines spoken by Lady M. *during* her Sleepwalking Scene (5.1)

- "Hell is murky" (5.1.38).

- "Fie, my lord, fie, a soldier and afeard?" (5.1.38–9).

- "Yet who would have thought the old man to have had so much blood in him?" (5.1.41–2).

- "The Thane of Fife had a wife. Where is she now?" (5.1.44–5).

- "What, will these hands ne'er be clean?" (5.1.45).

- "Wash your hands. Put on your nightgown. Look not so pale" (5.1.65).

- "I tell you yet again, Banquo's buried; he cannot come out on 's grave" (5.1.66–7).

- "To bed, to bed. There's knocking at the gate" (5.1.69–70).

- "What's done cannot be undone" (5.1.71).

Macbeth in Act 5: Strutting and Fretting Toward His End, and . . . His Legacy Hereafter

Here's What We're Doing and Why

As a final tune-up before heading toward those summative final projects, in this lesson students will approach Macbeth's final soliloquy—his famous "Tomorrow and tomorrow and tomorrow" speech—in several different ways. These approaches include Choral Reading, Tone and Stress, 3D Lit, promptbooks, discussion, and annotation.

Students will also dig into Macbeth's state of mind. As we've traveled through *Macbeth*, students have used Folger Essentials as tools to explore the play and, among other aspects, how fear works in this play: where it shows itself and why, who fuels it and when, who are the victims of others' fears. They've examined language and action that suggests that many of Macbeth's actions, along with those of other characters in the play, are driven by fear: fear of losing power, fear of other characters, fear of not living up to his expectations of himself as a "real man," and more. In Act 5, students can ponder whether Macbeth fears his own death; at this point, his death seems inevitable.

Students will take an extended dive into the speech—investigating juicy words and line structures—then in small groups they will discuss more broadly the language, the power, and the legacy of the soliloquy. Specifically, they will focus on one example of that legacy—its prominence in *Hamilton*, an award-winning Broadway musical written by Lin-Manuel Miranda more than 400 years after Shakespeare wrote *Macbeth*.

It's all coming together! Be sure to remind them that next week is final project/summative performances week.

And be sure to check out your own homework assignment for next week at the end of this lesson. We've also included it in the first lesson for next week – **RESOURCE #5.1A**.

What Will I Need?

- Copies of the soliloquy (5.5.20–31) – **RESOURCE #4.5A**
- Copies of Questions on "Tomorrow . . ." to distribute or project – **RESOURCE #4.5B**
- Copies of excerpt from "Take a Break," *Hamilton*, Lin-Manuel Miranda – **RESOURCE #4.5C**
- Audio of "Take a Break," *Hamilton*, Lin-Manuel Miranda

How Should I Prepare?

- Familiarize yourself with the soliloquy and the questions
- Familiarize yourself with the song "Take a Break" from *Hamilton*
- Be sure to read your homework assignment for next week (**RESOURCE #5.1A**)

Agenda (~ 45-minute class period)

❏ Choral readings and reflections (20 minutes)

❏ Small group discussions (15 minutes)

❏ *Macbeth*'s Legacy (10 minutes)

Here's What Students Hear (From You) and (Then What They'll) Do

Part 1: Choral Readings and More

1. What's the context for this speech? What causes Macbeth to say it?

    We'll read it chorally a few different ways:

    - Choral reading at least 3 different ways, as we have been doing:
    - Choral reading whispering
    - Reading the last word of each line together
    - Choral reading getting louder with each sentence

    After each reading:

    - What did you notice?

    After all of the readings have been completed:

    - What are the effects of the different readings? What do they bring up for you?

2. Let's talk about "juicy" words. These are words that (a) have a lot of meaning, or (b) are fun to say, or (c) are poetic, beautiful, or striking in some interesting way. What other qualities make words juicy?

    Right now, highlight in the text what you feel are the 3–4 most "juicy" words from the speech. The last choral reading will be in a collective quiet voice, but say your "juicy" words with extra volume and emphasis. So our reading will be punctuated by juicy words from throughout the class.

    Afterward, we will reflect further:

    - How did this last reading feel to you? How did it sound?
    - Which words were the "juiciest" for the class? Do you think there's a reason for this?

Part 2: Further Exploration . . .

We'll get in small groups with **RESOURCE #4.5B**. Begin with the first question because it is perhaps the most important: What are your questions and thoughts after "living in" this speech for a little while? Address your questions and comments first, then choose 3 questions from the list and get busy. I'll move around and listen as you discuss. I don't want to miss anything.

Part 3: *Macbeth*'s Legacy and What We Can Learn from It

Next, we're going to leap ahead about 400 years to consider the big questions that the speech is asking.

We'll listen to a song from Lin-Manuel Miranda's musical *Hamilton*, "Take a Break," because it contains several *Macbeth* references. (You may know this musical or you may not. If not, don't worry.) At this point in the musical, Hamilton is in a conflict between joining his family at the lake house for the summer or remaining in Washington, DC, to get his political agenda through Congress. The main characters singing are Hamilton, his wife, Eliza, and his sister-in-law, Angelica. Listen carefully for the *Macbeth* references.

- What did you hear?

- Take a look at the language – **RESOURCE 4.5C**. What might these references mean?

- What point is Hamilton trying to make about how people perceive him and others?

- Do you know or can you take a guess about possible similarities between Macbeth and Hamilton? [**TEACHER NOTE:** One quick take—they are both very ambitious, very driven, and become less popular as the play goes on] Or between Macduff and Jefferson? Between Banquo and Madison? What does the Dunsinane Hill reference mean? In what ways does Eliza's line 115 allude to *Macbeth*?

- Overall, what does it mean that this speech is woven into a popular and groundbreaking musical?

As class ends, remind students that next week is final projects week! Ask students to quickly review how today's lesson helped prepare them for the summative performance, and what other tools they will be using as they create their projects.

[**TEACHER NOTE:** Look for use of choral reading, promptbooks, 3D Lit, tone and stress, and discussion with peers. All of these support students owning the text and being able to offer informed analysis and make informed performance choices.]

Here's What Just Happened in Class

- Students—using performance, stress and tone, and paired texts—have dug into the language and meaning of one of the most famous speeches in all of literature.

- Students took these insights into a deeper discussion of the speech.

- Students considered the prominence of *Macbeth* in *Hamilton* . . . what they can glean from the comparisons to Alexander Hamilton's situation as well as more generally the legacy of that speech.

- Students used and later reviewed some of the tools they will be using next week in their final projects.

RESOURCE #4.5A

5.5.20–31

MACBETH

   She should have died hereafter.   20
   There would have been a time for such a word.
   Tomorrow and tomorrow and tomorrow
   Creeps in this petty pace from day to day
   To the last syllable of recorded time,
   And all our yesterdays have lighted fools   25
   The way to dusty death. Out, out, brief candle!
   Life's but a walking shadow, a poor player
   That struts and frets his hour upon the stage
   And then is heard no more. It is a tale
   Told by an idiot, full of sound and fury,   30
   Signifying nothing.

Questions about "Tomorrow . . ."

Mark up your text as you go . . .

1. What questions or feelings do you have about the speech, or about Macbeth at this point?

2. What are Macbeth's feelings about his wife's death?

3. How does Macbeth use figurative language to suggest the futility of life?

4. How does Macbeth's reaction to his wife's death differ from Macduff's reaction (end of 4.3)?

5. Can you find the stage metaphor?

6. Does Macbeth fear death? Justify your response with evidence.

7. Who is the audience? Is it Seyton? Himself? The audience of the play? Someone else?

Be the director: If you were directing an actor playing Macbeth, how would you ask them to perform these lines?

• What shifts will you include in tone and volume, and why?

• Where would you have the longest pauses? Why?

• The speech has several examples of repetition, of both words and sounds. What effect does this have/could it have on an audience?

Excerpted from "Take a Break," from the Broadway Musical *Hamilton* Music and Lyrics by Lin-Manuel Miranda

HAMILTON

    My dearest, Angelica

    "Tomorrow and tomorrow and tomorrow   15

    Creeps in this petty pace from day to day"

    I trust you'll understand the reference to

    Another Scottish tragedy without my having to name the play

    They think me Macbeth, and ambition is my folly

    I'm a polymath, a pain in the ass, a massive pain   20

    Madison is Banquo, Jefferson's Macduff

    And Birnam Wood is Congress on its way to Dunsinane.

    . . .

HAMILTON

    I lose my job if I don't get my plan through Congress   110

    . . .

ANGELICA

    Screw your courage to the sticking place   115

    Take a break and get away

    Run away with us for the summer

ELIZA

    Let's go upstate   120

    Where we can stay

    . . .

HAMILTON

    I have to get my plan through Congress

    I can't stop until I get this plan through Congress   132

Teacher's Overview

Introducing the Final Week and the Final Project:
Make *Macbeth* Your Own

The Final Project's Learning Goals

This project is the culmination of everything your students have been doing all unit long: During this last week, students will work in groups to make a scene from Shakespeare entirely their own.

By the end of this project every student will have:

- Put together all the pieces of this unit, particularly essential practices like cutting a scene and creating a promptbook and 3D Lit

- Moved collaboratively through a complex process of reading, rereading, editing, adapting, embodying, imagining, re-editing, rehearsing, performing, deciding, and defending

- Used the text to make choices about how to edit, adapt, and stage the scene

- Created an original scene anchored in *Macbeth* and incorporating language from other sources (poetry, music, film, speech, etc.)

- Performed their original interpretation of the scene for an audience

- Written and presented a group rationale for the text-based decisions that led to this performance (edits, additions, staging, etc.)

- Written a brief personal reflection on the experience of completing this project

Both the students and you, the teacher, should walk away with resounding evidence that everyone in your class can make meaning from Shakespeare's language—from complex texts—on their own.

Advice and Reminders

Time. This learning experience is designed to take roughly 5 class periods of 45 minutes each. However, depending on your teaching context, it might take longer or shorter. If you have more time, and need more time, take more time!

Chaos. What is crucial for you, the teacher, to know is that it's all about turning the language and the learning over to the students, so expect the process to get somewhat messy and noisy. As long as students are making *their own way* through their scenes, it's all good. As you have been doing right along, resist the urge to explain the text to your students. Trust the process—and trust your students to ask questions, find answers, create interpretations, and make meaning on their own. (If they don't do this, then they're missing the deep learning and purpose of the project, and this whole *Macbeth* adventure, really.) All throughout this process, students are tracking their cutting, adding, and promptbooking decisions and preparing to present, along with their scene performance, an oral defense of their key decisions.

The following calendar is a suggestion.

DAY 1: What is this all about? The project, the purpose, the groups, the scenes. Groups begin reading their scenes aloud.

DAY 2: Cutting the scene

DAY 3: Adding outside texts to the scene and promptbooking the newly cut and adapted scene

DAY 4: Rehearsing the scene and writing the scene rationale

DAY 5: Performing scenes and presenting the defenses; whole-class "reflection round"

Time and Less Chaos. It works out best if you can decide how much time your schedule allows you for the final performances and scene rationales on the final day of the project. Then work backwards to schedule your groups within that time.

An example: If you have 45 minutes of class time and 20 students, you might have 5 performing groups with 4 students each. That could mean that each group would have 7–8 minutes to share their work (their performance + then defense of their decisions). Eight minutes x 5 groups = 40 minutes, leaving 5 minutes for a whole-class reflection round. If this feels tight to you, give each group 7 minutes.

Flexibility and Creativity. You'll see that on the menu of scenes for this project, some scenes involve more than 4 actors, and some fewer than 4 actors. Students will add their own creativity to the mix by double-casting parts, or using other means to make sure they have full participation.

Suggested Guidance on Assessing the Projects: A Seven-Point Checklist

1. Does the performance demonstrate a grasp of what the characters are saying and wanting?

2. Does the performance make strategic use of voice and body to convey effective tone and feeling?

3. Does the defense summarize the scene clearly, concisely, and accurately?

4. Does the defense comment on the scene's importance in the overall play and our world today?

5. Does the defense justify key decisions to cut, add, and perform language in this particular way? Is there strong and relevant textual evidence for this performance overall?

6. Does the defense describe how this process shaped new or different understandings of this play?

7. Does the personal reflection consider specific things that the student has learned, contributed, and discovered?

WEEK FIVE: LESSON 1

Your Final Projects!

Here's What We're Doing This Week and Why

Today kicks off the culminating project, the student-driven process of making Shakespeare thoroughly their own by collaborating on creating for each other great scenes from *Macbeth*. By the end of this lesson, students will understand what's expected of them and why—both as individuals and as project groups. They will also have gathered with their groupmates and have their assigned scene for this project. Although we've divided the final project into 5 days, it's really one unified, cumulative process, so please **make whatever pacing adjustments your students need**. Different groups might be at different steps of the process on different days, and that's OK.

What Will I Need?

- Final Project: The Teacher's Overview – **RESOURCE #5.1A** (Perhaps you got an early start and have read this already!)

- Final Project: The Student's Overview and Assignment – **RESOURCE #5.1B**

- The menu of *Macbeth* scenes for you to assign from, or for groups to choose from – **RESOURCE #5.1C**

How Should I Prepare?

- Make copies of the student's overview and assignment for everyone in class.

- Make a plan for grouping students.

- Make a plan for matching groups to scenes. (It's up to you whether you want to assign them the scenes we've provided, or scenes that you feel are key to the play, or to allow them to make their own choices.)

- Figure out how much time students will have for their scenes and their defense so you can let them know today. (See Teacher's Overview, **RESOURCE #5.1A**.)

- Prepare yourself to get out of the way and let students figure things out on their own. You're assessing their ability to do exactly that.

Agenda (~ 45-minute class period)

- ❏ Part 1: Intro to the assignment and scene menu: 20 minutes
- ❏ Part 2: Groups meet for the first time: 25 minutes

Here's What Students Hear (from You) and (Then What They'll) Do

Part One: Project Introduction

1. Give students the project assignment.

2. Check for understanding with reflection rounds:
   - I notice . . .
   - I wonder . . .

3. Assign scenes, answer any wonderings, and fill in any details that students missed.

Part Two: Group Work

Students work in their groups and get started!

Here's What Just Happened in Class

- Students met their final project and started working in groups to tackle the assignment!

- Every student read out loud some *Macbeth* new to them as groups and started to befriend their scenes.

Teacher's Overview

Introducing the Final Week and the Final Project:
Make *Macbeth* Your Own

The Final Project's Learning Goals

This project is the culmination of everything your students have been doing all unit long. Students will work in groups to make a scene from *Macbeth* entirely their own. By the end of this project, every student will have:

- Pulled together all the pieces of this unit, particularly essential practices like cutting a scene, creating a promptbook, and 3D Lit, in order to get inside of and create a scene from *Macbeth*.

- Moved collaboratively through a complex process of reading, rereading, editing, adapting, embodying, imagining, re-editing, rehearsing, performing, deciding, and defending.

- Used the text to make choices about how to edit, adapt, and stage the scene.

- Performed their original interpretation of their *Macbeth* scene for an audience.

- Written and presented a group rationale for the text-based decisions that led to this performance (edits, additions, staging, etc.).

- Written a brief personal reflection on the experience of completing this project.

- Grappled with the whole play through work in class up to now and more collaborative work across the whole play this week.

Both the students and you, the teacher, should walk away with resounding evidence that everyone in your class can make meaning from Shakespeare's language—from complex texts—on their own.

Advice and Reminders

Time. This learning experience is designed to take roughly 5 class periods of 45 minutes each. However, depending on your teaching context, it might take a longer or shorter time. For example, this plan is written with one day for final performance, but if you need more time and have the time, take it!

Chaos. Since it's all about turning the language and the learning over to the students, you can expect the process to get somewhat messy and noisy. As long as students are making *their own way* through their scenes, it's all good. As you have been doing right along, resist the urge to explain the text to your students. Trust the process—and trust your students to ask questions, find answers, create interpretations, and make meaning on their own, as they have been doing. (If they don't do this, then they're missing the deep learning and purpose of the project.) Throughout this process and this week, students are tracking their cutting, adding, and promptbooking decisions, and preparing to present (along with their scene performance) an oral defense of their key decisions.

Time and Less Chaos. It works out best if you can decide how much time your schedule allows you for the final performances and scene rationales on the final day of the project. Then work backwards to schedule your groups within that time.

An example: If you have 45 minutes of class time and 20 students, you might have 5 performing groups with 4 students each. That could mean that each group would have 7 to 8 minutes to share their work (their performance + then defense of their decisions). 8 minutes x 5 groups = 40 minutes, leaving 5 minutes for a whole-class reflection round. If this feels tight to you, give each group 7 minutes.

Flexibility and Creativity. You'll see that on the menu of scenes for this project, some scenes involve more than 4 actors, and some fewer than 4 actors. Students will add their own creativity to the mix by double-casting parts or using other means to make sure they have full participation.

Suggested Guidance on Assessing the Projects: A Seven-Point Checklist

1. Does the performance demonstrate a grasp of what the characters are saying and wanting?

2. Does the performance make strategic use of voice and body to convey effective tone and feeling?

3. Does the defense summarize the scene clearly, concisely, and accurately?

4. Does the defense comment on the scene's importance in the overall play and our world today?

5. Does the defense justify key decisions to cut, add, and perform language in this particular way? Is there strong and relevant textual evidence for this performance overall?

6. Does the defense describe how this process shaped new or different understandings of this play?

7. Does the personal reflection consider specific things that the student has learned, contributed, and discovered?

RESOURCE #5.1B

Student's Overview and Assignment

Introducing the Final Week and the Final Project
Make *Macbeth* Your Own

You will work in groups to make a scene from *Macbeth* entirely your own. This project is the culmination of everything you have been doing all unit long, and this week you will be demonstrating all that you have learned!

By the end of this project, you will have:

- Put together all the pieces of this unit, particularly essential practices like choral reading, cutting, creating a promptbook, and 3D Lit in order to get inside of and create a scene from *Macbeth*

- Moved collaboratively through a complex process of reading, rereading, editing, adapting, embodying, imagining, re-editing, rehearsing, performing, deciding, and defending

- Used the text to make choices about how to edit, adapt, and stage the scene

- Created an original scene anchored in *Macbeth* and perhaps incorporating language from other sources (poetry, music, film, etc.)

- Performed your original interpretation of the scene for an audience

- Written and presented a group rationale for the text-based decisions that led to this performance (edits, additions, staging, etc.)

- Written a brief personal reflection on the experience of completing this project

- Grappled with the play through work in class up to now and are completely focused on collaborative work this week

You, your classmates, and your teacher will walk away with resounding evidence that YOU can make meaning from Shakespeare's language—from complex texts—on your own.

What You Will Produce

- A performed scene from *Macbeth* (in a group)

- A defense of your scene, delivered orally and in writing (in a group)

- A personal reflection on this project (from you, as an individual)

Your Action Steps

1. **Get your group assignment** from your teacher.

2. Next, before anything else: With your group, **dive deeply into your scene**. Read it out loud as a group, just as we have done in class. Take notes on all of this—these will come in handy later. Collaboratively as a group, figure out:

- What's happening in the scene
- What the characters are saying
- What each of the characters want
- Why the scene is important in the play
- Why someone should care about this scene today

3. Next, **consider the end goal**: your group is making a scene of **X** minutes and an oral defense of the scene that is no longer than **X** minutes. Your teacher will tell you the timing that you—like any group of actors—must work with. Keep this in mind as you work through the scene.

4. Next, work to **be directors and put the scene on its feet**. Each member of the group should be creating a promptbook for the scene along the way so that you're all working from the same script with the same notes. Together, as you have been doing all along, make—and note—decisions about the following and be prepared to explain to your audience what in the text (and in your personal experience of reading it) motivated you to cut, add, and perform as you did:

   - **Cutting the scene.** Perhaps you must cut it so that it fits your time limit and still makes sense. What must stay? What can go?

   - **Locating the scene.** Where is it happening? What does this place look like? Feel like? Smell like? Sound like? How do you know this?

   - **Adding to the scene.** You may want to choose 1–2 outside texts to mash up with your scene. If you do, what is gained by putting these texts into your Shakespeare scene? What made you choose this/these text/texts? Why and where do they work best? If you choose to add outside texts, be sure that at least 80 percent of your scene is *Macbeth.*

   - **Getting ready to perform the scene.** Cast the parts. Which of you plays whom? Every group member must speak. What does each character want and think and feel? How can the audience tell? Who is moving where on what line, and why? Get on your feet and start moving, because some of these questions are answered when you get a scene on its feet. As you know, this is not about acting talent; it is about knowing what you are saying and doing as you bring life to this scene.

   - As you go, you're documenting your decisions and preparing your oral defense of the scene. What are the most significant or original decisions your group made? What drove those decisions? Let the audience into your interpretive process, your minds, ever so concisely. Your defense should involve every group member and do the following:
     - Summarize your scene
     - Comment on the scene's importance in the overall play
     - Justify your cutting, adding, and performing choices with textual evidence
     - Conclude by describing how the process of preparing this performance shaped new or different understandings of *Macbeth*

5. **Rehearse.** Yes, you should memorize your lines, though you can ask someone to serve as your prompter, as we think Shakespeare's company might have. Repeat: This is not about acting talent.

6. **Perform your scene and present your scene rationale** during your scheduled class period. After your performance, present your rationale for your scene. As with your performance, every group member must speak. Focus on just the most significant decisions and stick to your time limit. We will all watch all the final project scenes together so that we can celebrate wrapping up *Macbeth* with YOUR voices.

7. At that time, you will **submit the 2 written documents**:
   - The written version of your group's defense of your scene.
   - Your own individual reflection (400–500 words) on the experience— both the process and what you feel were your own contributions to the project.

Scene Menu—*Macbeth* – 15 options

Act & Scene	# of Characters and who they are
1.3	(5) Banquo, Macbeth, 3 witches (note: Ross & Angus appear toward end of scene, could also include them)
1.7	(2) Macbeth, Lady Macbeth
2.2	(2) Macbeth, Lady Macbeth
2.3	(7) Macbeth, Lady Macbeth, Lennox, Donalbain, Malcolm, Macduff, Porter
3.1	(5+) Lady Macbeth, Macbeth, Banquo, Servant, Murderers
3.4	(5+) Lady Macbeth, Macbeth, Ross, Lennox, Lords
4.1	(4+) 4 + 3 apparitions
4.2	(5+) Messenger, Ross, Lady Macduff, Son, Murderers
4.3	(4) Macduff, Malcolm, Ross, Doctor
5.1	(3) Lady Macduff, Gentlewoman, Doctor
5.2 & 5.4 & 5.6	(9) Menteith, Angus, Caithness, Angus, Lennox, Malcolm, Siward, Macduff, Young Siward
5.3 & 5.5	(5) Macbeth, Seyton, Doctor, Attendants, Messenger
5.7 & 5.8	(4) Macbeth, Young Siward, Macduff, Malcolm

Your Final Project: Making *Macbeth* Your Own

Here's What We're Doing and Why

We're here! Groups are making their way through the final project this week. They are working on scenes from *Macbeth* demonstrating as they go what they have learned in terms of making the language, characters, and action their own—all infused with their own energy and creativity. They are also presenting scenes to each other as we wrap up *Macbeth*.

Agenda for Lessons 2, 3, and 4 (~ THREE 45-minute periods)

Lesson 2:

❑ Introduction/Warm-up: 10 minutes

❑ Cutting the scene/Group Work: 35 minutes

Lesson 3:

❑ Introduction: 10 minutes

❑ Promptbook the newly edited scene and add outside texts if you choose to/ Group Work: 35 minutes

Lesson 4:

❑ Students' Choice/Warm-up: 10 minutes

❑ Rehearsing the scene and writing the scene rationale/Group Work: 35 minutes

What Will I Need for These Three Lessons?

- Some print copies of the Folger Shakespeare edition of the play for student reference

- A few dictionaries or Shakespeare glossaries for student reference

- Space and time for students to make their way through this project

- Strength to resist the urge to explain or interpret the text for students (you're a pro by now)

- Access to outside books, songs, poems, films, etc. if they choose to add outside material to their scene

- A discreet eye to observe students as they work

How Should I Prepare for These Three Lessons?

As long as every student understands the task at hand, you're good. Students are doing the hard work now!

Lesson 2: Here's What Students Hear (From You) and (Then What They'll) Do

Part One: Introduction/Warm-up

1. Choose your favorite line from your scene.

2. Count off by 4. Meet with the other students with the same number.

3. Toss your lines in a circle; everyone should say their line three times (say it differently each time!)

4. Discuss as a class: Given the lines you heard in your circle, what do you think is happening in the scenes we are performing? Which delivery of your line felt like the best fit for your character or scene? Why?

Part Two: Group Work

Groups are reading, rereading, and cutting their final scenes. They are also co-operating to compose a rationale for their unique performance of the scene. For a closer look at the steps in this process, please refer to the Student Overview – **RESOURCE 5.1B**.

[**TEACHER NOTE:** Students typically need to take this work home with them, especially the 2 writing tasks: the group rationale and the personal reflection. Check in with your students each day to see where they are in the process, and help them set realistic goals for homework and classwork.]

Lesson 3: Here's What Students Hear (From You) and (Then What They'll) Do

Part One: Introduction/Warm-up

1. In your groups, agree on a song that best represents your scene.

2. Discuss with your small group. Share with the class.

Part Two: Group Work

Groups are cutting, adapting, promptbooking, and rehearsing their final scenes. If they are including an outside text(s), they should decide what and how today. For a closer look at the steps in this process, please refer to the Student Overview – **RESOURCE #5.1B**.

[**TEACHER NOTE:** Once again, check in with your students in each class to see where they are in the process, and help them set realistic goals for homework and classwork, and be sure that they have a plan to complete the 2 writing tasks.]

Lesson 4: Here's What Students Hear (From You) and (Then What They'll) Do

Part One: Warm-up

- Teacher's choice or student choice!

Part Two: Group Work

Groups are rehearsing their final scenes. They are also cooperating to compose a rationale for their unique performance of their scene. For a closer look at the steps in this process, please refer to the Student Overview – **RESOURCE #5.1B**.

Students typically need to work at home on these, especially the 2 writing tasks: the group rationale and the personal reflection. Check in with your students each class to see where they are in the process, and help them set realistic goals for homework and classwork.

Here's What Just Happened in These Three Classes

- You observed a class full of students in a state of flow, deeply engaged in the process of making a scene from *Macbeth* their own!

- You watched peers help one another by asking good questions, building comprehension, citing textual evidence, and encouraging creativity.

The Final Project: Your Own *Macbeth*, Performed!

Here's What We're Doing and Why

It's showtime! Watch and listen as your students demonstrate their ability to grapple with, respond to, and perform Shakespeare's language. Hear why they staged things as they did. Celebrate how far your students have come, not just as Shakespeareans but as thinkers and readers and makers. Don't forget to save time for a whole-class reflection round after all the performances (this is often just as, if not more, enlightening as the scenes themselves). Celebrate your students, and make sure they celebrate each other!

Agenda (~ 45-minute class period)

- ❏ Groups get organized: 5 minutes
- ❏ Scenes performed and defenses presented: 30 minutes
- ❏ Whole-class reflection: 10 minutes

What Will I Need?

- Space and time for all groups to present their performances and rationales
- The "run of show" for today—which group performs when
- A notepad or digital doc to take notes on all the great learning you're witnessing. These notes will come in handy when you provide student feedback. (Revisit the 7-point checklist and the learning goals on your Final Project: Teacher Overview – **RESOURCE #5.1A** – when it's time for feedback.)
- Space and time for everyone to gather in a circle for a reflection round

How Should I Prepare?

- Create and share the "run of show" for today. As they enter class, groups should know when they're on and be reminded of how much time they have.
- It's always nice to have a lighthearted but clear way to call "time" on a scene, too. Some teachers rely on a timer, but maybe an exit pursued by a stuffed bear might be more fun. (Inside Shakespeare joke!) Your call.
- Arrange your space so everyone can see each scene. A giant circle is our favorite.

Here's What Students Will Do

Part One: Groups Get Organized

Students meet in their groups to organize props or make quick, last-minute changes to their scene.

Part Two: Performances

- Each group presents their work to thunderous applause

- Collect whatever project documentation you need to assess student learning

Part Three: Reflection Rounds

To conclude the performances, respond to the following prompts *thinking just about your work this week, including this performance experience*. With 10 or so minutes left, let's gather in a giant circle so that every student can reflect on the experience by finishing each of these sentences (finish each in ONE sentence!):

- Round 1: I noticed . . .

- Round 2: I discovered . . .

- Round 3: I will . . .

If responses stay focused on the language and activities, teachers should add: "What did you learn about yourself?"

Here's What Just Happened in Class

Revisit the 7-point checklist and the learning goals of the final project. You just saw them all in action. WOW!

Teaching Shakespeare—and *Macbeth*—with English Learners

Christina Porter

I am Christina Porter and for the past 20 years I have worked in an urban school community right outside of Boston, Massachusetts. I began as an English teacher, then a literacy coach, and currently I am the district curriculum director for the humanities. I first started working with English Learners in 2006 when I became a literacy coach. Prior to that, I had little experience with these phenomenal students.

Also prior to working with them, I knew the general assumptions about ELs. For as long as they have sat in U.S. classrooms, ELs most often have been considered "other," having many "deficits" that need to be overcome. The "deficits" tend to be their native language and culture—seen as roadblocks that should be surmounted so that EL students can more closely match prevailing assumptions of "American" culture—white, middle-class, and English-speaking. In my work with EL students, I soon learned that this mindset can manifest itself in many ugly ways in schools, and that can be both culturally and academically destructive.

Something I observed early on was that while our white, middle-class, English-speaking students were reading Shakespeare—the real thing, not that watered-down summarized stuff—our English Learners were not. Not even a watered-down version of Shakespeare! By "real Shakespeare" I mean his words in all their glorious Early Modern English (both with the full text of a play as well as in edited scenes from a play). Initially, I had the incorrect assumption myself: I assumed, like so many others, that because students were developing English, Shakespeare was probably too difficult for them to handle. I learned that this is incorrect. What I learned instead was that once we adults dismissed our own deficit-based thinking—and allowed our EL students to read, create, design, and imagine—the results were tremendous, with Shakespeare as well as with many other complex texts.

Coinciding with my start as a literacy coach, I spent a summer at the Folger Library's Teaching Shakespeare Institute. I learned about so many of the student-centered, get-them-on-their-feet methods that are one of the backbones of this book. As the new literacy coach at the high school, I was so excited to get into a classroom and use these, especially because I had the unique opportunity to work with many teachers in the building. One of the first colleagues to reach out was an English as a Second Language (ESL) teacher. We met to brainstorm, and I described how I had spent my summer at the Folger Library learning all of these innovative methods of engaging students. She was immediately onboard. Specifically, she wanted to tackle Shakespeare (again, REAL Shakespeare). Over the course of several years, we taught many plays together, and I did the same with other colleagues in the ESL department. Our ELs consistently destroyed any concern I or others could have had about their ability to read and perform something as intricate and complex as Shakespeare. Just one example: one of the first things I learned was that these students are uniquely attuned to the intricacy of language; it's how they exist on a daily basis! Sometimes when teaching a play with my native speakers, I found that they would want to rush. In this rushing, they would miss the depth and beauty of the words. ELs, on the other hand, take time with language— with the word, the line, the speech, and the scene. This is only one of the many strengths these students bring to working with Shakespeare, and other authors too.

Because the Folger understands the importance of ELs, I have been asked to share some of the knowledge I've gained working with these unique, intelligent, and resilient EL students and Shakespeare. My suggestions are based on years of scholarly research regarding second language acquisition coupled with my knowledge and experience working with ELs, Shakespeare, and the Folger Method. I am excited to share both what I've taught and what I've learned from EL students!

One important and perhaps obvious note here is that English Learners are not a monolith. You may have students in your class who have had exposure to English in their native country, you may also have students who have experienced gaps in schooling, and more. Though most of this chapter is focused on ELs generally, when I have found an approach that is particularly helpful for a specific subgroup of ELs, I point that out.

I build here on principles and classroom practices that you will find throughout this book and this series. Since teachers are the busiest people on the planet, this material is organized so that you can find what you need quickly:

❏ **Part One: ELs at Home in the Folger Method**

❏ **Part Two: Shakespeare with English Learners**

❏ **Part Three: *Macbeth* with English Learners**

Part One: ELs at Home in the Folger Method

Many of the Folger Essentials are *already* excellent supports for ELs. Folger Essentials like choral reading, rereading, focusing on single words and lines and then building to speeches and scenes—all of these support fluency and comprehension. In addition, these Teaching Guides include plot summaries and play maps, and the lesson plans include lots of other active instructional approaches.

When reading Shakespeare with ELs, I always give the option to read the scene summary in advance. I do this because it balances accessibility with giving them a chance to grapple with a complex text. Remember, Shakespeare borrowed most of his plots, so the plot is the least of our concern. We never want the story to become the roadblock to working with the words. The Folger Shakespeare, both in print and online, includes brief play and scene synopses for all the plays. The play maps may be helpful to ELs who may have had interruptions in their prior schooling or ELs who have not previously read a drama. It can be another structural support to "unveil" the characters and plot. You may choose to spend some time deconstructing the structure of a drama—discussing, for example, scenes, acts, and character lists. For some students, drama may be completely new, for others this quick activity can serve as an activator of prior knowledge.

Understanding text features is a solid support for comprehension. It is easy to assume that by high school, when most students are reading this play, they have been exposed to drama, but this is not always the case, depending on the backgrounds of individual students.

Part Two: Shakespeare with English Learners

With the Folger Method as my base, I build in additional resources to support English Learners in my urban school. This is because working with ELs *is* different from working with native English speakers. Equity is removing barriers. Equity is giving students what *they* need to be successful. Thus, I have come to four Truths that prevail when diving into Shakespeare—and other complex texts too—with EL students:

- TRUTH #1: **ELs need support with classroom practices.** We cannot assume that our ELs have had the same experience in classrooms as our other students. We need to offer specific guidance and support for common classroom practices such as having a small group discussion, acting out a piece of drama, or other Folger Essentials. Being clear in our expectations, our directions, and offering scaffolds (for example, sentence starters for small group discussions) is good for all students and essential for ELs.

- TRUTH #2: **ELs need additional support in order to grapple with complex texts.** ELs are capable of reading Shakespeare. ELs also need supports for language comprehension. Important supports include: chunking a scene/speech into smaller parts and using edited scenes or plays. To be clear, we always use Shakespeare's text (rather than the "simplified" versions), and we want to offer accessibility to those words through appropriate support for students who are in the process of acquiring English.

- TRUTH #3: **ELs need to have space for their unique language and culture to live in our classrooms.** Students' funds of knowledge are an asset, not a deficit. They need to bring their selves and their whole native culture to Shakespeare. This truth echoes the Folger principle about the importance of student voice.

- TRUTH #4: **ELs need support with the specific aspects of the English language and how words function** (individually, in a sentence, and more). This helps them build academic vocabulary, in written as well as oral language.

Continuing from Truth #4 and parts of the Folger Method, I introduce my students to what I call the "actor's arsenal"—a toolbox of 5 elements of communication that actors (and all of us) have at their disposal in English: stress, inflection, pause, nonverbal communication, and tone. At its simplest, it looks like this, and my students appreciate this visual:

STRESS: Emphasis placed on a **WORD** (or word, or ₘₒᵣd)

INFLECTION: The way the voice goes ᵘᵖ or ₔₒwₙ when a word is pronounced

PAUSE: A break . . . . . in reading for emphasis

NONVERBAL COMMUNICATION: Without words, the gestures, posture, presence or absence of eye contact

TONE: The *emotional* sound in your voice

These five tools deserve attention because *they are not the same in all languages*. In some languages, some of these tools are nonexistent or used in different ways than they are in English. I have a distinct memory of teaching a lesson on tone for the first time to a class of ELs. Generally, students really enjoy practicing a word/line with varying tones of voice. In this class, I couldn't help but notice one student who had a puzzled look on his face. I didn't want to embarrass him in his small group, so I sought guidance from the ESL teacher I was working with. She explained to me that tone did not work the same way in his native language as it did in English. In some languages—Hmong, for example—tone alone literally changes the meaning of a word, while in other languages—English, for one—tone accompanied by nonverbal communication alters the subtext of a word/phrase.

When working with students who have varying language backgrounds, additional attention to tone and nonverbal communication is very helpful. I typically introduce this "arsenal" as a part of our pre-reading. Tone and Stress, the first Folger Essential, includes visuals and practice rounds, and is recommended for all students beginning their journey with Shakespeare's language. Learn more about it in the Folger Method chapter. What I describe here can be an additional and introductory support for EL students.

I often begin this communication work by asking students to consider a universal teenage dilemma—having a disagreement with your parents or caregivers. (I have found, after working with students from all over the world, this is one of the few situations that transcend language and culture for most adolescents.) I then ask them to brainstorm all the different ways they can "show" their displeasure with words or actions. The list they generate generally includes items like volume, eye rolling, silence, additional gestures, and tone of voice. I then introduce the concept of tone vocabulary and include visuals with each element to further support comprehension. We pay particular attention to tone, as the English language offers infinite options for impacting the meaning of a word or phrase with tone alone. We define tone as the emotional sound in your voice, and I offer a specific list of tones for students' reference: love, hate, anger, joy, fear, and sorrow. While certainly not comprehensive of all the tones available in English, these six seem to capture the fundamentals. Students always enjoy taking a phrase like "That's great!" and applying these tones in small groups. For students coming from language backgrounds where tone is not utilized in the same way as it is in English, this activity offers additional practice in and added awareness of how tone functions in English. Using the Folger Essential, students practice with the word *Oh!*, saying it in a variety of tones (happy, sad, angry, surprised, and more). Students on their own will automatically add accompanying nonverbal communication, crossing their arms if the tone is angry, for example.

In addition, you can use a film clip of a scene from a Shakespeare play to further explore tone. (There is a wide variety of clips on sites like YouTube, or check out www.folger.edu.) Initially, I hand out to the students a copy of the scene, and I play the clip *audio only*. Students can work individually or they can work in small groups. They listen to the audio only, following along with the lines. As they listen, I instruct them to focus on one character and note any tone of voice they hear (anger, love, joy, and more). Next, we watch the scene *video only*, with no audio at all. They continue to track the same character and note any nonverbal communication. Finally, we watch the scene *with audio and video*, and add any additional notes on tone, stress, nonverbal communication, inflection, or pause. After this, students share their notes and findings either in a pair (if they have been working individually) or with another small group. Later, when we get up on our feet as a class, we are able to draw upon this kind of analysis to support our version of the play!

Part Three: *Macbeth* with English Learners

Truth #2—ELs need additional support with complex texts—led me to create supports with the plot of the play (remember what I said above about Shakespeare stealing all of his plots!). Truths # 1, 3, and 4 inform the ways in which I support ELs with staging a scene. Born from these Truths and backed up by the Folger Method, I share here approaches and practices that I have used most frequently when reading *Macbeth* with EL students. You will find that these strategies are useful for all students but *essential for ELs!*

Pantomime Pre-reading for *Macbeth*

In teaching any of the plays to ELs, I tend to spend a good amount of time dedicated to pre-reading. The goal here is simple . . . before we get into the words, I want to make sure my students are familiar with the story and the characters. We never want the story to be the thing that prevents them from accessing the language! Elizabethan audiences would have already been familiar with the play and the characters. You know your students the best and are able to determine what level of background knowledge will help them in being successful with this play. Prior to reading *Macbeth*, I want them to be familiar with the plot and who the characters are.

To access the plot, I created an activity I call the "Pantomime Pre-Reading." I have a pantomime pre-reading for each play we read. For this activity, small groups of students are given an important event from the play to pantomime (act out with actions and without sound) for their class. As students act, a narrator reads the events on the card out loud to the class. The purpose here is really twofold: 1. share some major plot points in advance, 2. immediately get students up on their feet and performing.

PANTOMIME PRE-READING DIRECTIONS

1. Divide students into small groups (ideally three to five students per group) and assign each group one or two "event cards" that describe specific incidents from the play.
2. Explain to students that they have a few minutes to come up with a pantomime (no words or sounds) for the events on the card. It can be helpful to show a quick video of a pantomime if students are new to the concept.
3. They may use items in the class as props, but props are not necessary.
4. When everyone is ready, the teacher or a student volunteer reads the list of events from the card in order as the groups perform their actions for the class. I generally give students 20–30 minutes to work on their pantomime.
5. After the pantomime is complete, ask students to make predictions for what will happen in the play. You may also provide students with stem starters to make their predictions: "I predict that . . . ," "I wonder if . . ."

Examples of responses for #5 above include: "I wonder if the witches are prophets or devils," "I predict that the play will be a game of thrones," and "I guess there will be a power struggle." Card #4 is displayed below.

PANTOMIME CARD FOR *MACBETH*
Card #4 *(6–8 actors and a narrator)*

- The Nobleman
- The Nobleman's Wife
- A Lord
- Prince #1
- Prince #2
- The Crowd of Nobles

It is morning in THE NOBLEMAN'S house and EVERYONE is gathered in a great room talking. A LORD notices that the King (a guest in the house) has not gotten out of bed yet. A LORD asks THE NOBLEMAN to show him to the King's bedroom so he can wake him up. A LORD and THE NOBLEMAN exit to wake the King while THE CROWD OF NOBLES remains chatting.

A moment later, A LORD reenters followed by THE NOBLEMAN. A LORD is screaming and pointing and *totally* flipping out! EVERYONE rushes to A LORD to see why he is flipping out. He points to the bedrooms and tells them all that the King has been murdered! PRINCE #1 and PRINCE #2 look shocked at the news of their father's death. THE NOBLEMAN announces that the guards must have killed the King so he killed the guards. THE CROWD OF NOBLES looks shocked . . . why would he do such a thing???? Suddenly, THE NOBLEMAN'S WIFE faints and everyone turns their attention to her. THE CROWD OF NOBLES helps THE NOBLEMAN'S WIFE to her feet and everyone exits except PRINCE #1 and PRINCE #2. They are shocked and talk about what they should do next . . .

Staging a Scene from *Macbeth* with Language Supports—Text/Subtext

Shakespeare was written to be performed. While the pantomime pre-reading serves as a wonderful "performance precursor," EL students benefit from additional language supports for the performance of a scene/act or entire play (Truth #4!). In order to build upon some of the truths I mentioned above (as well as the actor's arsenal), I want to walk you through some supports for reading and performing a scene in *Macbeth* with ELs.

Specifically, I want to introduce the idea of working with text and subtext as an actor. Simply put, the subtext is the meaning that exists below a character's written dialogue. The actor can utilize some of the tools already discussed (nonverbal gestures or tone, for example) to communicate the subtext. In working with ELs, I have, again, discovered that the concept of meaning (beyond literal meaning) changes with students' languages and cultural backgrounds.

While Shakespeare utilizes text/subtext in all of his plays, it is an integral part of many scenes in *Macbeth*, especially in the relationship between Macbeth and Banquo.

Scene and Characters	Featured text/subtext exchanges
1.3: Macbeth and Banquo	After the three witches make their predictions and disappear, Macbeth and Banquo converse about the predictions (and possible implications). **begins line 84 in the Folger Shakespeare**
1.5: Macbeth and Lady Macbeth	Lady Macbeth has read her husband's letter with the predictions of the witches/new titles from the king. They have a conversation about the upcoming visit of the king. **begins line 59 in the Folger Shakespeare**
2.1: Macbeth and Banquo	Macbeth and Banquo again discuss the prophecies. Macbeth tries to figure out if Banquo would conspire with him. **begins line 13 in the Folger Shakespeare**
3.1: Macbeth and Banquo	Macbeth tries to figure out when and where Banquo will be alone. **begins line 21 in the Folger Shakespeare**

I introduce the idea of subtext with this visual:

Text and Subtext

*Have you ever **said** one thing and **thought** another?*

1. What do you think the student in the orange shirt is thinking?

2. What does that student **say** or **do** that helps you to understand what they are thinking?

EL students benefit from visual representations! Remember, depending on the language and cultural backgrounds of the students, subtext may be communicated in different ways (i.e., through tone of voice, gestures, OR not at all). I like to use visuals with this topic to give students the time to examine an image that represents the concept. In the image above, students point out the nonverbal and verbal cues that the student in the orange shirt is using to communicate displeasure with their classmate's request (hands on the hips and head, the use of the word *umm* with the pause indicated by the ellipses).

The next support I introduce is the context organizer. This brief organizer serves as a refresher to who is in the scene, how they are connected, and what happened before this scene occurred. This is useful for actors in any scene they plan to stage! In thinking about how to "act" out the subtext, I always use this organizer first. Depending on the language development level, you can also add stem starters to this organizer, for example, "This scene takes place . . ." or "The important events that have already happened are 1. _____, 2. _____."

Play: _____

Act/Scene: _____

Who is in the scene? _____

Where does the scene take place? _____

What **important events** happened before this scene_____

_____

What do we need to know about the **relationships between the characters** in the scene?

_____

_____

Once students have this organizer filled in, I offer them the scene summary in advance (if they would like it). We give the scene an initial read and then I remind them of subtext as an important tool in the play *Macbeth*. I typically give them another visual to work with prior to getting the scene up on its feet. The visual below is from 3.1 of *Macbeth*. Students work in small groups to fill in the thought bubbles for Macbeth and Banquo. To determine the subtext, they have the context organized (shown above) and the visuals (shown below). We then stage this scene (again, in small groups) and experiment with using our actor's arsenal (featured on page 219) and various types of blocking to communicate the subtext. I have seen students come up with some brilliant ideas for this particular scene, including having Macbeth deliver the lines on a swing, going back and forth and jumping off on the line, "Is't far you ride?" I had another group of students seat Banquo in front and have Macbeth standing behind him so that both actors could add facial expressions the other could not see (not to mention the ominous feel of Macbeth looming over Banquo!). Yet another group had them kicking a soccer ball back and forth and had Macbeth score a goal toward the end of the exchange . . . just brilliant!

All of what we have discussed here will make for a rich experience with *Macbeth* and more broadly with Shakespeare—for EL students and for you too! Working with ELs and Shakespeare (and the Folger too) is a joy. You're on your way!

Teaching Shakespeare— Including *Macbeth*—to Students with Learning Differences

Roni DiGenno

I am Roni DiGenno, a special education teacher with 10 years' experience teaching ninth- through twelfth-grade English in a District of Columbia public high school. My students' reading levels range from pre-primer to college level and their special education classifications include specific learning disabilities, ADHD, auditory disabilities, autism, as well as intellectual and emotional disabilities. I teach self-contained, pull-out classes, each of about fifteen students, all with IEPs (Individualized Education Programs). Sometimes I have a teaching assistant, but most often I do not.

I love teaching. I love my students. And I love teaching Shakespeare to my students. I put to use what I have learned at the Folger; I use Shakespeare to inspire my students to believe in themselves. Most importantly, my students begin to see themselves as learners because I trust them with the hard stuff, the challenging content. I believe we can do it together, and my students know this. My passion for teaching these kids, who at times seem unreachable, comes from my own experience growing up with a reading difficulty. I could not sound out words, but this had nothing to do with my value or my intellect. My students, and all students, deserve the best, most engaging, intellectually stimulating lessons possible.

Shakespeare Rewrites How Students See Themselves Learning

For the past several years, I have taught exclusively some of the most difficult students in my school—those with very large learning gaps, usually reading 5–8 years below grade level, and with emotional disturbances that make it difficult to build positive peer and adult relationships. They arrive in my classroom plagued with low expectations of themselves and of school, because for years other people have had low expectations of them. They are used to passing just by showing up and doing minimal work. Some have been through the criminal justice system, which adds another layer of low expectations. My first priority is to help my students see themselves as capable and valued members of our classroom community. I do this by teaching lessons that empower them—lessons based on the Folger's philosophy. As a result, my students grow in exciting and surprising ways that no one could have anticipated.

I teach students like Armando, who had serious trust issues. He cut class frequently and was involved in groups that negatively influenced him in school. He repeated grades because he refused to do the work and he cursed teachers out regularly. In addition to being in and out of the criminal justice system, he was also a target of violent crime, which left him hospitalized for weeks and suffering from post-traumatic stress disorder. Through our class's collaborative work using Folger methods, Armando slowly began to discover and enjoy his strengths. He felt welcomed into the learning process and started to trust himself and others. He eventually became a peer leader who helped facilitate lessons.

I also taught Martin, a student who had such severe dyslexia that early on in my class he was reading at kindergarten level. He was withdrawn and shied away from participating for fear of judgment. Here again, by incorporating Folger principles and practices, I was able to give Martin the safe learning environment that he needed and the confidence to try reading aloud. He learned to trust his peers and he began to take risks—reading parts, participating, and giving amazing insight into discussion topics.

The Folger Method supports students like Armando and Martin, who have vastly different learning needs but who may also be in the same class. The teaching strategies offer students multiple entry points—tactical, visual, and aural—through which to engage and enjoy complex texts. Differentiation and scaffolding are built into the Folger's interactive lessons so students build a positive association with challenging texts. This is hugely important for students with learning differences and emotional difficulties. If content or concepts are overwhelming, or not taught in a way that they can grasp them, students will build a negative association. No one wants to struggle or feel like they can't learn something, which is often the root cause of behavior issues within classrooms. The Folger Method meets students' social and emotional learning needs through building a supportive and collaborative classroom community. Through the process, students begin to work through conflict, solve problems, and accept and support one another's learning differences.

How the Folger Method Works for Students with IEPs

In the Folger Method chapter and in the *Macbeth* lessons in this book, you'll find the Folger Essentials that will throw your students right into the text through powerful practices like tossing words and phrases, two-line scenes, choral reading, and 3D Lit. Each Essential gives students exposure to the language and removes a barrier to learning and comprehension. Each builds on the others, increasing cognitive demand. Students master each step before moving to the next—words before lines, lines before scenes, choral reading before acting and reading parts solo. They don't feel left behind, because they learn the content and the skills simultaneously so that they understand more comprehensively.

Every year, my students look forward to our unit on Shakespeare. Typically about 10 weeks long, the unit allows us to slow down and dig into the text. Instead of skipping over difficult parts, we want to conquer them! It is important for us to embrace the struggle because it is an inevitable part of the learning process. In the Folger work, struggle is about joyful investigation and thinking hard together rather than a feeling of inadequacy. Students question, try out, and connect with the words and each other, and so they learn that there is no one right answer but rather a whole new way to discover a text. The Essentials get the language in the students' mouths, encourage collaboration, and shift focus away from the teacher so that students can practice navigating themselves through their learning. It's a different way of teaching and a different way of learning. At first, they are hesitant: They resist, they laugh, they feel weird, they are unsure, they can't believe they are talking this much in class—and I am encouraging all of it. Within a week or two, students are more willing to experiment and take risks with the language by reading really strange words they have never seen or heard before. And soon, students are reading Shakespeare and enjoying it.

Reading Shakespeare can be a great equalizer. While scholars and directors and actors never tire of decoding, interpreting, and defining Shakespeare, the truth is that no one knows exactly what Shakespeare really meant. He left no diary or notes. Everyone is entitled to their own interpretation. We also have no idea how the words were pronounced because we have no audio recordings of the performances in the Globe Theatre. The "funny" English (my students' term) in Shakespeare's works puts us all on the same playing field. Be vulnerable, mess up some words, and have fun! The students will ask, "How do you say this word?" and my only response is, "Not sure, let's figure it out." It's okay to do your best and sound "funny." We are all in this together and repeating that idea to students builds bridges.

The Folger Method gives students the scaffolding and tools needed to launch them from struggling readers to invested readers. Martin, my student with severe dyslexia and on a Beginning Reader level, struggled with sight words. As the rest of his class became more comfortable reading Shakespeare's words, he remained unsure. Could he read and understand Shakespeare? But he can't read! But he has a learning disability! But . . . nothing! Martin found his voice and his courage to try to read, and read he did. One day we were using the Folger Essential 3D Lit to explore a scene, and when his turn came to read, he chose not to pass. Previously, he'd always politely declined to read aloud, and the class and I obliged. On this day, though, he did not pass. Slowly, he began to read the words. Fumbling often, he kept reading, with the encouragement and support of his peers. They helped him sound out words when he didn't know how to start. He finished reading, and the room applauded him. Martin entered center stage that day because he had developed both belief in himself and trust in his peers. He wanted to join them and believed he could do it. Shakespeare is truly for everyone, and everyone is capable of "getting it." Martin "got it," not because he read the text flawlessly and was able to analyze the motifs in an essay. He got it because he was able to understand the text through a series of activities that led to his comprehension.

Shakespeare and other excellent complex texts are so important, especially for students who have IEPs, because they deserve an enriching learning experience with real, challenging content. Giving students access to appropriate, grade-level material is essential to meeting their IEP goals, regardless of the educational setting (resource, pull-out, or inclusion). More than teaching Shakespeare, the Folger Method is also about instilling confidence in the students about the reality that they can do much of this work themselves. Even if it takes a while, even if they need a little help here and there— *they can do it.*

My Students and *Macbeth*

Connecting the Play to Their Own Lives

In general, multiple connections to any text build interest and improve comprehension. I have found that when my students connect elements of Shakespeare's plays to their own lives, they become more engaged in what they read and build stronger bonds to the text. In my classes, through the Folger approach, we have been building a safe, trusting community all along that makes it possible to explore these big ideas in the text.

Macbeth offers students any number of connections to their own lives. Here are a few, and ways in which you might use these in class.

Fate/Personal Responsibility: The beginning of the play starts with the premonition of three witches who tell Macbeth that he will become king. Once he knows this, Macbeth schemes to ensure that his path to the throne happens as quickly as possible, thus making the vision true. This creates a teaching opportunity to visit the duality of fate and personal responsibility. Macbeth is both responsible for making himself king and for the acts that have put him there, including the murders. Regardless of the witches' prophecy, it is Macbeth who is responsible for the murderous acts that put him on the throne.

Idea for Class: Following the reading of Act 1, Scene 3, the class can have a debate about whether fate exists. First, start by examining the witches with the class. Display the text for the class focused on line 50 or so. What are the three proclamations the witches make? If the prophecies come true, will it be because of fate or personal responsibility? Fate means because the witches proclaimed it will happen, it will happen. Personal responsibility means it will happen only as a result of Macbeth's beliefs and actions.

The class can then be split into two groups and brainstorm Macbeth's options after hearing the witches.

Power and Gender in *Macbeth*: Neither Lady Macbeth nor Macbeth fall into absolute gendered roles in the play. The language tells us that while Macbeth does show manly bravery on the battlefield, he lacks courage when it comes to murder. Meanwhile, Lady Macbeth plays a subservient role to her husband while also being the brains behind the murder plot. Another rich question to consider about their relationship is "Who has the power?" *Macbeth* presents a great opportunity for students to get with the language and to examine gender and power.

Idea for Class: In 1.7, look at lines 39–88 and as a group, analyze the scene closely to determine who has the power in the conversation. One way to shed some light on this is to count the number of lines Lady Macbeth has versus Macbeth. The students should be able to determine that Lady Macbeth speaks more during this section. Next, students can practice reading this section out loud using different tones to illustrate their sense of the meaning. The first time, half the students read Lady Macbeth in a gentle voice, sweet, and the other half read Macbeth as forceful. Debrief what students believe happened in this section. Next, half the students read Lady Macbeth in a forceful, demeaning voice and the other half read Macbeth in an afraid, unsure voice. Debrief again and discuss which one they believe makes the most sense for them.

Relationships/Loyalty: The issues are relatable and timely to teach, helping students develop their own social/emotional skills along with literary analysis skills. One issue in *Macbeth* is the powerful relationship between Macbeth and Lady Macbeth and where loyalty comes into play.

Idea for Class: Have a discussion with students about Macbeth's options. Students can engage in a structured Socratic seminar about these issues. Give students the questions beforehand so that they can prepare their answers and come up with examples from the text or their own lives to support their responses. You can include questions such as: Can anyone be a "Macbeth"? Who has the power in the relationship between Macbeth and Lady Macbeth? How badly does Macbeth want to be king? Can pressure cause someone to do something that turns out to be the wrong thing or a bad thing? Can anyone be susceptible to peer pressure, and how? Do you believe everyone has control over their choices? What does loyalty mean to you?

Focus on Key Scenes

The lessons in this book focus on key scenes and use the Folger Essentials to actively and immediately involve students. Those scenes are great ones, and there are others too that I find work really well with my students. These might be key for you and your students: the witches' prophecies (1.3); Lady Macbeth persuades Macbeth (1.7); Duncan's murder (2.1 and 2.2); the witches' riddles (4.1); Lady Macbeth's sleepwalking scene (5.1), and the final scene—swordfight! (5.8).

IMPORTANT GUIDELINES In working with scenes, I pay attention to these important guidelines:

Keep the original language. Always use Shakespeare's original language and *not* the modernized, made-easy versions. Do not substitute simplified language to make it easier. For one thing, it doesn't make it easier. More importantly, students with IEPs need to be given access to the original language and be able to make sense of it. And they can.

Prioritize depth over breadth. It is more important that students learn the skills to dig deep into a text, especially independently, than it is to read every line in the play. It may take your class of students with IEPs the same amount of time to analyze four key scenes as it takes your general education class to analyze seven. That's okay. Give your students the time they need to do this important work rather than rush through the text. The scripts we create and use in class are without footnotes or explanatory glosses. This allows students to decipher meaning on their own or collaboratively, and removes distractions that impede their understanding.

For example, feel free to delete the discussion about capturing the Irish. While important in the historical context (Scottish vs. Irish territory wars), it does not advance the plot of Macbeth killing his way to the throne. By cutting the scenes, you are choosing to forgo breadth in favor of depth. By cutting (which directors and editors and actors do all the time), you are offering students the ability to dive deep into Shakespeare's words to determine their own meaning. Feel free to use summaries to ensure students understand the whole story, but don't feel the need to explain every detail.

Shorten the scenes if you need to. You can cut key scenes to include just the most important information. To guide you, ask yourself these questions: What do I want students to understand from this scene? In what part of the scene does that idea happen? The following is a cut version of 1.3 that I have used in my class.

The cut version of *Macbeth* 1.3 below is about 36 lines; the original scene is 175 lines. You can find the full text here: folger.edu/macbeth/read and you can download it for your own editing. Because the scene is brief, students can focus on meaning, setting, and characters on their own without getting lost. The cutting keeps the most important parts of the plot and character. Using the free Folger Shakespeare online makes finding and cutting scenes easy.

FIRST WITCH Where hast thou been, sister?

SECOND WITCH Killing swine.

THIRD WITCH Sister, where thou?

FIRST WITCH
Look what I have.

SECOND WITCH Show me, show me.

FIRST WITCH
Here I have a pilot's thumb,
Wracked as homeward he did come.
                              Drum within.

THIRD WITCH
A drum, a drum!
Macbeth doth come.
                    Enter Macbeth and Banquo.

MACBETH Speak if you can. What are you?

FIRST WITCH
All hail, Macbeth! Hail to thee, Thane of Glamis!

SECOND WITCH
All hail, Macbeth! Hail to thee, Thane of Cawdor!

THIRD WITCH
All hail, Macbeth, that shalt be king hereafter!

BANQUO
Good sir, why do you start and seem to fear
Things that do sound so fair?
You greet with present grace and great prediction
Of noble having and of royal hope.

FIRST WITCH Hail!

SECOND WITCH Hail!

THIRD WITCH Hail!

FIRST WITCH
Lesser than Macbeth and greater.

SECOND WITCH
Not so happy, yet much happier.

THIRD WITCH
Thou shalt get kings, though thou be none.
So all hail, Macbeth and Banquo!

FIRST WITCH
Banquo and Macbeth, all hail!

MACBETH
Stay, you imperfect speakers. Tell me more.
With such prophetic greeting. Speak, I charge you.
                              Witches vanish.

BANQUO
Whither are they vanished?

MACBETH
Into the air, and what seemed corporal melted.

BANQUO
Were such things here as we do speak about?

MACBETH
Your children shall be kings.

BANQUO
You shall be king.

MACBETH
And Thane of Cawdor too. Went it not so?

MACBETH, *aside*
If chance will have me king, why, chance may
   crown me
Without my stir.

ANNOTATE THE TEXT When I say "annotate," I mean making any notes about what is happening in the text; this practice helps students remember what is happening. Some may call this "marking the text." It's all the same. Encourage students to take notes directly on the text during discussions because it leads them to analysis. **Make it purposeful.** Ensure that each time students annotate, they relate the underlined parts of the text to what is happening in the discussion. The annotations can be used for writing assignments.

   Show them what an annotated scene or speech looks like and how it's useful. Model for students by annotating and thinking aloud with them. You can do this by using a projector or smartboard, or by distributing copies of your own annotations. The following example is a student's annotation of Act 5, Scene 1.

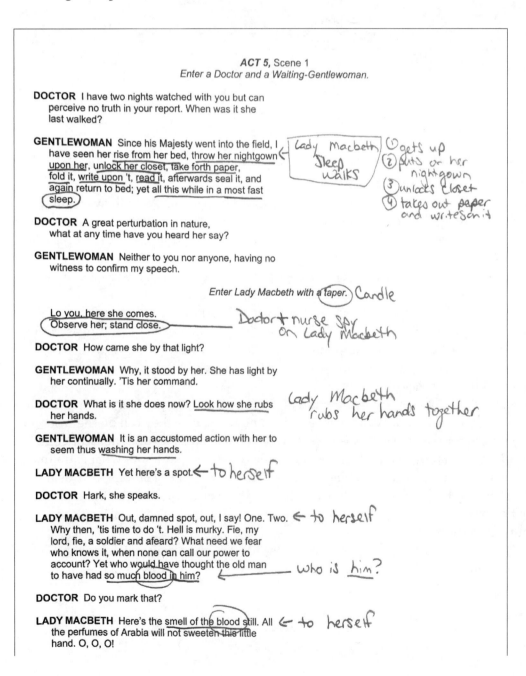

DOCTOR This disease is beyond my practice. Yet I have
known those which have walked in their sleep,
who have died holily in their beds.

LADY MACBETH Wash your hands. Put on your nightgown. ← to herself
Look not so pale. I tell you yet again, Banquo's
buried; he cannot come out on 's grave.
To bed, to bed. There's knocking at the
gate. Come, come, come, come. Give me your
hand. What's done cannot be undone. To bed, to
bed, to bed.

talking to herself about Banquo's death.

Lady Macbeth exits.

DOCTOR Will she go now to bed?

GENTLEWOMAN Directly.

DOCTOR
Foul whisp'rings are abroad. Unnatural deeds
Do breed unnatural troubles. Infected minds ← *People sometimes tell*
To their deaf pillows will discharge their secrets. *their secrets in their*
I think but dare not speak. *sleep.*

GENTLEWOMAN Good night, good doctor.

They exit.

Spread the Shakespeare Love

You and your students are on a Shakespeare journey together. As with everything you teach, the energy you give is the energy you get back. The more you LOVE teaching Shakespeare, the more your students will love it too. Keep in mind that it may take time, so fake it until you make it. When I started using the Folger Method, my students thought I was way too excited about Shakespeare. Over time, the energy is contagious, and they are just as excited to learn as I am to teach. Shakespeare has always been my favorite unit because it demonstrates that powerful literature belongs to them, and my students look forward to it because it is fun. From calling each other "greasy onion-eyed nut-hook" and "rank rump-fed giglet" to fake swordplay with foam weapons, and adding "thee" and "thou" to those words, I can see through their actions that they have fallen for Shakespeare as well.

Starting this journey with your students isn't always easy, but it is worth it. You are expecting more from them and teaching them more. Believe they can do the work and they will start to believe in themselves. Forgive yourself if a day does not work out. We are all works in progress, and it may take some tweaking to find out what extra things your students may need. Teaching Shakespeare or any other complex text using the Folger Method may be an adjustment to the way you teach now, so the more you do it, the better you will get at it. Students will become the drivers of the classroom, so get yourself ready for the show.

So, to my students who pop in to ask, "Hey Ms. DiGenno, you still doing that Shakespeare thing?" "Yes, I am, and so are you," I always say back as they rush out of the class again. Usually their last word: "Cool!"

Pairing Texts:
Macbeth Off the Pedestal and in
Conversation with Other Voices

Donna Denizé

Something wildly important happens when we teach two very different works or authors together—like *Macbeth* and writings of Frederick Douglass; *Hamlet* and something by Claudia Rankine; *Othello* and the poetry of George Moses Horton, or *Taming of the Shrew* and the poems of Audre Lorde.

Paired texts are two texts that you and your students dive into at the same time. Both texts have equal weight; each is strong and can stand fully on its own. You can pair whole works or segments of works, selected narratives, scenes, or stanzas. But there is no "primary" and "secondary" or "supplemental" hierarchy—ever. Two voices, two points of view, two writing styles, two characters . . . and each will illuminate the other.

It's important to note here, since we are in the world of Shakespeare, that a Shakespeare play and an adaptation of a Shakespeare play or plot are *not* paired texts. That's a primary text and most often some kind of supplemental one. Together, they don't have the power or the payoff of a set of paired texts.

Why pair texts? Because, taken together, they illuminate each other in powerful and surprising ways. Looking closely at paired works gives kids a sense of the sweep of literature and allows them to consider together two authors who wrote in vastly different times, places, cultures, genders, races, religions—you name it. These juxtapositions allow them to notice that in many cases, writers have been asking the same big questions for some time: about human identity—how we define ourselves through culture, our moral choices, or how we navigate power or powerlessness, and more. In other instances, they are on very different wavelengths . . . and what might be the reasons for that?

I developed my love for paired texts in my thirty-eight years teaching in a variety of secondary school settings—public, private, urban, and rural—and in serving a term on the advisory board for all vocational schools in the state of Virginia. I currently teach at St. Albans School for Boys in Washington, DC, where I chair the English department. I love working with paired texts because two strong texts working together produce something marvelous in class: They create a space for meaningful conversations that come from students' experiences and questions, and this creates not just good analysis but empathy. Since students today must navigate an incredibly complex global society, they can only benefit by considering a sweep of literature that helps them deepen their empathy for others.

I've found that the more specific or particular the pairing, the better, since this inspires students' creativity and establishes new ways of thinking about both texts. It also strengthens students' analytical skills and increases their capacity for understanding complexity—qualities that are essential for navigating current human challenges and the promise of an ever-evolving world—and the worlds students inhabit.

The following section is designed in two parts: the first to give you an example and a fuller sense of how paired texts work together, and the second to recommend three text pairs that include *Macbeth*, and that in my experience work very well with students.

Part One: An Example of a Pair of Texts and How They Have Worked in Class

Pairing **Iago's speech in** *Othello* (3.3.367–382, he plots to use Desdemona's handkerchief to stoke Othello's jealousy) with **"Troubled with the Itch and Rubbing with Sulphur," a poem by George Moses Horton**, a contemporary of Frederick Douglass. This is a pairing that focuses on language.

A note here on George Moses Horton (ca.1798–ca.1883): He was an enslaved man in North Carolina who taught himself to read with the help of spelling books, a Bible, and a book of hymns. His master soon realized that there was money to be made sending Horton on errands to deliver produce to students and staff at the University of North Carolina in Chapel Hill. That is where Horton became a little like a celebrity; students befriended him because he created love poems that enabled them to get dates. Since Horton could not yet write, the students would write the poems down as he dictated them; they paid him in either money or books. In this way he acquired a complete works of Shakespeare, a collection of works by Lord Byron, Samuel Johnson's *Dictionary*, Homer's *Iliad*, and many more. Once paid, Horton tried to save enough to purchase his freedom, but his attempt was unsuccessful. Horton lived long enough to see the end of slavery, though, so he was freed eventually. After his first book, *Poems by a Slave* (1837), newspapers began calling him "the colored bard of Chapel Hill." In 1997, Horton was named "Historic Poet Laureate" of Chatham County, North Carolina.

Othello (3.3.367–382) by William Shakespeare	*"Troubled with the Itch and Rubbing with Sulphur"* by George Moses Horton

IAGO
 	
    Be not acknown on 't
I have use for it. Go, leave me.
 	
                    Emilia exits.
 	
I will in Cassio's lodging lose this napkin
And let him find it. Trifles light as air
Are to the jealous confirmations strong
As proofs of holy writ. This may do something.
The Moor already changes with my poison;
	'Tis bitter, yet 'tis sweet;
	    Scratching effects but transient ease;
	Pleasure and pain together meet
	    And vanish as they please.
	
	My nails, the only balm,
	    To every bump are oft applied,
	And thus the rage will sweetly calm
	    Which aggravates my hide.

Dangerous conceits are in their natures poisons,
Which at the first are scarce found to distaste,
But with a little act upon the blood
Burn like the mines of sulfur.

Enter Othello.

I did say so.
Look where he comes. Not poppy nor mandragora
Nor all the drowsy syrups of the world
Shall ever medicine thee to that sweet sleep
Which thou owedst yesterday.

It soon returns again:
  A frown succeeds to every smile;
Grinning I scratch and curse the pain
  But grieve to be so vile.

In fine, I know not which
  Can play the most deceitful game:
The devil, sulphur, or the itch.
  The three are but the same.

The devil sows the itch,
  And sulphur has a loathsome smell,
And with my clothes as black as pitch
  I stink where'er I dwell.

Excoriated deep,
  By friction played on every part,
It oft deprives me of my sleep
  And plagues me to my heart.

In class, we read both pieces aloud first, and then I asked students to look up the word *sulfur* and its purposes. From various online sources, both medical and agricultural, they learn that, at least in the Delta, sulfur has been an important substance in yielding maximum cotton crops. Yet, applied to the skin, sulfur can both cause pain *and* provide relief from itching and burning and rashes, even though as Horton points out, it stinks.

I asked students to make as many connections between the two texts as possible. Where does sulfur come in? What does sulfur do?

- Sulfur can heal or burn, or both.

- In both texts, it seems like the thing that is meant to heal and at first brings relief (sulfur) is also the thing that brings the pain again.

I had to do little to keep the discussion going. My students had this to say about Horton:

- Even if he's free, which means he can make his own choices and his own money, Horton is still not a citizen, not part of society, and the self is torn between two worlds—as an established reader and writer in a world that denies Blacks literacy and education.

- Horton has no way to vote or own property. In fact, he's part of a larger society where slavery exists and the laws, as well as the social practices, deny his equality with white citizens.

- For the whites, Horton's existence is problematic: he's supposed to be inferior intellectually and morally, but he has demonstrated the opposite, and it's difficult to reconcile the contradiction he creates through the racial lens. This creates moral dilemmas. Irrational Othello, on the other hand, is looking to solve a moral dilemma, seeking a way out of his suffering, and believing Iago is the one to heal his fears and insecurity about Desdemona's infidelity. Students saw pretty quickly that Othello thinks that Iago will bring freedom from these worries, but in reality, Iago is the cause—the sulfur that burns, and not the healing balm.

In both cases, my students saw clearly the corrosive effects of prejudice, of racism; so with matters of prejudice, whether it's class, gender, race, or religion, there are no quick solutions, no easy balms to apply. Moreover, if we do not see the "other," we cannot see the self and cannot understand the self.

Part Two: Pairing Various Texts with *Macbeth*

1. Pairing *Macbeth's* **"If it were done" soliloquy** (1.7.1–28, Macbeth weighs plans to murder King Duncan) with the passage from **Frederick Douglass's *Narrative of the Life of Frederick Douglass: An American Slave*** in which Douglass sits on a hillside watching freely moving passing ships while his movements are confined by slavery, its laws, and its customs.

Macbeth 1.7.1–28 **by William Shakespeare**	*Narrative of the Life of Frederick Douglass* by Frederick Douglass
MACBETH If it were done when 'tis done, then 'twere well It were done quickly. If th' assassination Could trammel up the consequence and catch With his surcease success, that but this blow Might be the be-all and the end-all here, But here, upon this bank and shoal of time, We'd jump the life to come. But in these cases We still have judgment here, that we but teach Bloody instructions, which, being taught, return To plague th' inventor. This even-handed justice Commends th' ingredience of our poisoned chalice To our own lips. He's here in double trust: First, as I am his kinsman and his subject, Strong both against the deed; then, as his host, Who should against his murderer shut the door, Not bear the knife myself. Besides, this Duncan Hath borne his faculties so meek, hath been So clear in his great office, that his virtues Will plead like angels, trumpet-tongued, against The deep damnation of his taking-off; And pity, like a naked newborn babe Striding the blast, or heaven's cherubin horsed Upon the sightless couriers of the air, Shall blow the horrid deed in every eye, That tears shall drown the wind. I have no spur	Our house stood within a few rods of the Chesapeake Bay, whose broad bosom was ever white with sails from every quarter of the habitable globe. Those beautiful vessels, robed in purest white, so delightful to the eye of freemen, were to me so many shrouded ghosts, to terrify and torment me with thoughts of my wretched condition. I have often, in the deep stillness of a summer's Sabbath, stood all alone upon the lofty banks of that noble bay, and traced, with saddened heart and tearful eye, the countless number of sails moving off to the mighty ocean. The sight of these always affected me powerfully. My thoughts would compel utterance; and there, with no audience but the Almighty, I would pour out my soul's complaint, in my rude way, with an apostrophe to the moving multitude of ships:— "You are loosed from your moorings, and are free; I am fast in my chains, and am a slave! You move merrily before the gentle gale, and I sadly before the bloody whip! You are freedom's swift-winged angels, that fly round the world; I am confined in bands of iron! O that I were free! O, that I were on one of your gallant decks, and under your protecting wing! Alas! betwixt me

To prick the sides of my intent, but only Vaulting ambition, which o'erleaps itself And falls on th' other—	and you, the turbid waters roll. Go on, go on. O that I could also go! Could I but swim! If I could fly! O, why was I born a man, of whom to make a brute. The glad ship is gone; she hides in the dim distance. I am left in the hottest hell of unending slavery. O God, save me! God, deliver me! Let me be free! Is there any God? Why am I a slave? I will run away. I will not stand it. Get caught, or get clear, I'll try it. I had as well die with ague as the fever. I have only one life to lose. I had as well be killed running as die standing. Only think of it; one hundred miles straight north, and I am free! Try it? Yes! God helping me, I will. It cannot be that I shall live and die a slave. I will take to the water. This very bay shall yet bear me into freedom. The steamboats steered in a north-east course from North Point. I will do the same; and when I get to the head of the bay, I will turn my canoe adrift, and walk straight through Delaware into Pennsylvania. When I get there, I shall not be required to have a pass; I can travel without being disturbed. Let but the first opportunity offer, and, come what will, I am off. Meanwhile, I will try to bear up under the yoke. I am not the only slave in the world. Why should I fret? I can bear as much as any of them. Besides, I am but a boy, and all boys are bound to some one. It may be that my misery in slavery will only increase my happiness when I get free. There is a better day coming." Thus I used to think, and thus I used to speak to myself; goaded almost to madness at one moment, and at the next reconciling myself to my wretched lot.

In class, we started with a definition of *ambition*: Kids looked it up in various dictionaries. They came up with definitions like these:

- an earnest desire for some type of achievement or distinction, as power, honor, fame, or wealth, and the willingness to strive for its attainment

- the object, state, or result desired or sought after

- to seek after earnestly

- aspire to

I asked a few simple questions to start them off:

1. What is the ambition of each man? What's driving him toward it? What is he seeking?

2. What are they both wrestling against and with—morally and socially?

3. What solutions, if any, does each one reach?

A discussion developed that connected the word *ambition* with some of the other topics that they found in both texts: isolation; self-perception; moral dilemmas; questions about freedom and justice. My students came up with valuable comparisons and contrasts that I list here in no particular order:

- Both are wrestling in the mind, the imagination alive, the struggle with consequences, moral right and wrong.

- In *Macbeth*, the moral wrong is in the individual; in the Douglass text, the moral wrong is in the larger society.

- Both bring isolation, pain, and suffering. Macbeth's isolation leads to his destruction; Douglass's isolation leads him to being an orator and a major voice in the fight for the abolition of slavery.

- Macbeth's ambition has a negative outcome while Douglass's has a positive outcome.

- Both search for justice—Macbeth to avoid it and Douglass to have justice manifest.

- Macbeth has social and political power, while Douglass—a slave—is marginalized, without social and political power.

- Both are seeking freedom. Macbeth imagines freedom from consequences. Douglass imagines the consequences of freedom.

These two texts—Shakespeare's *Macbeth* and Frederick Douglass's *Narrative of the Life of Frederick Douglass: An American Slave*—are separated by time, space, culture, and geopolitics—and yet my students made wonderful connections between both texts, identifying isolation, self-perception, and moral dilemmas. They also asked big questions about freedom and justice, the function of human imagination, and ambition.

2. Pairing **Lady Macbeth's "Your face, my thane, is as a book"** (1.5.71–82, Lady Macbeth advises Macbeth to mask their plan to commit regicide) with **Paul Laurence Dunbar's poem "We Wear the Mask,"** in which Dunbar advises African Americans to hide their true feelings and humanity from the pain of racial oppression by white Americans.

Macbeth, 1.5.71–82 **by William Shakespeare**	*We Wear the Mask* **by Paul Laurence Dunbar**

LADY MACBETH
 	
  O never
Shall sun that morrow see!
Your face, my thane, is as a book where men
May read strange matters. To beguile the time,
Look like the time. Bear welcome in your eye,
Your hand, your tongue. Look like th' innocent
    Flower,
But be the serpent under 't. He that's coming
Must be provided for; and you shall put
This night's great business into my dispatch,
Which shall to all our nights and days to come
Give solely sovereign sway and masterdom.
	We wear the mask that grins and lies,
	It hides our cheeks and shades our eyes,—
	This debt we pay to human guile;
	With torn and bleeding hearts we smile,
	And mouth with myriad subtleties.
	
	Why should the world be over-wise,
	In counting all our tears and sighs?
	Nay, let them only see us, while
	We wear the mask.
	
	We smile, but, O great Christ, our cries
	To thee from tortured souls arise.
	We sing, but oh the clay is vile
	Beneath our feet, and long the mile;
	But let the world dream otherwise,
	We wear the mask!

Again, we started with the definition for *mask* in various dictionaries, and they came up with these:

- A covering for all or part of the face, worn as a disguise, or to amuse or terrify other people

- To conceal (something) from view; to make (something) indistinct or imperceptible

- A grotesque or humorous false face

- A covering for all or part of the face, worn to conceal one's identity, not show their real feelings or character

- A covering for part of the face, worn to protect one from disease

Once more, I asked a few questions to start discussion:

1. What is the purpose of the mask for Lady Macbeth and Macbeth?

2. What does Dunbar mean, and why does he think African Americans should wear a mask?

3. How do the Macbeths' reasons for masking differ from Dunbar's?

The discussion developed into topics that identified comparisons and contrasts in both texts:

- Both Macbeth and Dunbar are engaging in a performance.

- Both have more than one face.

- Both result in a type of erasure of true identity.

- For both, the mask enables them to operate from different positions materially and mentally.

- Macbeth's mask enables him to think he's become another person, one who struggles with identity and the human *potential* to be moral; Dunbar's mask forces him to become another person, struggling with identity, and the moral struggle that he can no longer show his true humanity or potential to the larger society.

- Macbeth's mask increases his agency, making him feel more powerful socially and materially; Dunbar's decreases his agency, making him feel dejected, less powerful socially and materially due to prejudice/Jim Crow laws.

- For both, the mask is a type of erasure, erasing human identity and hiding true feelings, but for different reasons.

- Macbeth's mask is freely chosen, giving him temporary power both social and material; Dunbar's mask has been imposed upon him by a larger society to limit his social and material power.

- As a celebrated hero, Macbeth's mask marginalizes, but functions as a (perfect) cover for social and moral corruption that moves him further away from understanding complexity and moral truth; Dunbar's marginalized social position increases his capacity for understanding complexity and for moral growth.

- For both, the mask holds a hidden danger: The masking and unmasking of self can cause difficulty in distinguishing what's true from what's false.

Once again, these two texts—Shakespeare's *Macbeth* and Paul Laurence Dunbar's "We Wear the Mask"—are separated by time, space, culture, and social politics—and yet my students made inspiring connections between both texts, defining and identifying equivocation and isolation, discussing how language can mask human identity, morality, and justice, and perhaps their most surprising connections between both texts: identifying the dangers of prejudice in the human imagination and the blindness that comes with a superficial understanding of reality.

3. Pairing the **Captain's speech "Doubtful it stood"** (1.2.9–25, the Captain reporting Macbeth's heroism in battle to King Duncan) with a passage from **Eudora Welty's short story "A Worn Path"** (the difficult journey of Phoenix Jackson, a frail, elderly Black woman who makes the long journey on foot from her home in rural Mississippi into Natchez to get medicine for her grandson).

Macbeth, 1.2.9–25 **by William Shakespeare**

CAPTAIN

> Doubtful it stood,
> As two spent swimmers that do cling together
> And choke their art. The merciless Macdonwald
> (Worthy to be a rebel, for to that
> The multiplying villainies of nature
> Do swarm upon him) from the Western Isles
> Of kerns and gallowglasses is supplied;
> And Fortune, on his damnèd quarrel smiling,
> Showed like a rebel's whore. But all's too weak;
> For brave Macbeth (well he deserves that name),
> Disdaining Fortune, with his brandished steel,
> Which smoked with bloody execution,
> Like Valor's minion, carved out his passage
> Till he faced the slave;
> Which ne'er shook hands, nor bade farewell to him,
> Till he unseamed him from the nave to th' chops,
> And fixed his head upon our battlements.

"A Worn Path" **by Eudora Welty**

It was December—a bright frozen day in the early morning. Far out in the country there was an old Negro woman with her head tied in a red rag, coming along a path through the pinewoods. Her name was Phoenix Jackson. She was very old and small and she walked slowly in the dark pine shadows, moving a little from side to side in her steps, with the balanced heaviness and lightness of a pendulum in a grandfather clock. She carried a thin, small cane made from an umbrella, and with this she kept tapping the frozen earth in front of her. This made a grave and persistent noise in the still air that seemed meditative, like the chirping of a solitary little bird.

She wore a dark striped dress reaching down to her shoe tops, and an equally long apron of bleached sugar sacks, with a full pocket: all neat and tidy, but every time she took a step she might have fallen over her shoelaces, which dragged from her unlaced shoes. She looked straight ahead. Her eyes were blue with age. Her skin had a pattern all its own of numberless branching wrinkles and as though a whole little tree stood in the middle of her forehead, but a golden color ran underneath, and the two knobs of her cheeks were illumined by a yellow burning under the dark. Under the red rag her hair came down on her neck in the frailest of ringlets, still black, and with an odor like copper.

Now and then there was a quivering in the thicket. Old Phoenix said, 'Out of my way, all you foxes, owls, beetles, jack rabbits, coons and wild animals! . . . Keep out from under these feet, little bob-whites . . . Keep the big wild hogs out of my path. Don't let none of those come running my direction. I got a long way.' Under her small black-freckled hand her cane, limber as a buggy whip, would switch at the brush as if to rouse up any hiding things.

On she went. The woods were deep and still. The sun made the pine needles almost too bright to look at, up where the wind rocked. The cones dropped as light as feathers. Down in the hollow was the mourning dove—it was not too late for him.

The path ran up a hill. 'Seem like there is chains about my feet, time I get this far,' she said, in the voice of argument old people keep to use with themselves. 'Something always take a hold of me on this hill—pleads I should stay.'

After she got to the top, she turned and gave a full, severe look behind her where she had come. 'Up through pines,' she said at length. 'Now down through oaks.'

Her eyes opened their widest, and she started down gently. But before she got to the bottom of the hill a bush caught her dress.

Her fingers were busy and intent, but her skirts were full and long, so that before she could pull them free in one place they were caught in another. It was not possible to allow the dress to tear. 'I in the thorny bush,' she said. 'Thorns, you doing your appointed work. Never want to let folks pass—no, sir. Old eyes thought you was a pretty little *green* bush.'

Finally, trembling all over, she stood free, and after a moment dared to stoop for her cane.

'Sun so high!' she cried, leaning back and looking, while the thick tears went over her eyes. 'The time getting all gone here.'

At the foot of this hill was a place where a log was laid across the creek.

'Now comes the trial,' said Phoenix. Putting her right foot out, she mounted the log and shut her eyes. Lifting her skirt, leveling her cane fiercely before her like a festival figure in some parade, she began to march across. Then she opened her eyes and she was safe on the other side.

'I wasn't as old as I thought,' she said.

But she sat down to rest. She spread her skirts on the bank around her and folded her hands over her knees. Up above her was a tree in a pearly cloud of mistletoe. She did not dare to close her eyes, and when a little boy brought her a plate with a slice of marble-cake on it she spoke to him. 'That would be acceptable,' she said. But when she went to take it there was just her own hand in the air.

So she left that tree, and had to go through a barbed-wire fence. There she had to creep and crawl, spreading her knees and stretching her fingers like a baby trying to climb the steps. But she talked loudly to herself: she could not let her dress be torn now, so late in the day, and she could not pay for having her arm or her leg sawed off if she got caught fast where she was.

At last she was safe through the fence and risen up out in the clearing. Big dead trees, like black men with one arm, were standing in the purple stalks of the withered cotton field. There sat a buzzard.

'Who you watching?'

In the furrow she made her way along . . .

She passed through the old cotton and went into a field of dead corn. It whispered and shook, and was taller than her head. 'Through the maze now,' she said, for there was no path.

Then there was something tall, black, and skinny there, moving before her.

At first she took it for a man. It could have been a man dancing in the field. But she stood still and listened, and it did not make a sound. It was as silent as a ghost.

'Ghost,' she said sharply, 'who be you the ghost of? For I have heard of nary death close by.'

But there was no answer, only the ragged dancing in the wind.

She shut her eyes, reached out her hand, and touched a sleeve. She found a coat and inside that an emptiness, cold as ice.

'You scarecrow,' she said. Her face lighted. 'I ought to be shut up for good,' she said with laughter. 'My senses is gone. I too old. I the oldest people I ever know. Dance, old scarecrow,' she said, 'while I dancing with you.'

She kicked her foot over the furrow, and with mouth drawn down shook her head once or twice in a little strutting way. Some husks blew down and whirled in streamers about her skirts.

Then she went on, parting her way from side to side with the cane, through the whispering field. At last she came to the end, to a wagon track where the silver grass blew between the red ruts. The quail were walking around like pullets, seeming all dainty and unseen.

'Walk pretty,' she said. 'This the easy place. This the easy going.' She followed the track, swaying through the quiet bare fields, through the little strings of trees silver in their dead leaves, past cabins silver from weather, with the doors and windows boarded shut, all like old women under a spell sitting there. 'I walking in their sleep,' she said, nodding her head vigorously.

In a ravine she went where a spring was silently flowing through a hollow log. Old Phoenix bent and drank. 'Sweet gum makes the water sweet,' she said, and drank more. 'Nobody know who made this well, for it was here when I was born.'

The track crossed a swampy part where the moss hung as white as lace from every limb. 'Sleep on, alligators, and blow your bubbles.' Then the cypress trees went into the road. Deep, deep it went down between the high green-colored banks. Overhead the live oaks met, and it was as dark as a cave.

A big black dog with a lolling tongue came up out of the weeds by the ditch. She was meditating, and not ready, and when he came at her she only hit him a little with her cane. Over she went in the ditch, like a little puff of milkweed.

Down there, her senses drifted away. A dream visited her, and she reached her hand up, but nothing reached down and gave her a pull. So she lay there and presently went to talking. 'Old woman,' she said to herself, 'that black dog come up out of the weeds to stall you off, and now there he sitting on his fine tail, smiling at you.'

A white man finally came along and found her—a hunter, a young man, with his dog on a chain.

'Well, Granny!' he laughed. 'What are you doing there?'

'Lying on my back like a June bug waiting to be turned over, mister,' she said, reaching up her hand.

He lifted her up, gave her a swing in the air, and set her down. 'Anything broken, Granny?'

'No sir, them old dead weeds is springy enough,' said Phoenix, when she had got her breath. 'I thank you for your trouble.' . . .

'On your way home?'

'No sir, . . . I bound to go to town, mister,' said Phoenix. 'The time come around.'

He gave another laugh, filling the whole landscape. 'I know you old colored people! Wouldn't miss going to town to see Santa Claus!'

But something held Old Phoenix very still. The deep lines in her face went into a fierce and different radiation. Without warning, she had seen with her own eyes a flashing nickel fall out of the man's pocket onto the ground.

'How old are you, Granny?' he was saying.

'There is no telling, mister,' she said, 'no telling.'

Then she gave a little cry and clapped her hands and said, 'Git on away from here, dog! Look! Look at that dog!' She laughed as if in admiration. 'He ain't scared of nobody. He a big black dog.' She whispered, 'Sic him!'

'Watch me get rid of that cur,' said the man. 'Sic him, Pete! Sic him!'

Phoenix heard the dogs fighting, and heard the man running and throwing sticks. She even heard a gunshot. But she was slowly bending forward by that time, further and further forward, the lids stretched down over her eyes, as if she were doing this in her sleep. Her chin was lowered almost to her knees. The yellow palm of her hand came out from the fold of her apron. Her fingers slid down and along the ground under the piece of money with the grace and care they would have in lifting an egg from under a setting hen. Then she slowly straightened up; she stood erect, and the nickel was in her apron pocket. A bird flew by. Her lips moved. 'God watching me the whole time. I come to stealing.'

The man came back, and his own dog panted about them. 'Well, I scared him off that time,' he said, and then he laughed and lifted his gun and pointed it at Phoenix.

She stood straight and faced him.

'Doesn't the gun scare you?' he said, still pointing it.

'No, sir, I seen plenty go off closer by, in my day, and for less than what I done,' she said, holding utterly still.

He smiled, and shouldered the gun. 'Well, Granny,' he said, 'you must be a hundred years old, and scared of nothing. I'd give you a dime if I had any money with me. But you take my advice and stay home, and nothing will happen to you.'

'I bound to go on my way, mister,' said Phoenix. She inclined her head in the red rag. Then they went in different directions, but she could hear the gun shooting again and again over the hill.

She walked on. The shadows hung from the oak trees to the road like curtains. Then she smelled wood smoke, and smelled the river, and she saw a steeple and the cabins on their steep steps. Dozens of little black children whirled around her. There ahead was Natchez shining. Bells were ringing. She walked on.

In the paved city it was Christmas time. There were red and green electric lights strung and crisscrossed everywhere, and all turned on in the daytime. Old Phoenix would have been lost if she had not distrusted her eyesight and depended on her feet to know where to take her.

I began by asking my students to write down three qualities that make a hero in their opinion. Their answers looked like these:

- A traditional hero is *usually* a young man or male

- A good person

- A trailblazer, someone who is the first to do something, a pioneer

- A person who does something out of the ordinary that most people would not do

And then I asked students to describe a "traditional hero," and if they were less familiar with this term, I'd offer the following descriptive from literature like Homer's *The Odyssey*:

- A man who is on a journey/quest of some kind and who encounters many dangers

- A selfless man who works to serve the community, and does not act for glory

- A man who is courageous, is physically strong, and endures suffering with dignity

I asked a few more questions to start discussion:

1. Compare and contrast your own definition or description of a hero with the more traditional definition; what did you find?

2. Is present-day society less concerned with a hero's morality and more concerned with a hero's fame and image? If so, why?

3. Does present-day society's definition of a hero need to be redefined?

The discussion that followed opened surprising avenues of connection between both texts, broadening their understanding of who is most often identified as a hero and raising questions about how, why, and if this definition has become more restricted and limiting over time. Their observations are in no particular order:

- Both Macbeth and Phoenix Jackson do something that would frighten others, and so both show a form of courage.

- Macbeth's courage causes pain and grief that results in a loss of human dignity, his own and others'; Phoenix Jackson's courage elevates human dignity, her own and others', as she has endured pain and grief with dignity.

- Both are clever, resourceful.

- In age, Macbeth is in his prime; Phoenix is in the decline of age.

- Macbeth is physically strong and morally weak; Phoenix Jackson is physically frail but spiritually strong.

- Macbeth's motives for action are self-serving and expedient, causing him to be foolhardy, apathetic toward others, irrational, and cruel; Phoenix Jackson's motivation for action is selfless, showing patience, good sense/judgment, wisdom, and compassion, even toward those who have been condescending or oppressive toward those of her ethnic origin.

- Both move through time, but differently: Phoenix is patient, knowing human limitation; Macbeth is impulsive/impatient and tries to exceed human limitations.

The connections students made between these texts—Shakespeare's *Macbeth* and Eudora Welty's "A Worn Path"—engaged them in big questions: What is love and how does true love behave? What is justice and what limits human judgment? And finally, what actions transform and elevate moral character, bringing new perspectives to light about what it means to be humane, and fully human?

Sources

Horton, George M. (1845). *The Poetical Works of George M. Horton, the colored bard of North-Carolina: to which is prefixed The life of the author, written by himself.* Hillsborough, North Carolina.

Douglass, Frederick. *Narrative of the Life of Frederick Douglass: An American Slave.* New York: Penguin Books, 1968. Print. https://docsouth.unc.edu/neh/douglass/douglass.html.

Dunbar, Paul Laurence. "We Wear the Mask." From *The Complete Poems of Paul Laurence Dunbar*. New York: Dodd, Mead and Company.

PART FOUR

Five More Resources for You

- *Folger Teaching*—**folger.edu/teach**—The Folger's online universe for teachers! Search lesson plans, podcasts, videos, and other classroom resources. Connect with like-minded colleagues and experts. Access on-demand teacher workshops and participate in a range of live professional development opportunities from hour-long sessions to longer courses, all offering CEU credit. Complete access to *Folger Teaching* is one of many benefits of joining the Folger as a Teacher Member.

- *Folger Shakespeare* online—**folger.edu/shakespeares-works**—Shakespeare's complete works free and online, and all downloadable in various formats that are particularly useful for teachers and students. The Folger texts are the most up-to-date available online; behind the scenes, they have been encoded to make the plays easy to read, search, and index. Also available here are audio clips of selected lines performed.

- *Folger Shakespeare* in print—Shakespeare's plays and sonnets in single-volume paperbacks and in ebooks. The texts are identical to those of *Folger Shakespeare* online; the books, however, are all in a format featuring the text on the right-hand page with glosses and definitions on the left. Used in many, many classrooms, the *Folger Shakespeare* in print is published by Simon & Schuster and available from booksellers everywhere.

- *The Folger Shakespeare Library*—**folger.edu**—The online home of the wide world of the Folger Shakespeare Library, offering all kinds of experiences and resources from the world's largest Shakespeare collection. We're waiting for you, your class, and your family! Explore the Folger collection, enjoy the magic of music and poetry, participate in a workshop, see a play! We're a great opportunityfor lively and satisfying engagement with the arts and humanities.

- *Shakespeare Documented*—shakespearedocumented.folger.edu—A singular site that brings together digitized versions of hundreds of the known primary source documents pertaining to Shakespeare—the playwright, actor, and stakeholder; the poet; and the man engaged in family and legal matters. A destination for curious students! Convened by the Folger, this collection is a collaboration among the Folger and Shakespeare Birthplace Trust, the National Archives of Great Britain, the Bodleian Library at Oxford, and the British Library.

ACKNOWLEDGMENTS

Seven or eight years ago, Mark Miazga, an exceptional high school teacher from Baltimore—and a Folger teacher—said, "We should make a series of books where we lay out for teachers key specifics about the play, and then how to teach the whole play using the Folger Method."

Ignition.

An important idea with a huge scope: five books, each focused on a single play—*Hamlet*, *Macbeth*, *Romeo and Juliet*, *Othello*, and *A Midsummer Night's Dream*. Each one a pretty revolutionary dive into basic info, scholarship, and the how of teaching each of the plays to *all* students. *Every* student. This demanded assembling an extraordinarily strong array of knowledge, expertise, and experience and moving it into action.

It is finally time to name and celebrate this crowd of people who, with generosity of all kinds, had a hand in creating the book that you are reading right now:

Folger director Michael Witmore, a deep believer in the importance of learning, teaching, and the power of the Folger to support both for all and at all levels, has been a fan and a wise advisor from the start.

The generosity of the Carol and Gene Ludwig Family Foundation—and in particular our fairy godmother, Carol Ludwig—has fueled every part of the creation of this series, including making certain that every English teacher in Washington, DC, has their own set of books *gratis*. I express the gratitude of the Folger as well as that of teachers in DC and beyond.

None of these volumes would exist without Folger Education's extraordinary Katie Dvorak, who, from the first minute to the last, herded not cats but our many authors, contracts, editorial conferences, publisher meetings, the general editor, and a series of deadlines that *never ever* stopped changing. Much of this was accomplished as Covid covered all lives, work, families, everything. Katie's persistence, along with her grace, humor, empathy, and patience kept us moving and was the glue we never did not need.

We appreciate the support and guidance of our team at Simon & Schuster: Irene Kheradi, Johanna Li, and Amanda Mulholland.

All along, the overall project benefited from the wisdom and support of these key players: Skip Nicholson, Heather Lester, Michael LoMonico, Corinne Viglietta, Maryam Trowell, Shanta Bryant, Missy Springsteen-Haupt, and Jessica Frazier . . . and from the creative genius of Mya Gosling.

Major gratitude to colleagues across the Folger who contributed to building these books in terms of content and business support. Our thanks to Erin Blake, Caroline Duroselle-Melish, Beth Emelson, Abbey Fagan, Esther French, Eric Johnson, Adrienne

Jones, Ruth Taylor Kidd, Melanie Leung, Mimi Newcastle, Rebecca Niles, Emma Poltrack, Sara Schliep, Emily Wall, and Heather Wolfe.

We are in debt to the schoolteachers and scholars who generously shared their time and wisdom as we got started, helping us to map our path and put it in motion—all along the intersections where scholarship and teaching practice inform each other. Massive gratitude to Patricia Akhimie, Bernadette Andreas, Ashley Bessicks, David Sterling Brown, Patricia Cahill, Jocelyn Chadwick, Ambereen Dadabhoy, Eric DeBarros, Donna Denizé, Ruben Espinosa, Kyle Grady, Kim Hall, Caleen Sinnette Jennings, Stefanie Jochman, Heather Lester, Catherine Loomis, Ellen McKay, Mark Miazga, Noémie Ndiaye, Gail Kern Paster, Amber Phelps, Katie Santos, Ian Smith, Christina Torres, and Jessica Cakrasenjaya Zeiss.

It's impossible to express our thanks here without a special shout-out to Ayanna Thompson, the scholarly powerhouse who has been nudging Folger Education for the last decade. Know that nudges from Ayanna are more like rockets . . . always carrying love and a challenge. We could not be more grateful for them, or for her.

With endless admiration, I give the close-to-last words and thanks to the working schoolteachers who authored major portions of these books. First here, we honor our colleague Donnaye Moore, teacher at Brookwood High School in Snellville, Georgia, who started on this project teaching and writing about *Othello* but succumbed to cancer far too soon. None of us have stopped missing her or trying to emulate her brilliant practicality.

I asked working teachers to take on this challenge because I know that no one knows the "how" of teaching better than those who do it in classrooms every day. The marvels I am about to name were teaching and living through all the challenges Covid presented their own lives *and* thinking about you and your students too, putting together (and testing and revising) these lessons for you who will use these books. Over a really loud old-fashioned PA system, I am shouting the names of Ashley Bessicks, Noelle Cammon, Donna Denizé, Roni DiGenno, Liz Dixon, David Fulco, Deborah Gascon, Stefanie Jochman, Mark Miazga, Amber Phelps, Vidula Plante, Christina Porter, and Jessica Cakrasenjaya Zeiss. You rock in every way possible. You honor the Folger—and teachers everywhere—with your wisdom, industry, and generosity.

Finally, I wrap up this project with humility, massive gratitude to all, for all, and—perhaps amazingly in these complicated days in which we are publishing—relentless HOPE. Hamza, Nailah, and Shazia O'Brien, Soraya Margaret Banta, and gazillions of children in all parts of the world deserve all we've got. Literature—in school, even!—can get us talking to, and learning from, one another in peace. Let's get busy.

—Peggy O'Brien
General Editor

ABOUT THE AUTHORS

Dr. Ayanna Thompson is a scholar of Shakespeare, race, and performance. She is the author of many books, including *Blackface and Passing Strange: Shakespeare, Race, and Contemporary America*. A Regents Professor of English and director of the Arizona Center for Medieval and Renaissance Studies, she was elected to the American Academy of Arts and Sciences in 2021. In addition to her scholarship, Thompson collaborates with many theaters and theater practitioners.

Dr. Christina Porter is a 2006 alumna of the Folger's Teaching Shakespeare Institute. She began her career as an English teacher and literacy coach for Revere Public Schools in Revere, Massachusetts. Currently, she is Director of Humanities for her school district. She is also a faculty member at Salem State University. She resides in Salem, Massachusetts, with her two precocious daughters.

Corinne Viglietta teaches Upper School English at The Bryn Mawr School in Baltimore, Maryland. From 2014 to 2022, Corinne was Associate Director of Education at the Folger Shakespeare Library, where she had the honor of exploring the wonders of language with thousands of amazing teachers, students, and visitors. Corinne played a key role in Folger's national teaching community and school partnerships. She has led workshops on the Folger Method for numerous organizations, including the Smithsonian, the National Council of Teachers of English, and the American Federation of Teachers. Corinne is a lifelong Folger educator, having first discovered the power of this approach with her multilingual students in Washington, DC, and France. She has degrees in English from the University of Notre Dame and the University of Maryland.

Dr. Catherine Loomis holds a PhD in Renaissance Literature from the University of Rochester, and an MA in Shakespeare and Performance from the Shakespeare Institute. She is the author of *William Shakespeare: A Documentary Volume* (Gale, 2002) and *The Death of Elizabeth I: Remembering and Reconstructing the Virgin Queen* (Palgrave, 2010), and, with Sid Ray, the editor of *Shaping Shakespeare for Performance: The Bear Stage* (Fairleigh Dickinson, 2016). She has taught at the University of New Orleans, the University of North Carolina at Greensboro, and the Rochester Institute of Technology.

Of Haitian American descent, **Donna Denizé** holds a BA from Stonehill College and an MA in Renaissance Drama from Howard University. She has contributed to scholarly books and journals, and she is the author of a chapbook, *The Lover's Voice* (1997), and a book, *Broken Like Job* (2005). She currently chairs the English Department at St. Albans School for boys, where she teaches Freshman English; a junior/senior elective in Shakespeare; and Crossroads in American Identity, a course she designed years ago and which affords her the opportunity to do what she most enjoys—exploring not only the cultural and intertextual crossroads of literary works but also their points of human unity.

Dr. Jocelyn A. Chadwick is a lifelong English teacher and international scholar. She was a full-time professor at Harvard Graduate School of Education and now occasionally lectures and conducts seminars there. In addition to teaching and writing, Chadwick also consults and works with teachers and with elementary, middle, and high school students around the country. Chadwick has worked with PBS, BBC Radio, and NBC News Learn and is a past president of the National Council of Teachers of English. She has written many articles and books, including *The Jim Dilemma: Reading Race in Adventures of Huckleberry Finn* and *Teaching Literature in the Context of Literacy Instruction*. Chadwick is currently working on her next book, *Writing for Life: Using Literature to Teach Writing*.

Liz Dixon began her English/Language Arts teaching career in 1998 in Charlotte, North Carolina, and has been at West Lafayette Junior/Senior High School (also her alma mater) in Indiana since 2003. Liz is an alum of the 2014 Folger Teaching Shakespeare Institute and has continued collaborating with the Folger ever since. She has co-directed fourteen high school musicals and eight Shakespeare plays. She has a master's degree in Literature from Purdue and aspires to a PhD someday. In her spare time, Liz loves to read, hang out with family, cook, knit, crochet, sew, and dabble in just about any other handicraft.

Mark Miazga, a National Board–certified English teacher, has taught and coached Varsity Baseball at Baltimore City College High School since 2001. The winner of the Maryland 2014 Milken Educator Award, Miazga participated at the Teaching Shakespeare Institute at the Folger Shakespeare Library in 2008. He has presented at NCTE conferences about connecting students to Shakespeare, as well as Steinbeck, Wilson, Baldwin, and Morrison. An advocate for urban education, Miazga currently also works as adjunct professor in the Urban Teachers program at Johns Hopkins University. After receiving his undergraduate degree at Michigan State University, Miazga received his master's in Secondary Education from Towson University.

Michael LoMonico has taught Shakespeare courses and workshops for teachers and students in 40 states as well as in Canada, England, and the Bahamas. He was an assistant to the editor for the curriculum section of all three volumes of the Folger's Shakespeare Set Free series. Until 2019, he was the Senior Consultant on National Education for the Folger. He is the author of *The Shakespeare Book of Lists*, *Shakespeare 101*, and a novel, *That Shakespeare Kid*. He was the

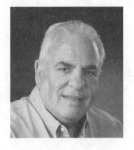

co-founder and editor of *Shakespeare*, a magazine published by Cambridge University Press and Georgetown University.

Dr. Michael Witmore is the seventh director of the Folger Shakespeare Library, the world's largest Shakespeare collection and the ultimate resource for exploring Shakespeare and his world. He was appointed to this position in July 2011; prior to leading the Folger, he was Professor of English at the University of Wisconsin–Madison and at Carnegie Mellon University. Under his leadership and across a range of programs and policies, the Folger began the process of opening up to and connecting with greater and more diverse audiences nationally, internationally, and here at home in Washington, DC. He believes deeply in the importance of teachers; also under his leadership, the Library's work in service of schoolteachers continues to grow in breadth, depth, and accessibility.

Mya Lixian Gosling (she/her) is the artist and author of *Good Tickle Brain*, the world's foremost (and possibly only) stick-figure Shakespeare comic, which has been entertaining Shakespeare geeks around the world since 2013. Mya also draws *Keep Calm and Muslim On*, which she co-authors with Muslim American friends, and *Sketchy Beta*, an autobiographical comic documenting her misadventures as an amateur rock climber. In her so-called spare time, Mya likes to read books on random Plantagenets, play the ukulele badly, and pretend to be one of those outdoorsy people who is in touch with nature but actually isn't. You can find her work at goodticklebrain.com.

Dr. Peggy O'Brien is a classroom teacher who founded the Folger Shakespeare Library's Education Department in 1981. She set the Library's mission for K–12 students and teachers then and began to put it in motion; among a range of other programs, she founded and directed the Library's intensive Teaching Shakespeare Institute, was instigator and general editor of the popular Shakespeare Set Free series, and expanded the Library's education work across the country. In 1994, she took a short break from the Folger—20 years—but returned to further expand the education work and to engage in the Folger's transformation under the leadership of director Michael Witmore. She is the instigator and general editor of the Folger Guides to Teaching Shakespeare series.

Roni DiGenno is a special education teacher at Calvin Coolidge Senior High School in Washington, DC. She earned her BA in Literature from Stockton University in Pomona, New Jersey, and her MA in English from Rutgers University in Camden, New Jersey. Her background in English and passion for special education led her to the educational mission of the Folger Shakespeare Library, participating in the Teaching Shakespeare Institute in 2016. She currently lives in Maryland with her husband, daughter, and two dogs.